AF606781

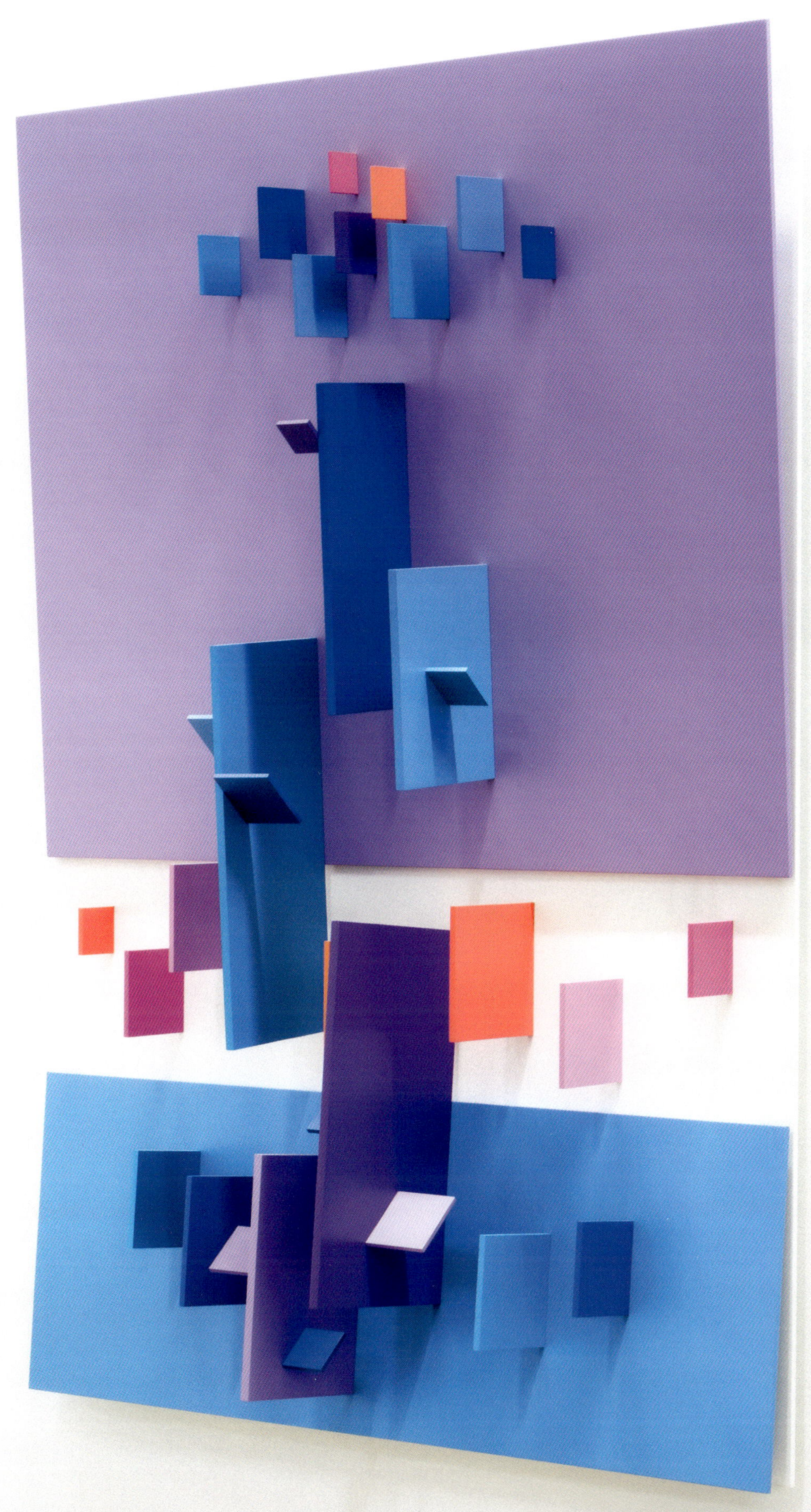

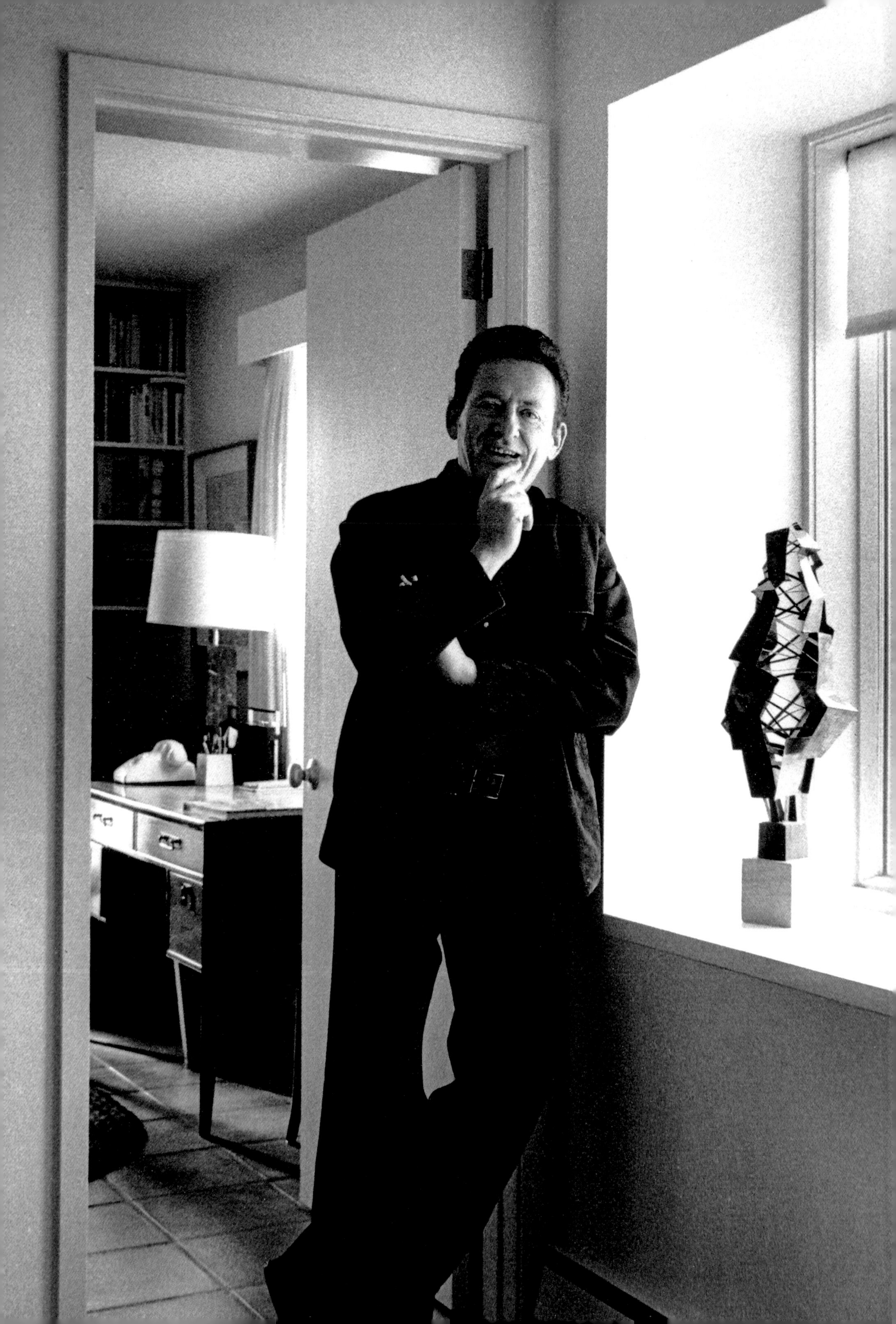

THE CANADIAN ART LIBRARY

Eli Bornstein

LIFE & WORK

By Roald Nasgaard

Contents

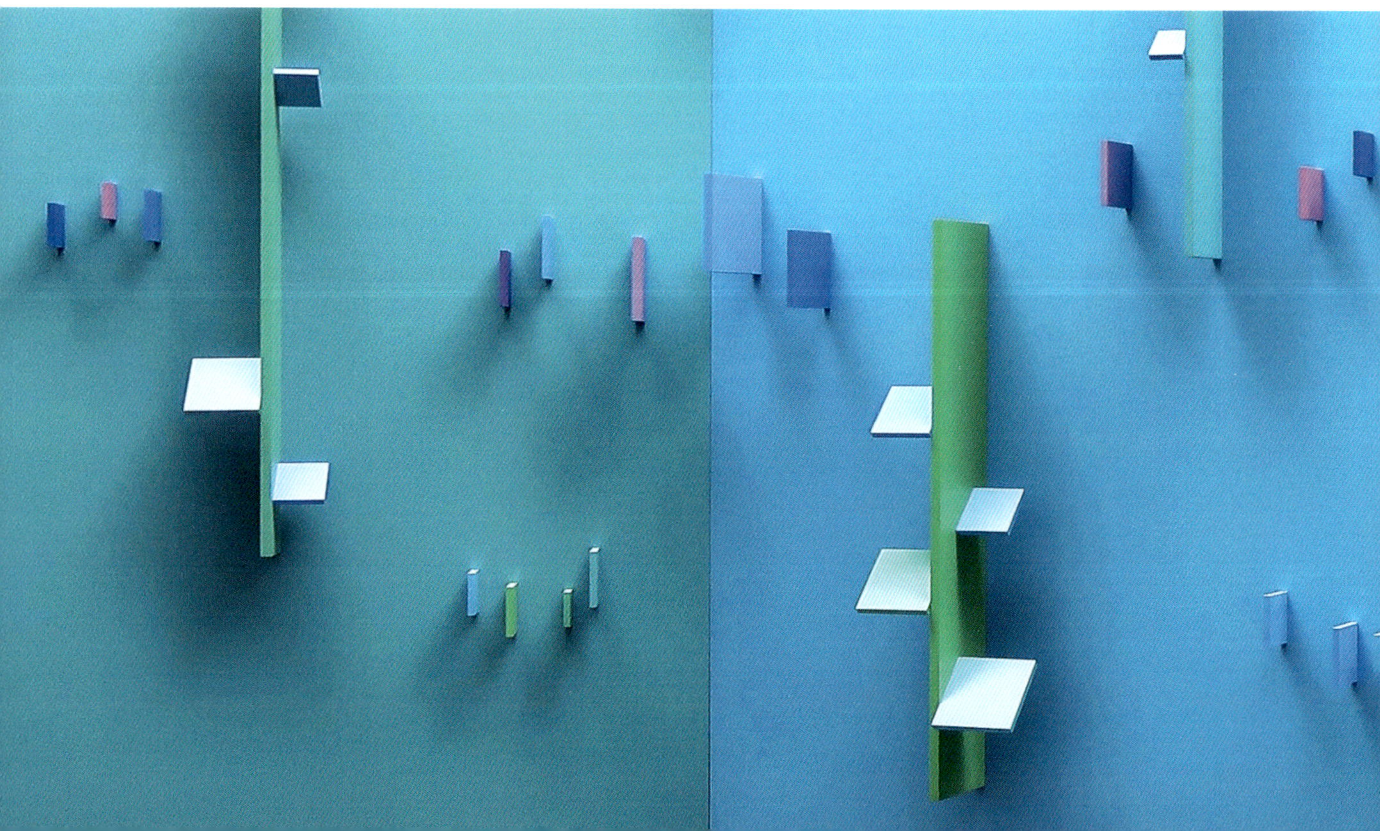

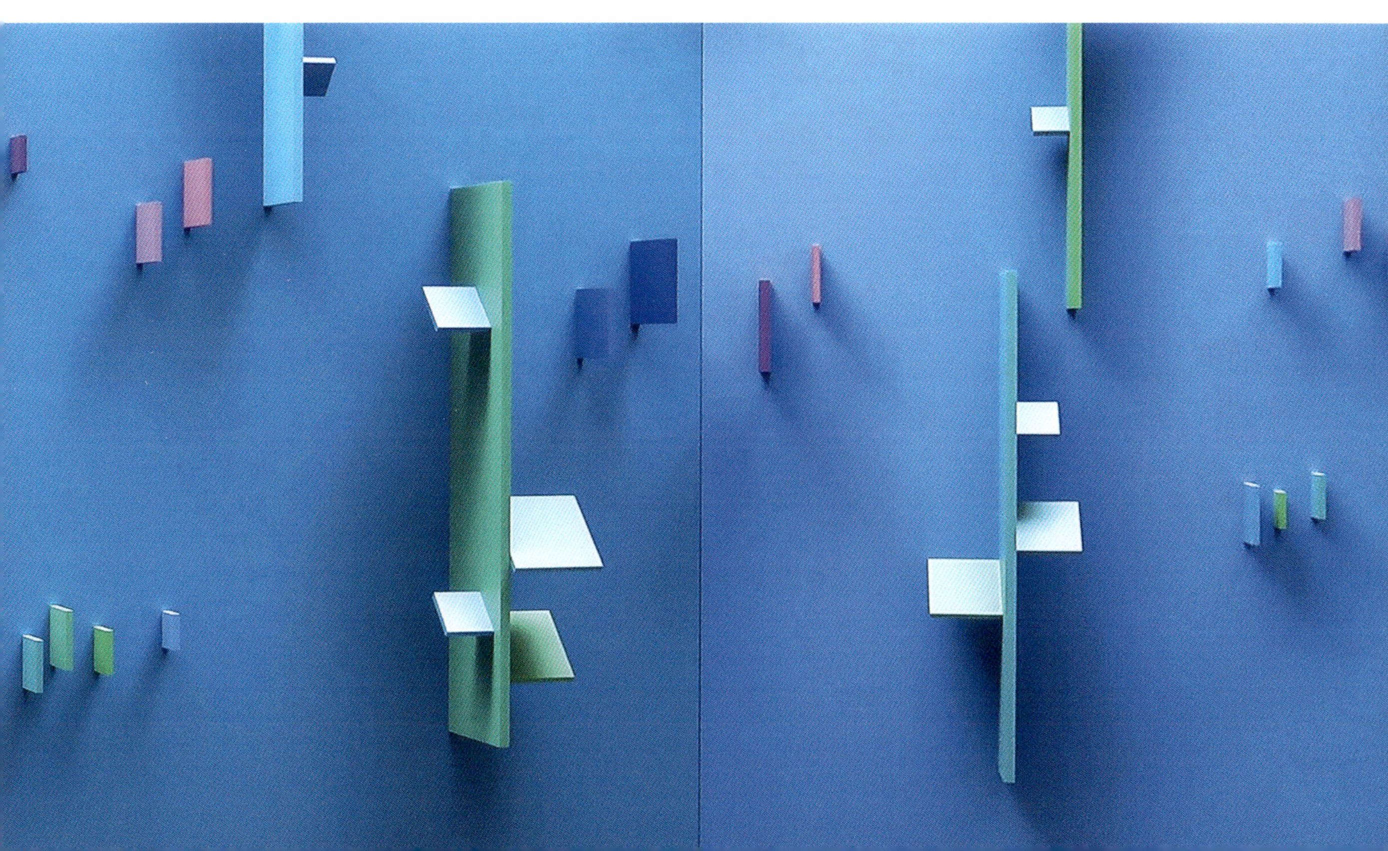

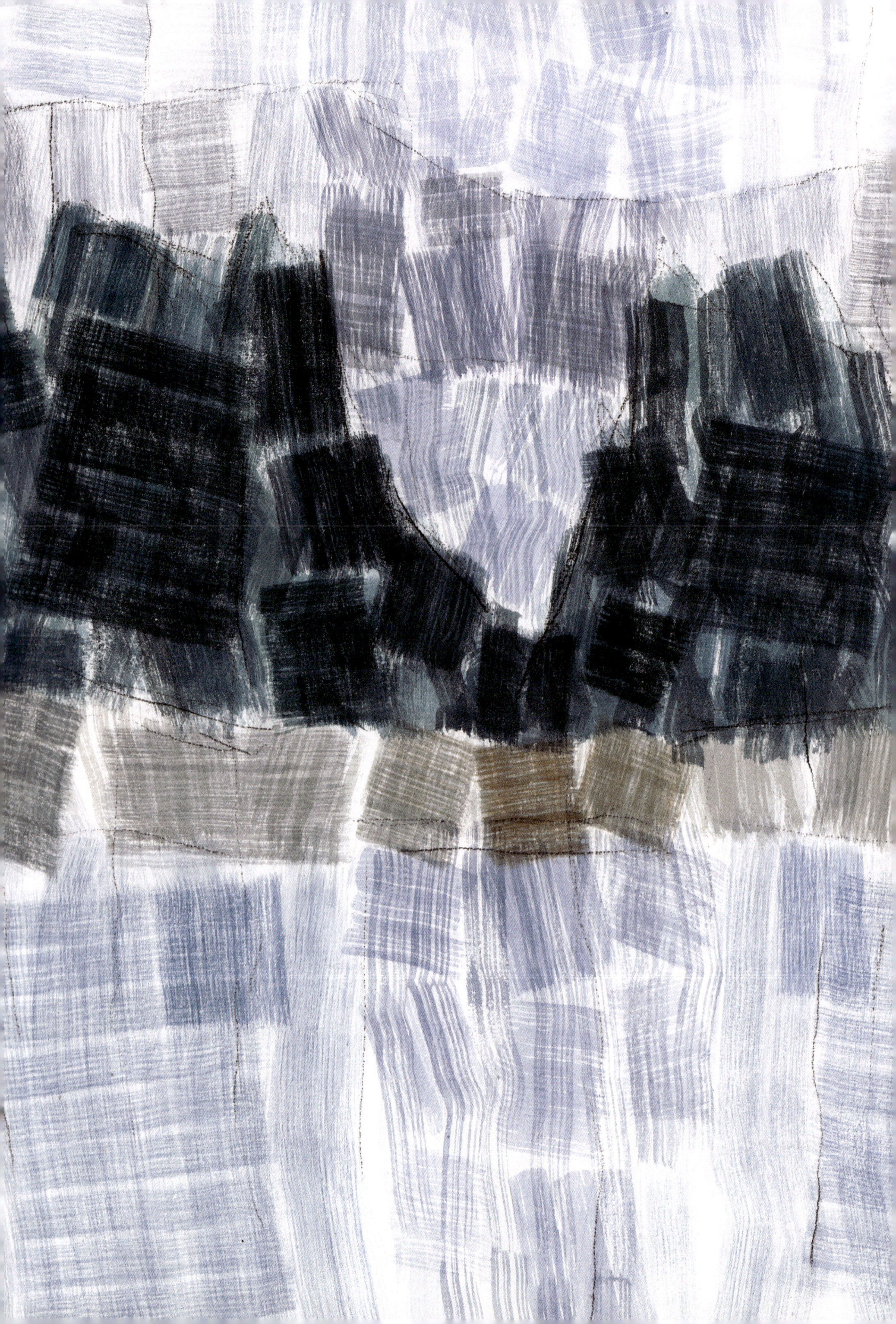

Introduction

With a career spanning seven decades, Eli Bornstein has defined for himself an exceptional place in the history of modern art in Canada. From the mid-1950s onward, the Saskatoon-based artist, educator, and writer set out on a singular creative journey, independent of other emerging trends in this country's art.

A student of European modernism, works of twentieth-century abstraction guided Bornstein as he created an art form that could express the vitality of the natural world with geometric shapes and vivid colours. One of the first artists in the province of Saskatchewan to produce abstract art, Bornstein launched a career in which he would earn accolades for his unique vision, combining elements of painting and sculpture to create something entirely new—an art form he would call the Structurist Relief.

In the following pages, author Roald Nasgaard, the leading expert on the history of abstract art in Canada, examines how Bornstein's extraordinary career developed through his reverence for nature and his conviction that the way forward for Canada's artists is to reinvent rather than to copy its forms. Over the years, Bornstein's Structurist reliefs have gone through many stylistic and material developments, but the resulting works are always rooted in the artist's close observation of a truly elemental Canadian focus: natural phenomena. As Nasgaard details, Bornstein's stylistic and technical shifts have culminated in his most celebrated body of work: a series of Structurist reliefs inspired by the Canadian Arctic.

Born in Milwaukee, Wisconsin, in 1922, Bornstein was encouraged by his parents to pursue creative interests from a young age. A passion for music in his youth became critical to defining his career. Playing drums in dance bands helped Bornstein pay for university. Jazz became an early influence that propelled him toward abstract art as well. At the Milwaukee State Teachers College, Bornstein began his study of the twentieth century's most important modern art movements, including Post-Impressionism, Cubism, and the innovative curriculum of the Bauhaus. In 1945, upon receiving his Bachelor of Science in art, Bornstein began his teaching career offering courses in drawing, painting, and sculpture at the Milwaukee Art Institute and the University of Wisconsin-Milwaukee.

After accepting a position at the University of Saskatchewan in 1950, Bornstein arrived in his new home of Saskatoon. It was a moment when Prairie artists—namely the Regina Five—were becoming interested in non-representational art. However, while Bornstein embraced contemporary styles, he chose a path different from that of his peers, who were moved by emerging trends in colour field and American Post-Painterly Abstraction. Working simultaneously in painting and sculpture, Bornstein looked to European artists for inspiration, including Constantin Brâncuși (1876–1957), Paul Cézanne (1839–1906), and Georges Seurat (1859–1891).

The year 1956 marked a turning point. Following his watercolour painting *The Island*, Bornstein's final representational painting before he began to exclusively produce abstract reliefs, he created works that would alter the course of his career. One of them, *Aluminum Construction (Tree of Knowledge)*, was a sculptural commission for

Opposite: Eli Bornstein, *The Island* (detail), 1956, watercolour on paper, 53.5 x 74 cm, collection of the artist.

the Saskatchewan Teachers' Federation. The first abstract public work installed in the city of Saskatoon, it marked Bornstein's foray into assembling rather than carving new forms. Also in 1956, Bornstein began corresponding with the American artist Charles Biederman (1906–2004), a painter who incorporated three-dimensional elements into his works and who provided inspiration for Bornstein's first relief works out of wood, including *Low Form Relief No. 10*, 1957, painted with white and primary colours.

In 1960, Bornstein further formalized his commitment to Structurist art. He founded and became the editor-in-chief of the periodical *The Structurist*, published out of the University of Saskatchewan, an internationally circulated journal that ran for sixty years and included Bornstein's own writings on ideas in architecture and the arts—including the connections between painting, sculpture, design, photography, music, and literature, as well as the relationship of art to science, technology, and nature.

Bornstein would continue to evolve the Structurist Relief, its formal elements becoming more differentiated and visually complex and the colours increasingly vibrant. Notable innovations with the art form include *Double Plane Structurist Relief No. 3*, 1967–69, which resembles a folded book jutting out from the wall; *Quadriplane Structurist Relief No. 4* (Sunset Series), 1997–99, which illustrates Bornstein's skill in colour gradation; and *Tripart Hexaplane Construction No. 2*, 2002–6, a free-standing public work installed on the University of Manitoba campus.

After two summer trips to Ellesmere Island in 1986 and 1987, Bornstein's Structurist Relief evolved again, this time to new, majestic heights. Between 1986 and 1998, his Arctic Series reliefs responded to his profound experience of the Canadian Arctic. In these works, Bornstein presented an intensified sensation of this frigid landscape by creating relief elements with pieces of transparent Plexiglas painted with hues of blue and green. The Arctic Series reliefs were born, as Nasgaard reveals, from Bornstein's belief that his Structurist methods could be enhanced to authentically embody his sensations of the Far North.

As we learn in *Eli Bornstein: Life & Work*, the artist's impressive oeuvre showcases a creative life of constant innovation and deep reverence for nature and modernity. Bolstered by his three decades spent as a professor in the Department of Art at the University of Saskatchewan, and as the editor-in-chief of *The Structurist*, Bornstein's career has been recognized with major honours, including the Saskatchewan Order of Merit in 2008 and the Order of Canada in 2019. His groundbreaking works are proof that nature remains an enduring influence on this country's artists.

Sara Angel, CM, PhD
Founder and Executive Director, Art Canada Institute
April 2025

Opposite: Eli Bornstein, *Low Form Relief No. 10*, 1957, tempera on composition board, 24.3 x 16.8 x 1.9 cm, collection of the artist.

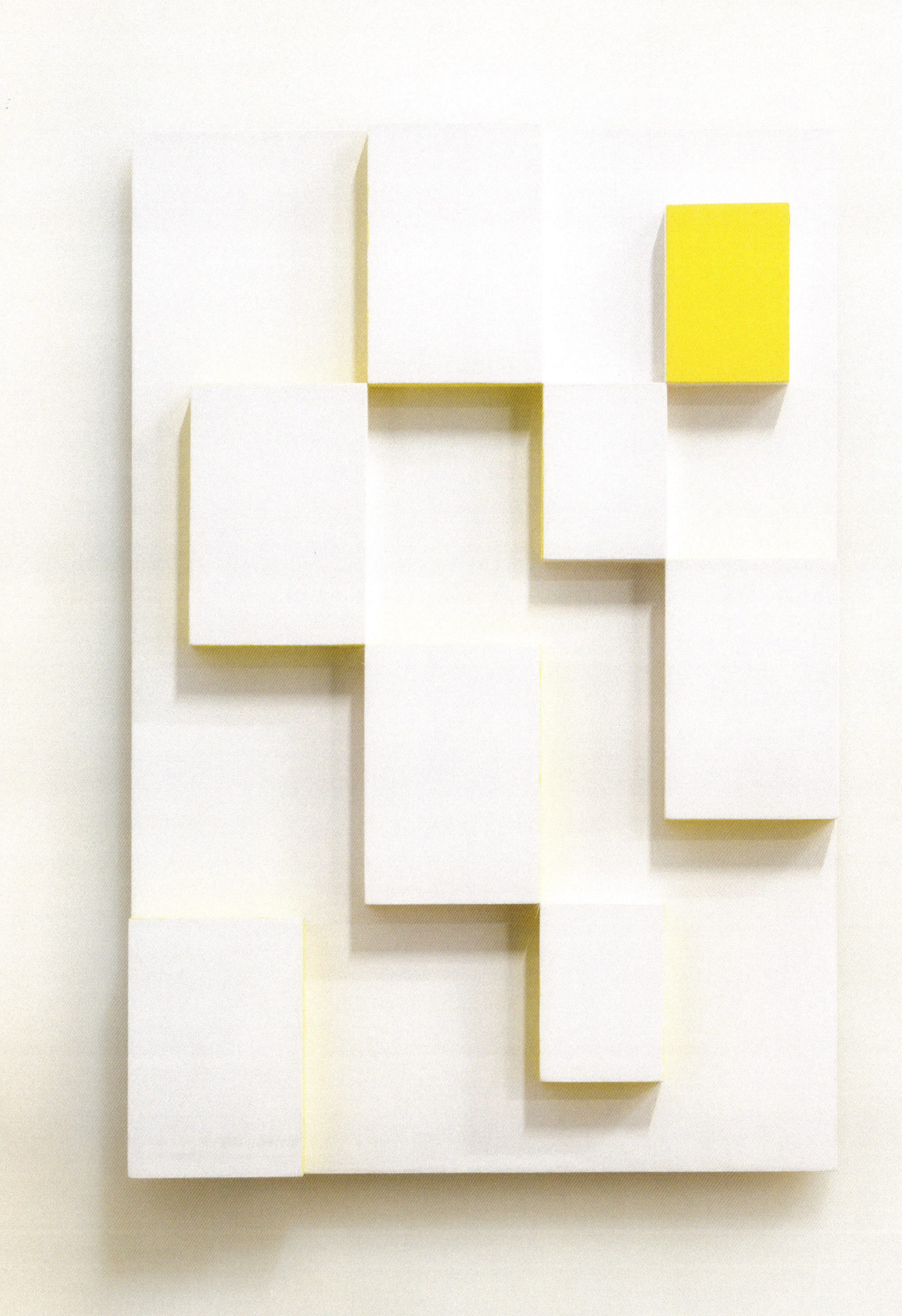

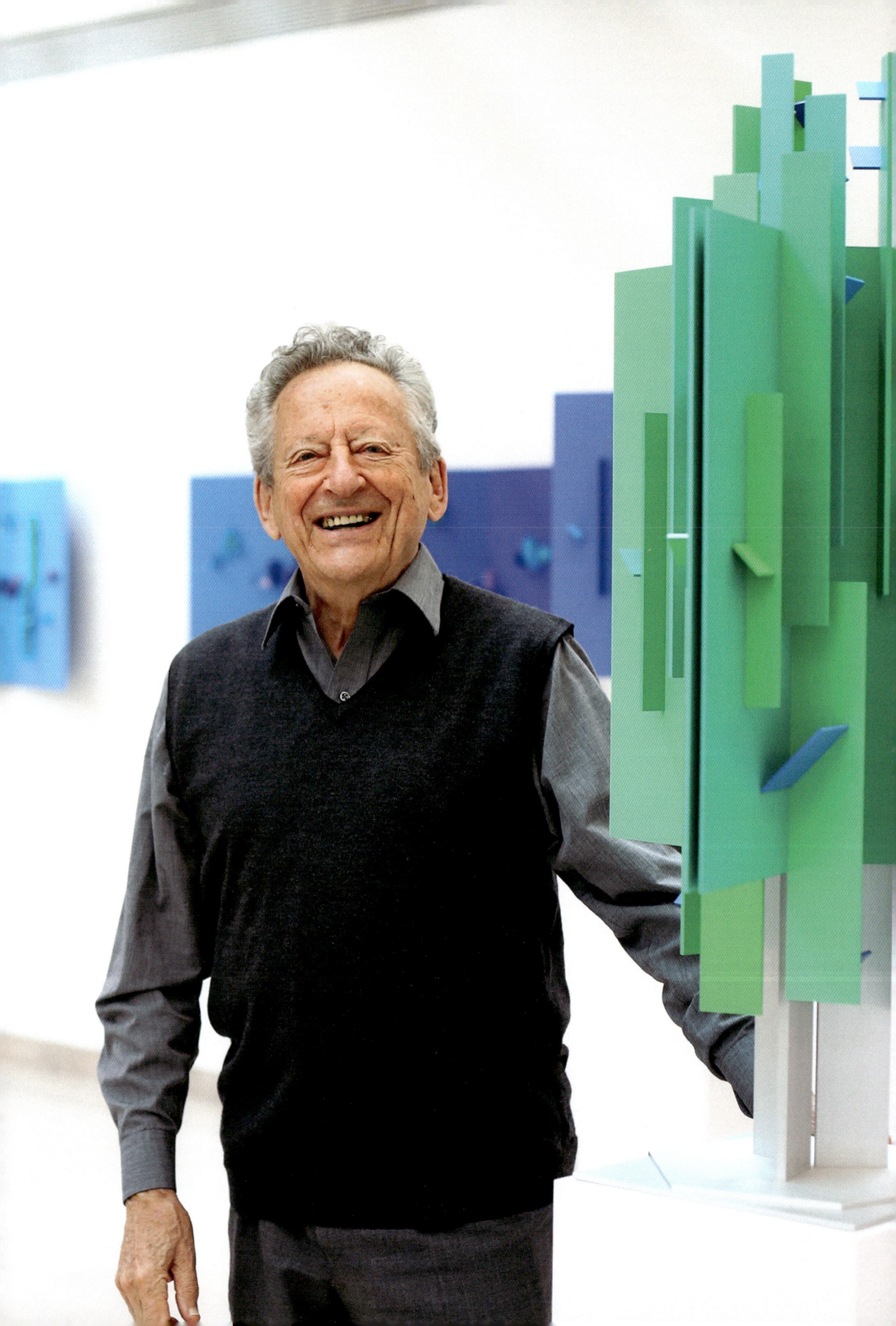

Biography

For the past half century, Eli Bornstein (b.1922) has been a unique contributor to abstract art in Canada. Born in Milwaukee, Wisconsin, he accepted a position at the University of Saskatchewan in 1950, Saskatoon becoming the base for his multi-faceted career. Initially both a painter and a sculptor, he soon combined these two practices into a lifelong commitment to what he would call the Structurist Relief, a three-dimensional art form that is simultaneously rigorously abstract and deeply rooted in the phenomena of the natural world. Both the prairie landscape and the Arctic have been constant inspirations for his creative thinking.

Early Years in Wisconsin

Eli Bornstein, future teacher, writer, and publisher, and ultimately the consummate Structurist artist, was born in Milwaukee, Wisconsin, on December 28, 1922. His parents came from Lithuania. They had arrived separately in the United States in 1904 and eventually met and married in Milwaukee. Bornstein knew little of their life before they immigrated other than that it was full of hardships, overburdened with work and poverty. Neither one, as he writes in a 1997 journal entry, had the privilege of a good education or the comfort of a close family life. And neither parent—both of whom were raised in Orthodox Jewish homes—"found solace in the Synagogue, in religious belief or practice [because] they could never overcome the hypocrisy they experienced from religious people, the bigotry, the fanaticism, intolerance and deceit."[1] Both his parents wanted to forget what they had left behind when they emigrated, looking ahead, instead, to America's promise of a better future in a free and democratic society.

The household Bornstein grew up in during the 1920s and 1930s was one that had to watch its pennies, but it was nonetheless a stimulating environment. Because his parents had turned their backs on religion, Bornstein was not educated in Hebrew or Judaism,

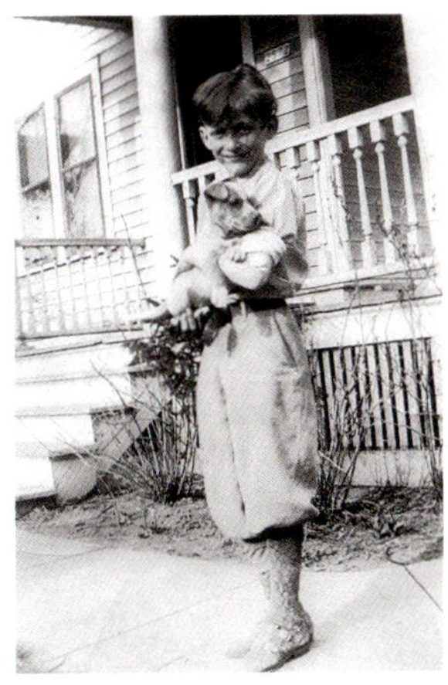

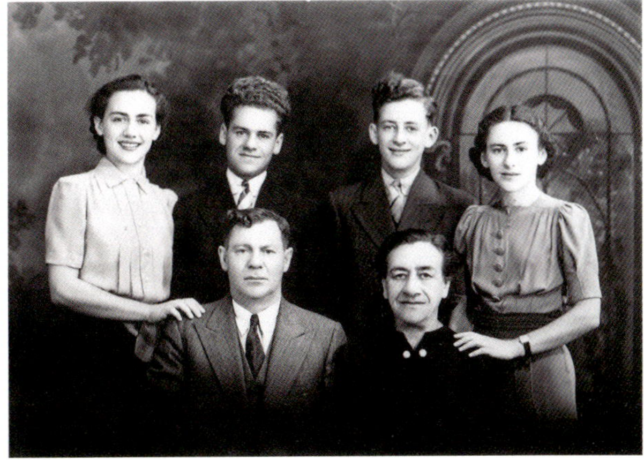

Opposite: Eli Bornstein with one of his Structurist reliefs in *An Art at the Mercy of Light: Recent Works by Eli Bornstein* at the Mendel Art Gallery, Saskatoon, 2013, photograph by Michelle Berg. Left: Eli Bornstein and his first dog, Skippy, 1932, photographer unknown. Right: The Bornstein family (*left to right*): sister Lilian, brother Fred, Eli, sister Dorothy; seated: father and mother, 1938–39, photographer unknown.

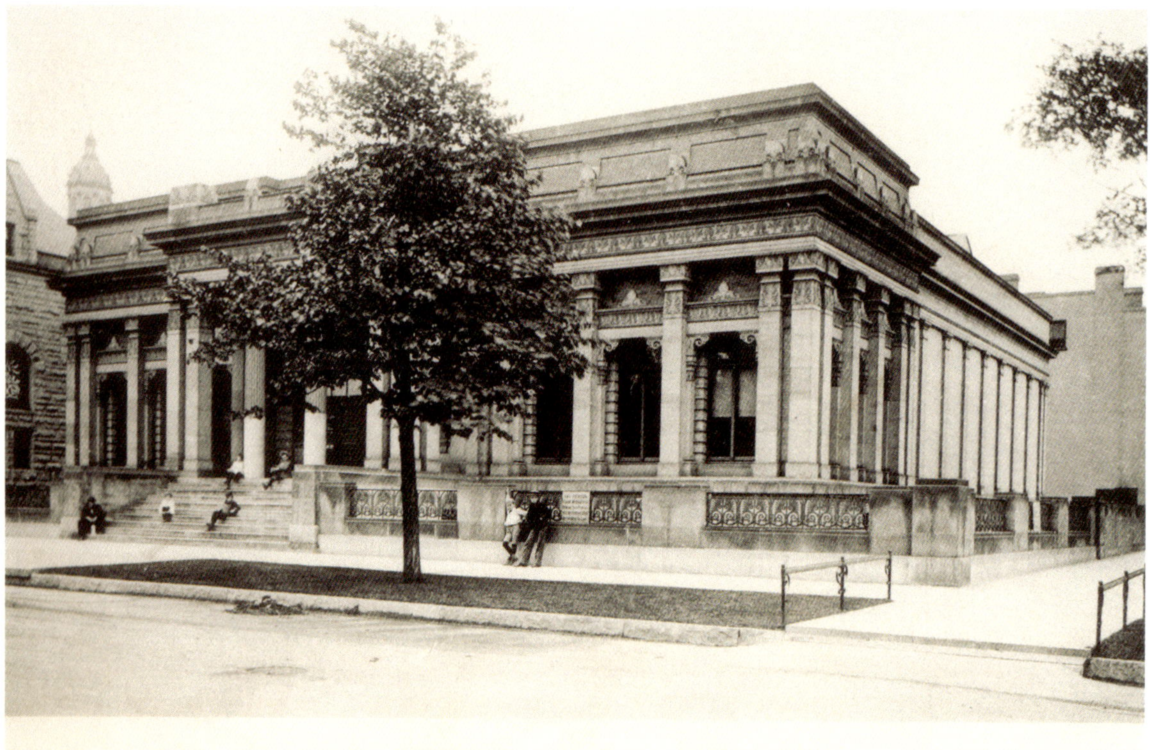

and he did not have a bar mitzvah. As he recalled to curator Jonneke Fritz-Jobse in her 1996 exhibition catalogue essay, his parents were religious freethinkers, pacifists, and attracted to socialism. Dinner conversations would engage in questions of ethics and philosophy. "We would talk about the existence of God and the meaning of life. We would talk about social and philosophical questions of every kind."[2]

The family home was filled with music. "My mother often said that 'here on earth, the closest we can get to God is through art'—meaning all the arts and human creativity and particularly music."[3] In a journal entry, Bornstein remembers how in the 1930s his older sister Dorothy would practise her piano lessons in the living room, playing Bach. He played the drums in his high school band, and then in dance bands as a way of earning money to pay for his college education. "I was in my late teens in Milwaukee in the late 30s and early 40s when I heard some of the best jazz bands and artists that were there often—Benny Goodman, Tommy Dorsey, Gene Krupa, Harry James, Les Brown, Earl "Fatha" Hines, Count Basie, Jimmie Lunceford, etc."[4] Although Bornstein finally quit the dance bands when evening and weekend performance schedules, as well as travelling, interfered too much with his schoolwork, his youthful music experiences were foundational to his art.

In a 2006 journal entry entitled "Jazz as an early influence toward abstract art," Bornstein analyzes vividly the analogies between music, especially jazz improvisation, and his future Structurist compositional practice, in works such as *Structurist Relief No. 1*, 1965. As he writes, "The physicality of jazz as it related to dance and movement ... [offered me] an early education of mind, senses, and body toward the animality of abstract visual art."[5] Jazz music was a common reference point for many modernist artists as they explored abstraction throughout the 1930s, 1940s, and 1950s.[6]

Exterior of the Layton Art Gallery, Milwaukee, 1895, photographer unknown, University of Wisconsin-Milwaukee Library.

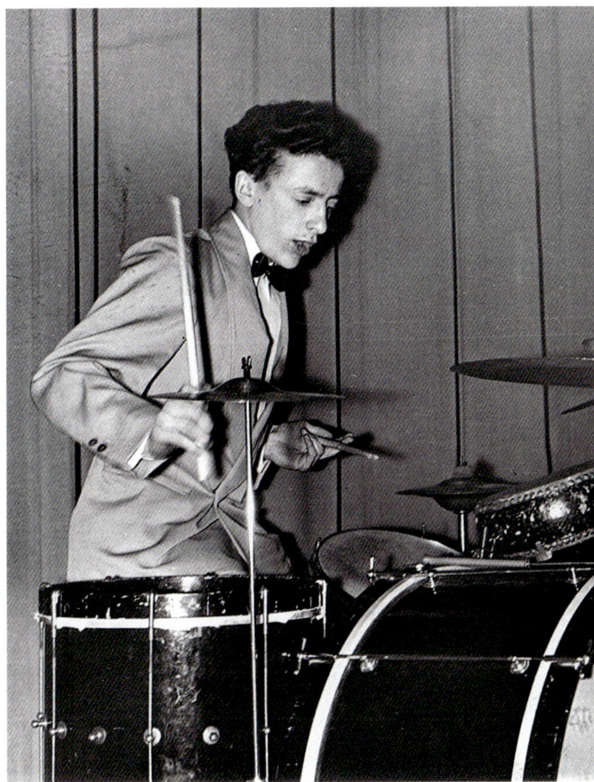

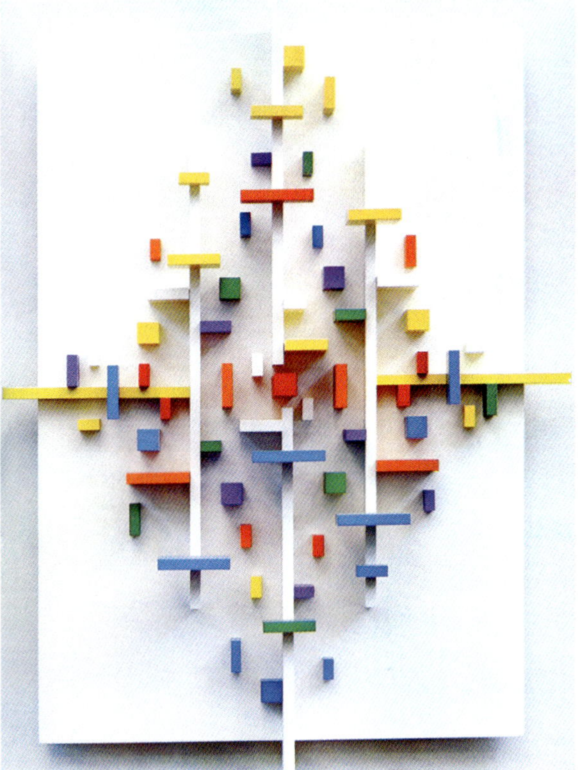

Bornstein made art even in kindergarten, and in his teens portrayed subjects from Milwaukee's Jewish community: "I recall making drawings and paintings of some of the marvelous old men with long beards or women wearing babushkas and long skirts whom I saw in the Jewish fish markets and butcher shops on Walnut Street when going shopping there with my mother."[7] His mother especially encouraged his creativity. When he was around twelve, she enrolled him in the Saturday morning art classes at the Layton Art Gallery (which merged with the Milwaukee Art Institute in 1957). Bornstein wrote: "I recall how struck I was by the Greek columns, the marble sculptures like *The Dying Gladiator*, and the huge paintings on the walls. Here was a temple to art. The tranquility and exalted atmosphere left a lasting impression."[8]

When Bornstein enrolled in his art courses at Milwaukee State Teachers College in 1941, the art world in Wisconsin was still quite conservative. But he remembers several teachers at the college who influenced him greatly: the historian F.E.J. Wilde, who guided him through the cultures of ancient Egypt and Greece; the German-born artist Robert von Neumann (1888–1976), who, although described as the quintessential Wisconsin Regionalist artist, introduced Bornstein to modern art from Impressionism to Cubism, with visits to the Art Institute of Chicago; and Howard Thomas (1899–1971), in whose design classes he learned about the Bauhaus and European abstract art. Thomas took his students to visit the School of Design in Chicago (founded in 1937 as the New Bauhaus), where they were introduced to its director, the Hungarian former Bauhaus professor László Moholy-Nagy (1895–1946)—an important future influence—who gave them an extensive tour of the school.

All in all, as Bornstein has recounted, his lessons at the Milwaukee State Teachers College aroused his interest in literature, philosophy, and history and stimulated his

Left: Eli Bornstein playing the drums, date unknown, photographer unknown. Right: Eli Bornstein, *Structurist Relief No. 1*, 1965, oil, aluminum, and Plexiglas, 99.1 x 73.7 x 17.1 cm, private collection.

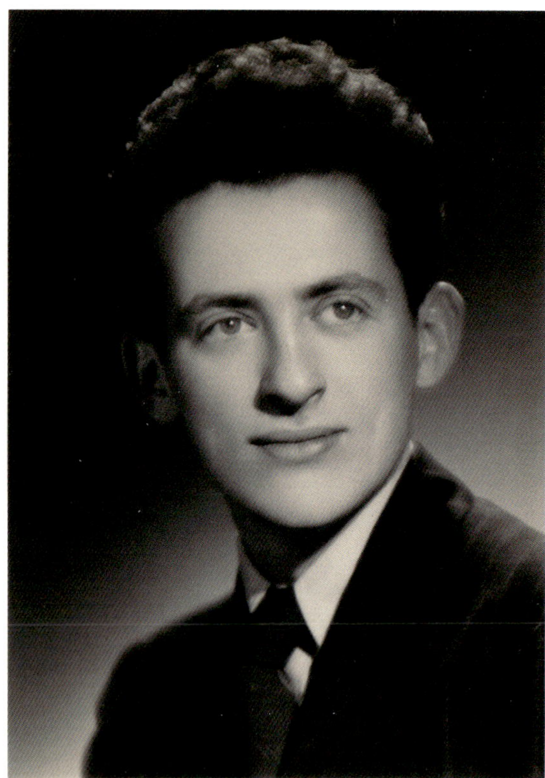

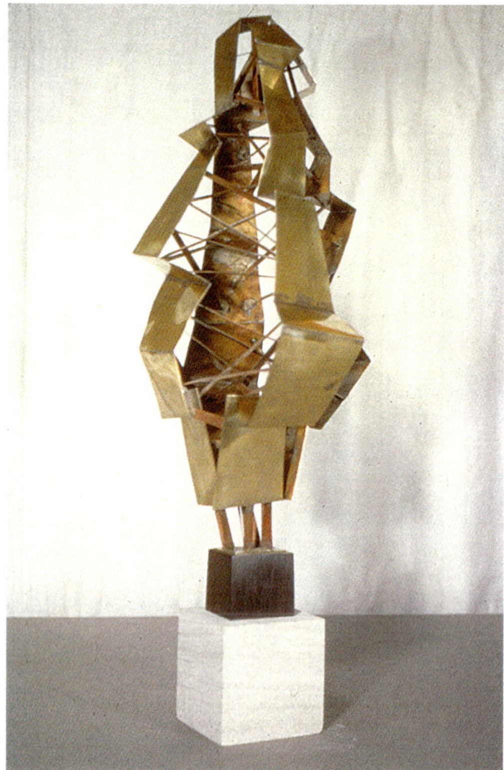

understanding of the relationships between art, philosophy, and religion.[9] As well, during his years at the college he developed a fascination with designing and building things: Bauhaus-inflected furniture such as a radio cabinet, a phonograph storage cabinet, and a bookcase.[10] In jewellery-making classes, Bornstein became adept at working with brass and bronze, skills that he would apply when he made his first constructed sculptures in the mid-1950s, such as *Growth Motif No. 4*, 1956.

At the outbreak of the Second World War, despite being a conscientious objector, Bornstein briefly served in the U.S. Army infantry in Texas before being honourably discharged in 1943. After his service, he moved to Chicago. He knew the city not only from school trips, but also from many family visits with relatives since he was a child. Attracted to its energy, Bornstein enrolled first at the School of the Art Institute and then at the University of Chicago, where he took classes in anthropology and history. But, as he recollects, he was restless and uncertain about how to get on with his life as an artist, and his short stay in the city as an art student while working as a part-time labourer handling railroad freight "was an unsatisfying and lonely time which led me back to my home in Milwaukee where I resumed my college education."[11]

In 1945, Bornstein received a bachelor of science in art from the Milwaukee State Teachers College, and for the rest of the decade he taught drawing, painting, sculpture, and design at the Milwaukee Art Institute and the University of Wisconsin-Milwaukee. In 1950, he accepted a position with the Department of Art at the University of Saskatchewan in Saskatoon. As he was pursuing a master of science degree in graphic techniques at the University of Wisconsin–Madison, he had to travel back and forth between the two cities. He graduated in 1954.

Left: Eli Bornstein on the occasion of his graduation from the Milwaukee State Teachers College, 1945, photographer unknown. Right: Eli Bornstein, *Growth Motif No. 4*, 1956, welded, silver-brazed, and tinned bronze and brass on limestone base, 22.9 cm (h), collection of the artist.

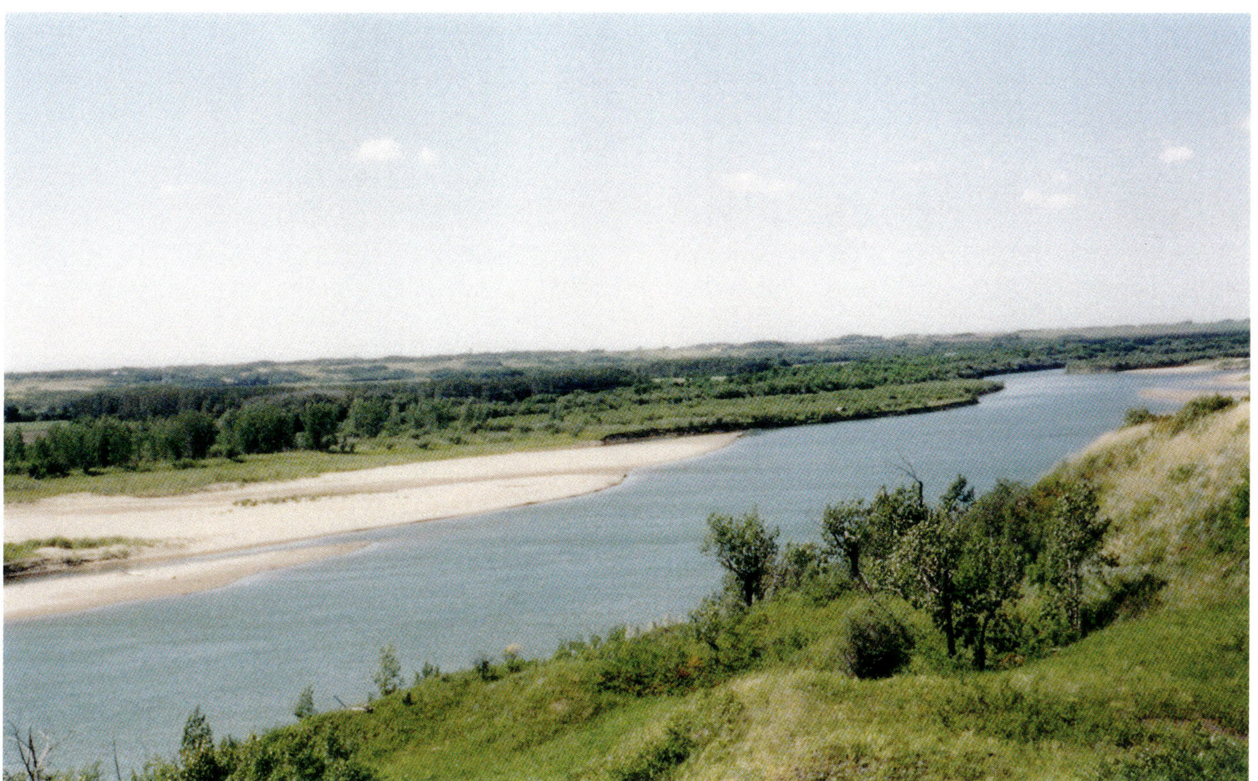

Move to Saskatchewan

When Bornstein first accepted his teaching job at the University of Saskatchewan in 1950, it was a one-year contract substituting for a faculty member on sabbatical leave. He was then offered a permanent position initially responsible for all the studio classes. In 1957, Bornstein was appointed associate professor, and in 1959, he introduced a new program of both theory and studio-based courses entitled "Structure and Colour in Space," as part of the Department of Art's undergraduate and graduate offerings. The program became an area of specialization unique in North America and attracted many pre-architecture students. In 1963, he was appointed professor and until 1971 served as head of the department. After nearly three decades working in higher education, Bornstein retired from teaching in 1990.

As Bornstein remembers it, his introduction to the landscape of the Saskatchewan prairies was in 1950, when he took the train across the Midwest, from Milwaukee to Saskatoon. "I was overwhelmed by the space and the light. The space at first was almost unbelievable in its flatness and endlessness."[12] It was a visual geography perhaps not unlike that of Lake Michigan, but his encounter with the vastness of the lake took place from its shore, looking off at a distant panorama. Instead, on the prairie, he was in the midst of it, "almost lost within it or consumed by it."[13] As he recollects, "The prairie light was almost equally overwhelming. Its brightness and unique character, the prominence of the sky, the far greater daily consciousness of the unobstructed sun and the moon and the dramatic changes through the seasons—these were to become one of my greatest attractions to the prairie that has continued to enthrall by its power and diversity."[14]

View of the South Saskatchewan River from Eli Bornstein's house, date unknown, photographer unknown. In the late 1960s, Bornstein built a home near the banks of the river. The feeling of endless space and light afforded by this landscape was a source of inspiration for his Structurist reliefs.

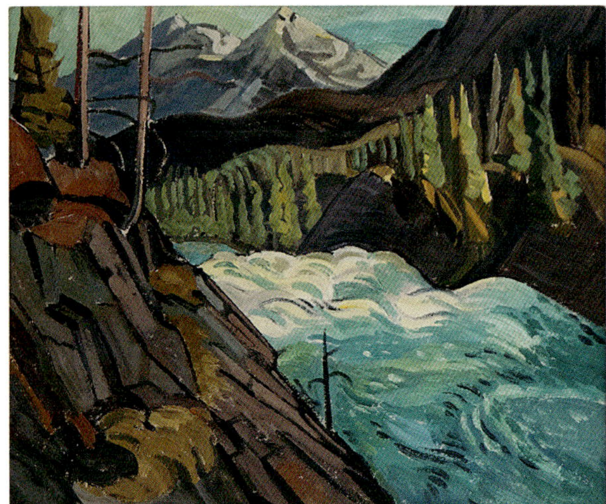

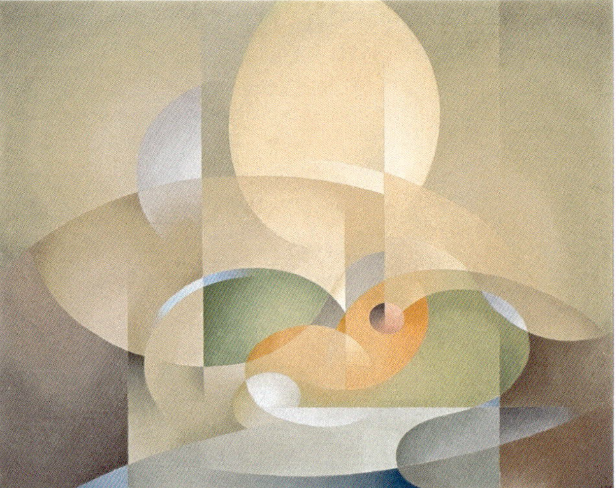

When Bornstein first arrived in Saskatoon, he found that artists on the prairies still mostly embraced some form of realism relatively untouched by the revolutions in art that had occurred in Europe. Artists such as the British-born Henry George Glyde (1906–1998), then the head of the painting division at the Banff School of Fine Arts (now the Banff Centre for Arts and Creativity), continued to work representationally using nineteenth-century British and European models, leavened with newer influences from the Group of Seven. There were, of course, exceptions. In 1950, when Bornstein arrived at the University of Saskatchewan, the newly formed art department at the University of Manitoba adopted modernist abstraction when it invited a small group of recent MFA graduates from the University of Iowa to form the faculty. The Winnipeg-based group included Richard Irving Bowman (1918–2001) and John Kacere (1920–1999), working variously in the modernist ways of the American Surrealist artist Gordon Onslow-Ford (1912–2003) and his circle; the printmaker Stanley William Hayter (1901–1988); and the Abstract Expressionists. There were other faculty members working in the style of Paul Cézanne (1839–1906) and Cubist modes, and the venerable Lionel LeMoine FitzGerald (1890–1956) also made his first abstract pictures in 1950. But the so-called Winnipeg Group flowered only briefly. While it received countrywide attention in the early-to-mid-1950s, the group faded from national sight with the departure of the Americans in 1953 and 1954 for warmer climates.[15]

In Saskatchewan, the principal factors of change that brought modern art to the province were Bornstein's appointment in Saskatoon in 1950 and the simultaneous hiring of Kenneth Lochhead (1926–2006) by the School of Art of Regina College (then a junior college affiliated with the University of Saskatchewan since 1934). But, because of Bornstein's imminent commitment to working in the Structurist Relief, the two artists' pathways would diverge dramatically. Over the next decade, Lochhead, through his faculty hires, brought together a group of artists—Ronald Bloore (1925–2009), Ted Godwin (1933–2013), Roy Kiyooka (1926–1994), Arthur McKay (1926–2000), Douglas Morton (1926–2004)—who eventually, as a consequence of a 1961 National Gallery of Canada exhibition, became known as the Regina Five.[16]

The Regina Five were dedicated to modernist abstraction, but emphasized the flatness of the painting medium. Their work, variously known as "colour field" or "Post-Painterly Abstraction," was, like Lochhead's *Dark Green Centre*, 1963, typically

Left: H.G. Glyde, *Above Bow Falls*, 1952, oil on board, 31 x 39 cm, Whyte Museum of the Canadian Rockies, Banff. Right: Lionel LeMoine FitzGerald, *Abstract: Green and Gold*, 1954, oil on canvas, 71 x 92 cm, Winnipeg Art Gallery.

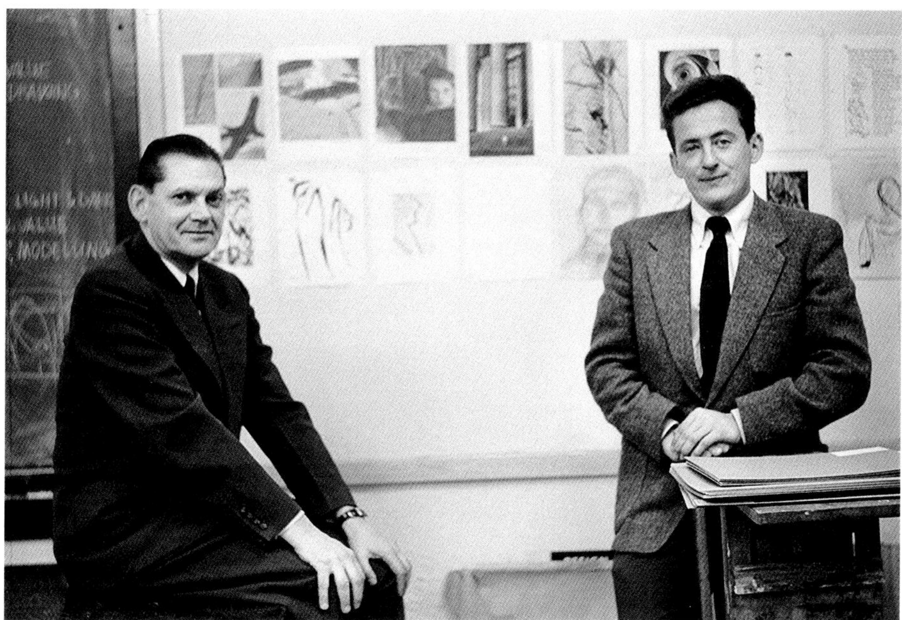

large-scaled and composed with flat expanses of colour, the paint thinly applied directly onto the raw canvas or stained into it. The terminology was devised by New York art critic Clement Greenberg (1909–1994), who for several decades exerted a pervasive if controversial influence on abstract painting practice as well as curatorial taste in the West, a context within which Bornstein, dedicated to relief construction, would be cast as a relative loner. This may explain why Bornstein chose not to participate in the two-week-long Emma Lake Artists' Workshops that Lochhead initiated in 1955 and which became for many decades an important fixture on the Canadian art scene. The workshops over the years were led by some of the most prominent Canadian and international artists including, famously, Barnett Newman (1905–1970) in 1959 and Greenberg in 1962.[17] Bornstein himself explained that his summers were reserved for research travel.

An Artist on His Own

Bornstein, with his metropolitan experiences of Chicago and Milwaukee, may initially have found himself a bit isolated when he first arrived in Saskatoon. He knew little about Canada or Saskatchewan. But he also remembers being amazed to discover how much interest and activity there was in art and music and drama in this prairie city of around fifty thousand people.[18] The university's Department of Art was headed by Gordon Snelgrove (1898–1966), painter, art historian, and one of the first people in Canada to receive a PhD in art history. (He retired in 1962 when Bornstein replaced him.) As well, there were departments of music and drama; the city supported an impressive public library; and, as a political bonus, the province was run by the pioneering socialist Co-operative Commonwealth Federation (CCF) party and its social justice premier, Tommy Douglas, whose government introduced the continent's first universal health care program.

The situation was further enriched when, two years later in 1952, Murray Adaskin (1906–2002) and his wife, Frances James (1903–1988), moved to Saskatoon. Adaskin, a musician and composer who was appointed head of the Department of Music at the University of Saskatchewan, helped make Saskatoon a major centre for the

Eli Bornstein and Gordon Snelgrove, c.1950–51, photographer unknown.

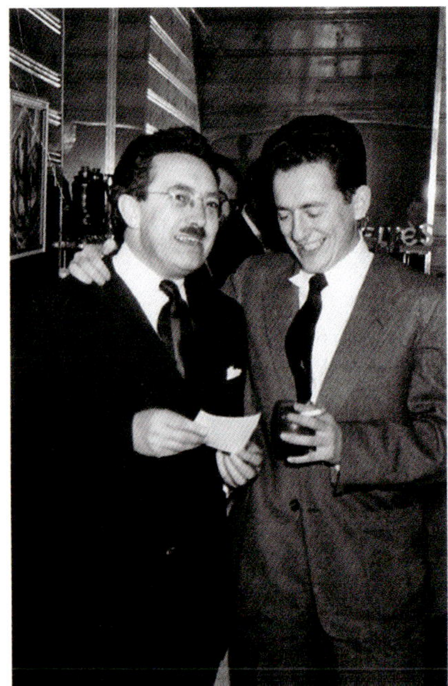

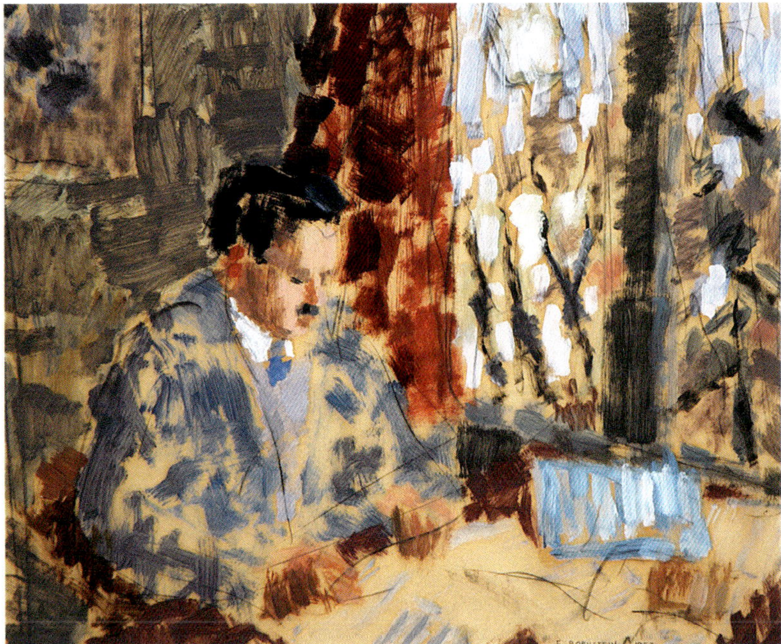

performance of contemporary Canadian music. James, in turn, was one of Canada's finest soprano singers. Her regular recitals on the CBC premiered songs by many modern composers, both international and Canadian.

How Bornstein met James and Adaskin shortly after their arrival forms an amusing anecdote. During high school while working his daily paper route delivering the *Milwaukee Leader*, Bornstein fell into the habit of whistling along the way. It was a practice he continued as he walked to the university every day, passing the Adaskins' house, "whistling away in the cold clear air of morning." One of those mornings, as Bornstein tells it:

> Murray came out on his front porch and stopped me. He wanted to know who was this young man that whistles Mozart so fluently.... That was the beginning of our life-long friendship and my admiration of those two extraordinary human beings from whom I learned so much about music, art, and life.[19]

Bornstein spent the summers of 1951 and 1952 in France (as did many American artists in the postwar years) on grants from the American government under the G.I. Bill. During the first summer he enrolled at the Académie de Montmartre in Paris, which since 1947 was directed by the Cubist painter Fernand Léger (1881–1955); and in 1952 at the Académie Julian. These institutions had long attracted a large number of foreign students, but in both cases, Bornstein found their offerings unsympathetic to his own developing concerns. He much preferred working independently, setting off on his own around Paris, working out of doors, or visiting museums, following up the interests in Impressionism and in French modernists Georges Seurat (1859–1891) and Paul Cézanne that he had cultivated at the Art Institute of Chicago. He also did some travelling outside Paris during these summers, venturing, as witnessed by the watercolour *Boats at Concarneau*, 1952, as far as the westernmost reaches of Brittany.

Left: Eli Bornstein and Murray Adaskin at a party hosted by Fred Mendel in Saskatoon, c.1954, photographer unknown. Right: Eli Bornstein, *Untitled (Murray Adaskin)*, 1953, oil on paper, 42.9 x 52.2 cm, Remai Modern, Saskatoon.

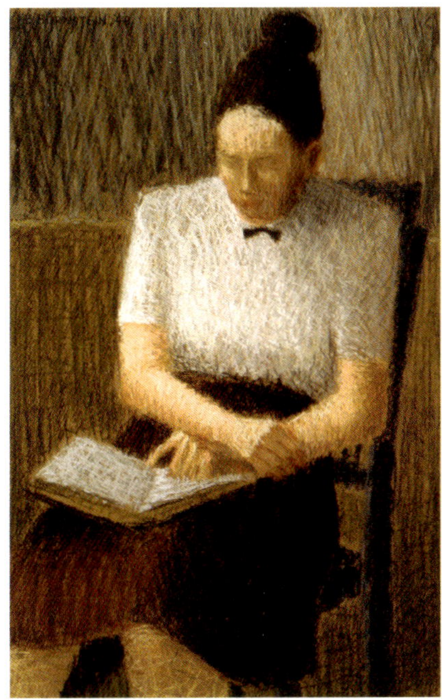

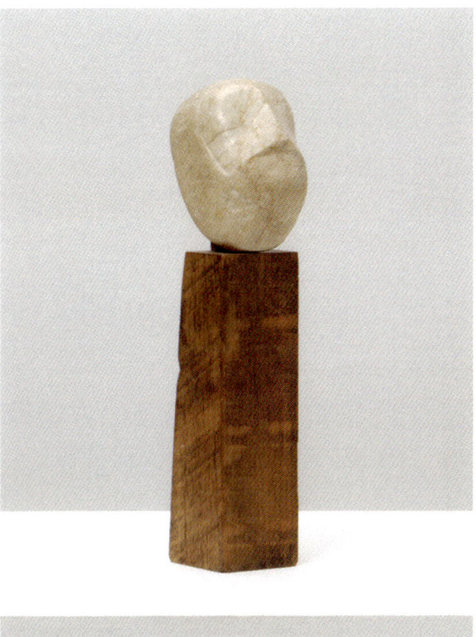

During the early 1950s, Bornstein's favourite subjects, which he executed in large-scale watercolour paintings and in various print media, were the single female figure observed in interior settings, as in the pastel on paper work titled *Girl Reading*, 1948, and then landscape and city motifs. His interest in the styles of Post-Impressionism and Cubism culminated in a watercolour, *The Island*, completed on the coast of Maine in 1956. Concurrently, Bornstein made sculptures influenced by Romanian sculptor Constantin Brâncuși (1876–1957) and the modern art movement known as Russian Constructivism. In 1947, his work *Head*—which was awarded a purchase prize by the Walker Art Center in Minneapolis—led to his monumental public commission, *Aluminum Construction (Tree of Knowledge)*, 1956. Despite this public recognition, no one from the art department supported Bornstein during a nasty letter campaign in the local newspaper that followed the installation of *Tree of Knowledge*. His public sculpture in front of the Saskatchewan Teachers' Federation Building in Saskatoon was attacked and deplored for being too abstract. Bornstein's detractors even demanded that he be fired from the university. It was Murray Adaskin from the music department who spoke out in defence of both the artist and his work.[20]

The Island and *Tree of Knowledge* would be Bornstein's last representational or quasi-representational works before he turned his full attention to constructing his signature abstract reliefs. The transformation was not as abrupt as it may seem but followed his study of art history through Impressionism to Cézanne, and then on to Piet Mondrian (1872–1944) and the Dutch artist's transition from nature-based imagery into pure abstraction, especially around 1916 and 1917. Then came Bornstein's encounter with American relief artist Charles Biederman (1906–2004) in the mid-1950s. All of these experiences and lessons came together during his European travels in 1957 and 1958, when Bornstein made his own first abstract reliefs.

During the early 1950s, Bornstein also began to build his professional career, successfully being accepted, on both sides of the border, into the major annual and biennial survey exhibitions that then were standard programming for art museums in

Left: Eli Bornstein, *Girl Reading*, 1948, pastel on paper, 50 x 32 cm, collection of the artist.
Right: Eli Bornstein, *Head*, c.1947, marble, 12.7 x 7.6 x 8.9 cm, Walker Art Center, Minneapolis.

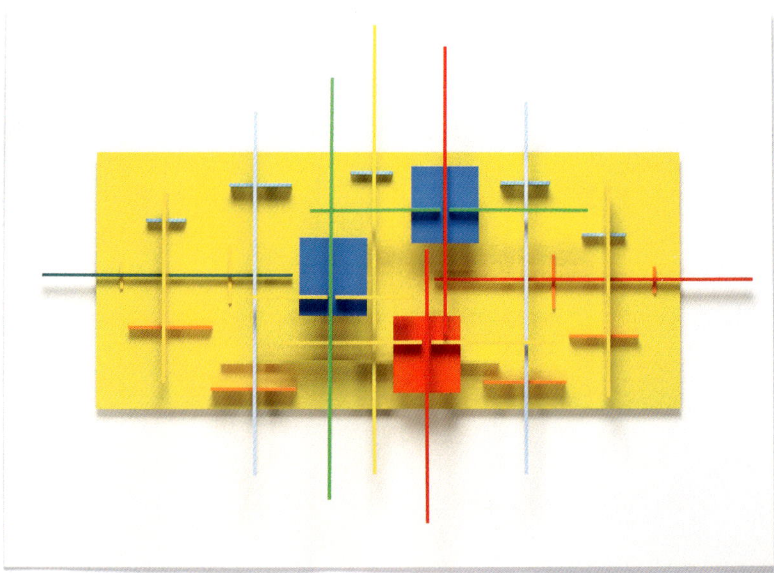

North America: at the Milwaukee Art Institute, the Walker Art Center in Minneapolis, the Art Institute of Chicago, the Pennsylvania Academy of the Fine Arts in Philadelphia, the National Gallery of Canada in Ottawa, the Montreal Museum of Fine Arts, and the Winnipeg Art Gallery, among others. His first solo show took place in 1954 at the University of Saskatchewan, followed by another in 1957. In 1956, the University of Toronto's Hart House (now the Justina M. Barnicke Gallery) held an exhibition titled *Eli Bornstein: Graphics*. Also that year, he received the Award of Merit from the Saskatchewan Arts Board in Regina.

Structurist Pathways

A decisive event of the mid-1950s was when Bornstein met the older American relief artist Charles Biederman, the pioneer, so to speak, of "Structurist art," the nature-based branch of abstract colour-relief sculpture of which he would soon become a leading practitioner. Bornstein had heretofore had doubts about Biederman's constructed reliefs, which he knew only in reproduction. But when in 1954 he read the latter's voluminous book on art history and theory, *Art as the Evolution of Visual Knowledge* (1948), and subsequently his *Letters on the New Art* (1951), he was deeply impressed. In the spring of 1956, Bornstein contacted Biederman and started corresponding with him. When he subsequently discovered that Red Wing, Minnesota, Biederman's home, was en route between Milwaukee and Saskatoon, Bornstein visited him on several occasions. Seeing Biederman's reliefs in person made Bornstein realize that they were in fact related to his own interests.

Three concepts in Biederman's writings particularly appealed to Bornstein. There was Biederman's systematic analyses of the evolution of modern art from its roots in Impressionism through to Constructivism and De Stijl, a pathway his own work had been negotiating. There was Biederman's ongoing commitment to nature—regretting how the Europeans in their formal pursuits had banished nature from art in favour of idealistic or metaphysical pursuits—an obligation that would make Structurist abstract relief art a uniquely North American phenomenon. As Biederman defined it, the task of the artist was to translate "the building method of nature into art possessing precisely

Charles Biederman, *#26, Red Wing, 1956–68*, 1956–68, painted metal, 81.3 x 114.3 x 14 cm, Minneapolis Institute of Art.

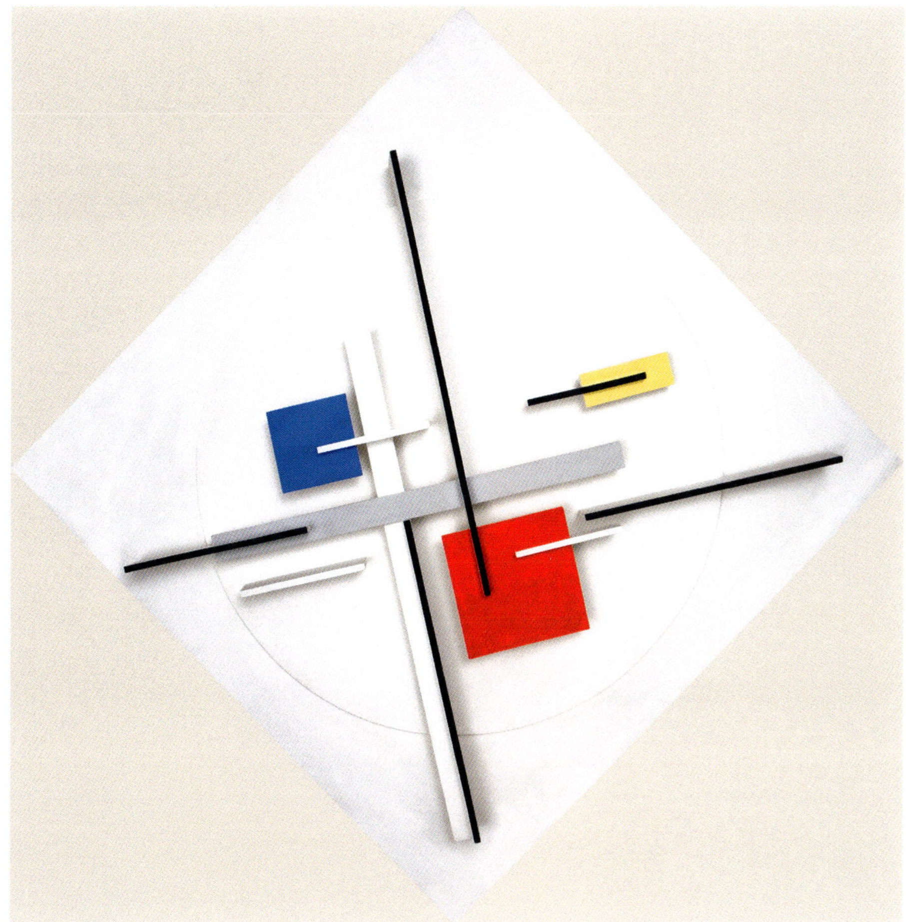

the palpable, corporeal qualities of nature—actual space forms."[21] And then there was how Biederman understood art as related to the larger society within which it was made: not art for art's sake, but art in a broader cultural sense, a conviction that Bornstein would support throughout his many writings and in his editorship of the periodical *The Structurist*, which he founded in 1960 and published for more than five decades.

While on sabbatical leave from teaching at the University of Saskatchewan, travelling in Europe during 1957 and 1958, with the specific purpose of studying Constructivism and De Stijl, Bornstein sought out many of the major European relief artists. In Paris, he visited Georges Vantongerloo (1886–1965), one of the founding members, along with Piet Mondrian, of De Stijl, an idealistic international alliance of artists, architects, and designers dedicated to creating an abstract visual vocabulary that, put to practical use, would communicate the way toward a peaceful and harmonious society. He also met Jean Gorin (1899–1981) who, in the mid-1920s, had pioneered relief constructions as an independent art form.

In London, he contacted the relief artists Kenneth Martin (1905–1984), Mary Martin (1907–1969), Victor Pasmore (1908–1998), and Anthony Hill (1930–2020); and in Amsterdam, Joost Baljeu (1925–1991). During Bornstein's sabbatical, he also travelled in England, Denmark, Norway, and Spain, and lived for a while in Punta Marina, a seaside resort near Ravenna in Italy, as well as in Amsterdam, where in 1957 he made his first relief constructions.

Jean Gorin, *Spatio-Temporelle #23*, 1966, oil on wood, 99.7 x 99.7 x 8.5 cm, University of Saskatchewan, Saskatoon.

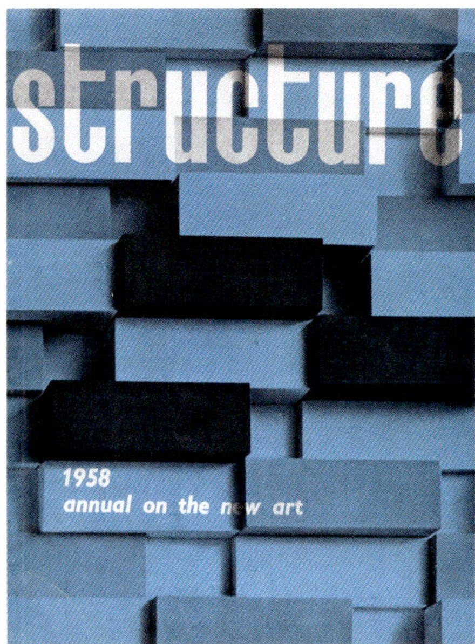

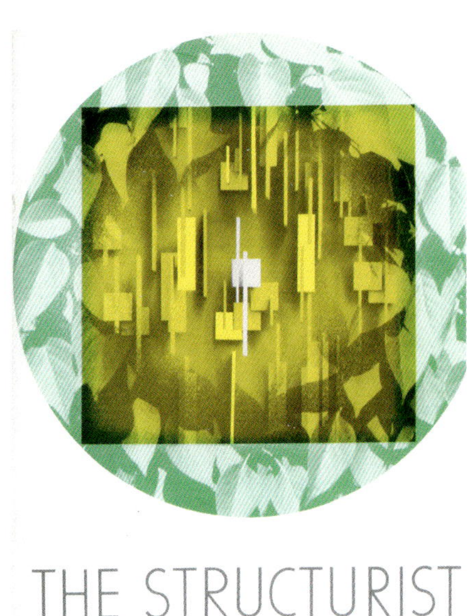

Throughout this period of travel abroad, Bornstein found himself dissatisfied with the abstract geometry of European artists' constructions. He saw Jean Gorin's work too defined by science and technology and too based on mathematical principles, and missing, as he wrote to Biederman, "a strong and necessary relationship to nature." In the same vein, Bornstein remarked on how the English confined themselves largely to unpainted industrial materials like plastic, Formica, stainless steel, and aluminum. While they took an interest in light effects, they had none in colour: that is, in colour as manifest in the structures of the natural world.[22] As Bornstein later recalled about finding his own way, it was during 1957 in Europe that his dual interests in painting and sculpture finally came together: to find resolution in an abstract constructed relief medium, which could embrace "the space, form and structure of sculpture and the colour and light of painting." [23]

First Reliefs

In 1958, following his breakthrough European sabbatical, Bornstein, back at the University of Saskatchewan, published an extensive iteration of his newly formulated aesthetic theories in the first issue of the periodical *Structure: Annual on the New Art*.[24] *Structure* was co-edited by Bornstein and the Dutch relief artist Joost Baljeu, who that year was a guest lecturer at the University of Saskatoon; also included were articles by Charles Biederman and the contemporary German composer Karlheinz Stockhausen (1928–2007). The issue was in effect a mission statement, if not a manifesto, for the "New Art," as they called it, until, later in the year, Bornstein adopted Biederman's terminology of the Structurist Relief.

After having co-edited the first issue of the periodical *Structure* in 1958, in 1960, he inaugurated his own internationally circulating journal, *The Structurist*, published out of the University of Saskatchewan, and appearing annually until 1972 and then biennially until 2000, with anniversary issues in 2010 and 2020. *The Structurist*, which drew on a roster of distinguished international writers, began, as Bornstein described it in retrospect, "as a forum dealing with the future of art and architecture, concerning interdisciplinary subjects related to many neglected considerations of how art evolved and was related to many other subjects such as science, technology, culture, education, music, etc."[25]

Left: Cover of *Structure: Annual on the New Art*, no. 1, edited by Eli Bornstein and Joost Baljeu (Saskatoon: University of Saskatchewan, 1958). Right: Cover of *The Structurist*, no. 1, "Structurist Origins/Developments," edited by Eli Bornstein (Saskatoon: University of Saskatchewan, 1960).

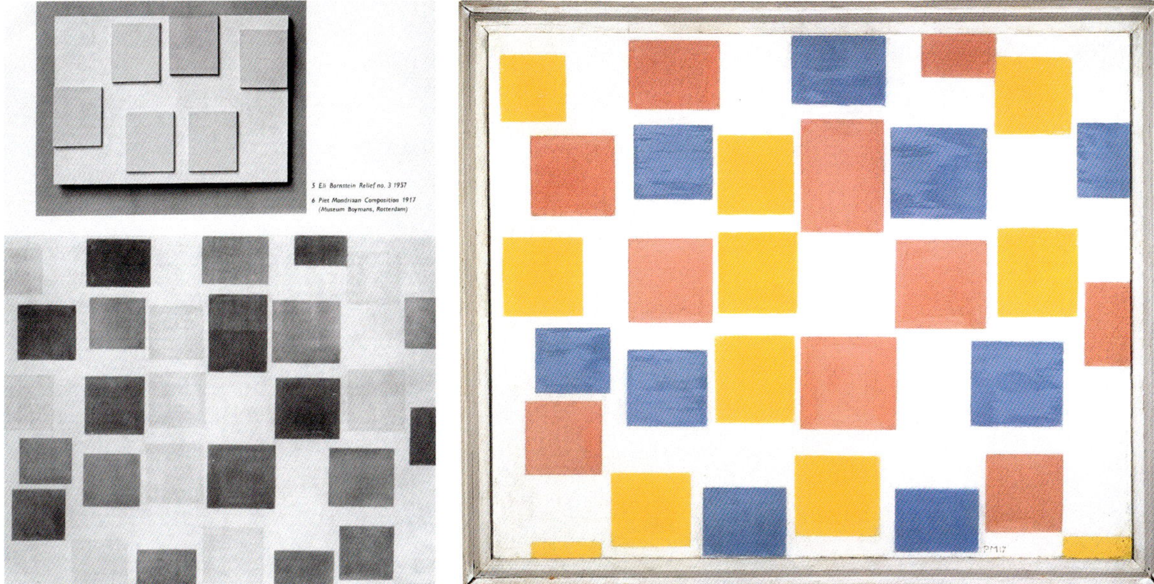

While the journal circulated Bornstein's ideas about Structurist art through the written word, his own reliefs had first been made the year before, in 1957. They were modestly constructed out of tempera in composition board or oil on wood, and composed of low, relatively large rectangles splayed out in asymmetrical compositions across a neutral background support plane. They are, as in *Structurist Relief No. 4*, 1957, mostly white on white with the addition of one or more primary colours. Their sensibility is Bornstein's own, but he does not yet stray far from the European De Stijl tradition, with its emphasis on colour and rectilinear geometry. Indeed, in the inaugural issue of *Structure*, on page 36, he tellingly juxtaposes one of his first 1957 reliefs to Piet Mondrian's *Composition with Color Planes* 2, 1917, a model he had already applied the year before in the across-the-surface dispersed composition of *The Island*, 1956.

Here was the start of what would be Bornstein's unwavering commitment to the evolution of the Structurist Relief as it launched the colour dynamics of painting into the sculptural world of space and light. Over the next six decades, he would steadfastly enhance its compositional potentials and enrich its expressive depths. Step by step his formal elements would become more diverse, their relationship and rhythmic interplay more complex and their colours more manifold, the reliefs increasingly resonant with the diversity of nature's unfolding, always the subject of his intense daily study.

The 1960s saw the first of many solo exhibitions of Bornstein's Structurist reliefs, including in 1965 and 1967 at the Kazimir Gallery on Michigan Avenue in Chicago. Kazimir Karpuszko (1925–2009) was a young art dealer, author, and curator who had become involved in the Structurist art movement. In 1968, he was instrumental in the group exhibition *Relief/Construction/Relief*, which opened at the Museum of Contemporary Art Chicago, and toured through the eastern United States. Karpuszko's commitment to Bornstein's work would persist into subsequent decades and, in 1982, he would curate *Eli Bornstein: Selected Works / Œuvres choisies, 1957–1982* for the Mendel Art Gallery, Saskatoon, an exhibition that toured to the Art Gallery of York University, Toronto, and other venues in eastern Canada, as well as to the University of Wisconsin in Milwaukee.[26]

Left: Page 36 of the inaugural issue of *Structure: Annual on the New Art* (1958), illustrating one of Eli Bornstein's first Structurist reliefs alongside Piet Mondrian's *Composition with Color Planes 2*, 1917. Right: Piet Mondrian, *Composition with Color Planes 2*, 1917, oil on canvas, 48 x 61.5 cm, Museum Boijmans van Beuningen, Rotterdam.

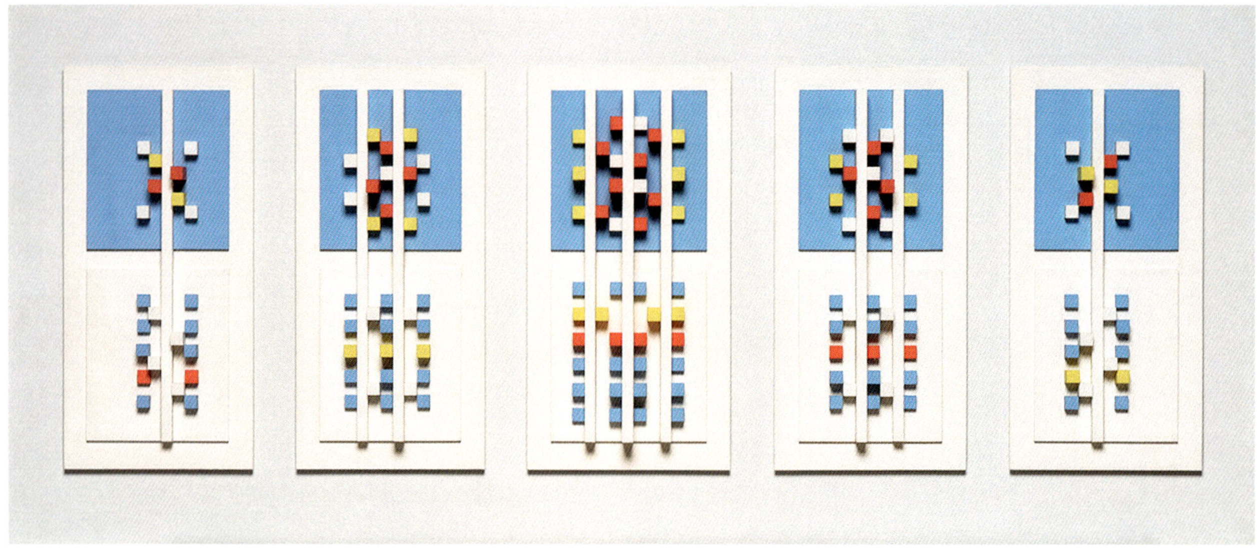

A Time of Innovation

As Bornstein's European journey in 1957 and 1958 had proven, summers and sabbaticals, unburdened by teaching and administrative duties, were valuable times for travel and research, and opportunities for concentrated creative innovation, which he took advantage of throughout the 1960s.[27] During this time period, Bornstein also constructed a federal government commission for the new Winnipeg International Airport, a work entitled *Structurist Relief in Fifteen Parts*, 1962. When the terminal was demolished some four decades later, the sculpture was removed, restored, refinished for exterior use, and reinstalled in 2014 on the facade of the Max Bell Centre at the University of Manitoba. A model version of the work, titled *Structurist Relief in Five Parts*, 1962, had been purchased by the National Gallery of Canada in 1965.

Innovation also came through the production of two important series created from 1964 to 1967: the Canoe Lake Series and the Sea Series. Both series exploited Bornstein's newly liberated colour palette, as the artist also honed his ways of making foregrounds and backgrounds conjoin and interact.

The Canoe Lake Series, begun in 1964 (and named after the celebrated place where Tom Thomson [1877–1917] painted), originated in Algonquin Park, where Bornstein spent the summer in a cabin owned by a friend of Murray Adaskin. The reliefs' layered constructions, their deep plays of light and shadow, and their colour orchestrations, now freed from the primaries, evoke lakeshores and the foliage of deep woods. Bornstein's growing propensity for colour complexities was something of a departure from more Structurist orthodoxies, which Charles Biederman had warned him about rushing into.[28] Fittingly, during that July, Bornstein met up with A.Y. Jackson (1882–1974) when the Group of Seven painter was on a short visit to Algonquin Park. A photograph shows the two artists in conversation seated before a window in Adaskin's own cabin.

As Structurist works of the early 1960s, the Canoe Lake Series reliefs are a little atypical for the period in that they quite squarely occupy the whole of their white background planes. In contrast, Bornstein's *Structurist Relief No. 1*, 1966, was more usual, its relief elements clustered toward the centre, leaving the support plane largely neutral, its corners empty. This was the common way to compose, as we can glean from the illustrations in an article titled "Structurist Art," published in May 1967 in the magazine *Chicago*

Eli Bornstein, *Structurist Relief in Five Parts*, Model Version, 1962, birch relief with oil paint, 54.7 x 130.5 x 7.1 cm, with non-integral mount, National Gallery of Canada, Ottawa.

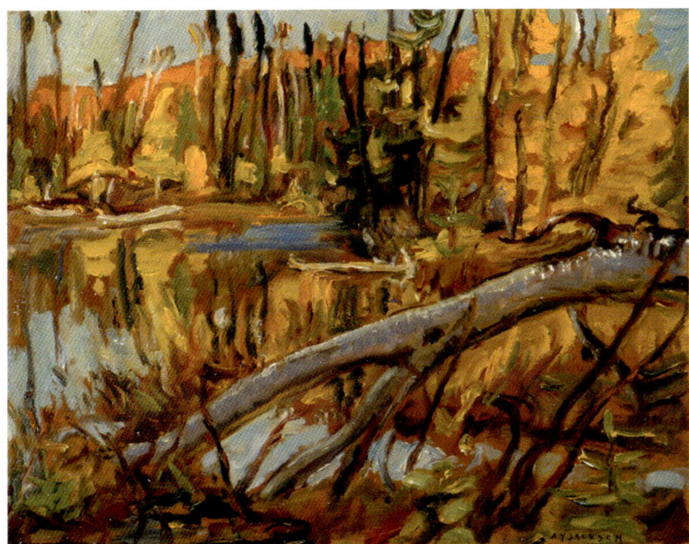

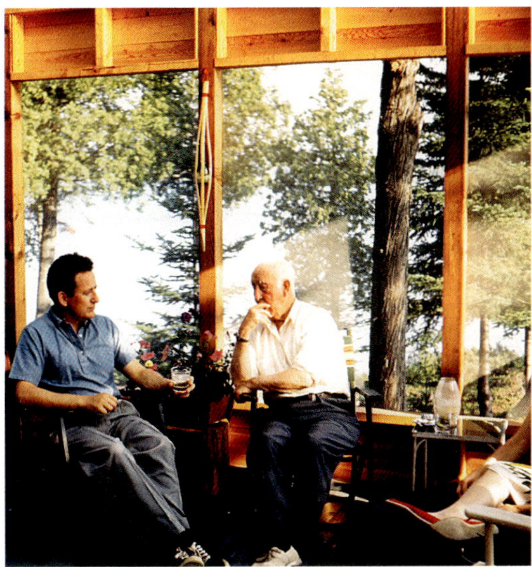

Omnibus. The article was dedicated to the new generation of artists who were following in the footsteps of Biederman and Bornstein. Working in the United States were William Jordan, David Barr (1939–2015), and Lawrence Booth; in Canada, Ron Kostyniuk (b.1941), Don McNamee (1938–1994), and Elizabeth Willmott (b.1928), the latter of the three among the most prominent of Bornstein's students. The *Chicago Omnibus* article further described the Structurist movement in 1967 as "a New World phenomenon now based at the University of Saskatchewan."

Another innovation came with Bornstein's Sea Series, in which the artist was clearly seeking new ways to animate his support planes. In these works, he stretches his now larger, flat component colour planes outward until they more fully occupy the background plane, reaching out into its four corners (see, for example, *Structurist Relief No. 3* [Sea Series], 1966–67).[29] Here Bornstein is not only taking another important step toward enlivening those ground planes, but he has also taken prescient steps toward defining the terms of his own individual stylistic and expressive pathway forward.

The Sea Series as well as the concurrent Double-Plane reliefs originated in 1966 to 1967, in California, where Bornstein spent a sabbatical year away from teaching, living near Big Sur on a mountaintop overlooking the Pacific Ocean. A journal entry recalls how his eyes "opened daily to an immense sky above and the great Pacific Ocean below that could as well have been the great prairie plane of Saskatchewan."[30] The solution of the Double-Plane reliefs was to fold his ground planes down the middle at 45 degrees as if they were half-opened books, in effect to enfold them and bring them inside. This seemed simple enough in its own way, but it complicated exponentially the task of composing the multiple colour components that were now nested between their also coloured pages, those thin tiles of colour that thrust themselves dynamically into space and were observable from multiple angles.

During this period of innovation, in 1969, Bornstein and his wife, Christina, née Girgulis, librarian and actress—they were married in 1965—built their modernist house, low and ground-flung in harmony with the prairie flatness. It featured long rectangular skylights above the major hanging walls that allow the changing daylight, from morn to dusk and through the seasons, to illuminate the reliefs installed below. The house was

Left: A.Y. Jackson, *Beaver Lake, Combermere*, 1961, oil on panel, 34.2 x 26.7 x 0.6 cm, Ottawa Art Gallery. Right: Eli Bornstein and A.Y. Jackson at Murray Adaskin's cabin at Canoe Lake, Ontario, 1964, photographer unknown.

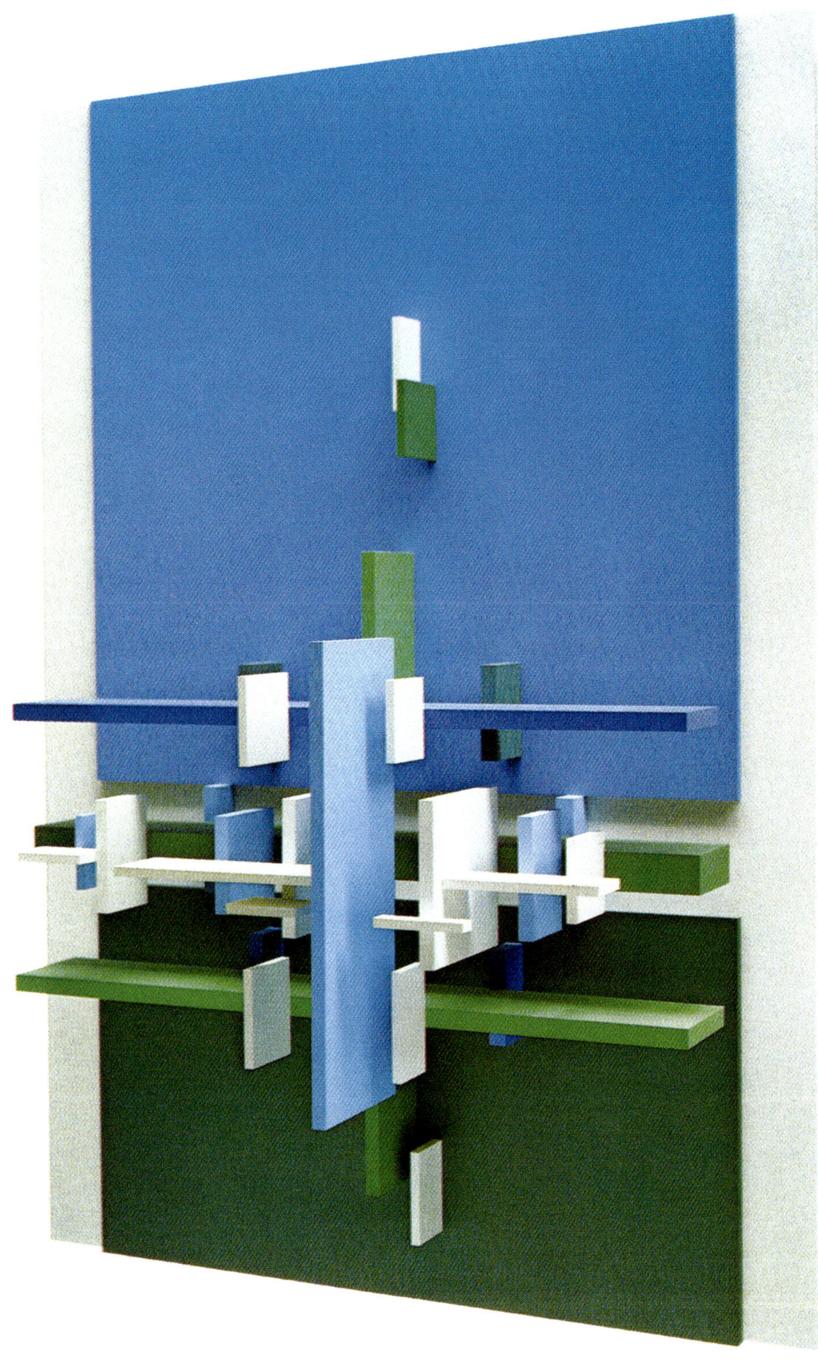

situated next to the South Saskatchewan River, which Bornstein describes as "an unfolding ribbon or screen of colour" that reflects back the continually changing phenomena of nature: slow and constant in its underlying geographical wholeness before which and within which life, light, and colour endlessly change. The prairie riverbank is "my school and my church," Bornstein writes.[31]

Eli Bornstein, *Structurist Relief No. 3* (Sea Series), 1966–67, enamel on Plexiglas and aluminum, 86.5 x 61 x 15.6 cm, collection of the artist.

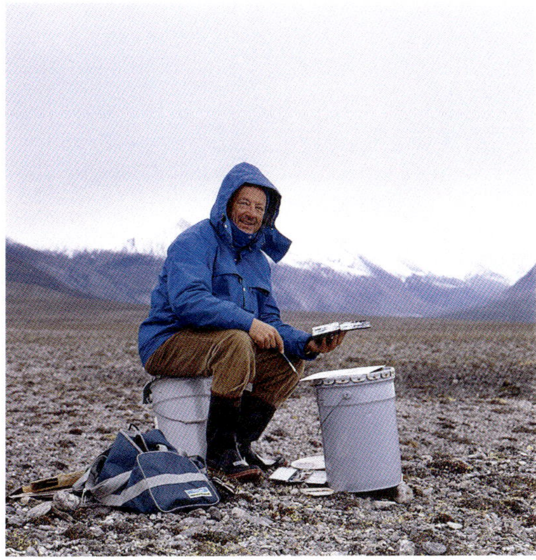

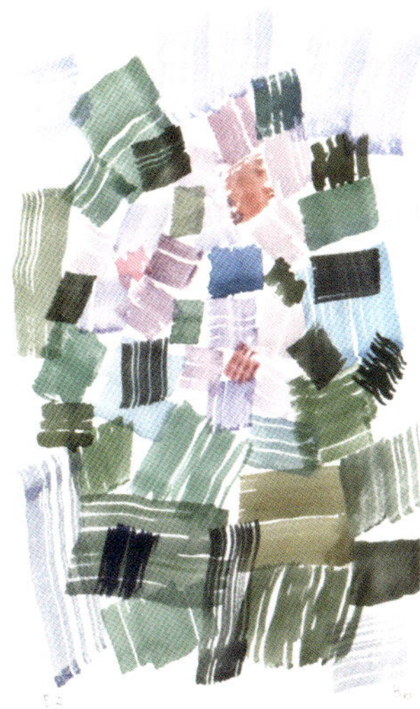

The Impact of the Arctic

Among Bornstein's travels were three foundational trips to the Canadian Arctic, the first in 1964 with Murray Adaskin and the anthropologist Bob Williamson. Subsequently, during the summers of 1986 and 1987, he returned to the Arctic again, this time with his University of Saskatchewan colleague the photographer Hans Dommasch (1926–2017). Out of those latter two summers emerged an exceptional body of drawings, paintings, and, back home in the studio, a series of Structurist reliefs such as *Hexaplane Structurist Relief No. 2* (Arctic Series), 1995–98. He kept a journal—the Arctic Journals, which eventually ran to some 24,000 words—in whose pages Bornstein recorded eloquently his explorations of the macro-landscape of the fjords, glaciers, and icebergs, and the micro-landscape of moss, lichens, and Arctic flowers.[32]

Bornstein kept a journal through most of his life, writing in longhand; but, beginning with the *Arctic Journals* from 1986 and 1987, he began to have it formally transcribed. His journal entries from 1990 up to 2017 run to 1,136 typewritten pages recording his thoughts on life, and on art in the context of the larger natural and human world. Rich in autobiographical reminiscences and eloquently poetic descriptions of nature, they form an intimate panorama of Bornstein's exterior and interior universes. In the concluding paragraphs of his *Arctic Journals*, he writes about the profound impact of his northern experiences:

> Somehow, clarity of vision and purpose seem more attainable in the Arctic. The wildness... or the wilderness... remain the ultimate hope for our survival or preservation in revealing what is most important. It makes or allows one to see more clearly that character is the supreme beauty. True character refers to genuine essence. It is a kind of identity that is unequivocal and fundamental—neither superficial nor pretentious—and as such is surely the highest form of beauty. The Arctic still has that power of essential character that can inform and instruct us without distraction. It can reveal to us a sense of identity with the earth and all living things that modern living tends to dispel.[33]

Left: Eli Bornstein painting at Ellesmere Island, 1986, photograph by Hans Dommasch. Right: Eli Bornstein, *Arctic Study No. 7*, 1986, watercolour on paper, 37.8 x 28.6 cm, collection of the artist.

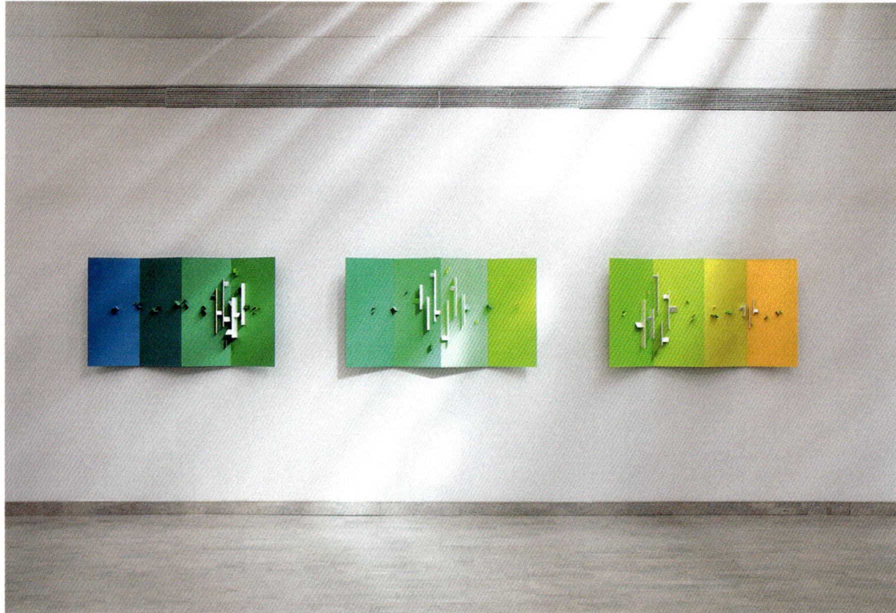

This is exalted language that rises into incantation, a kind of "inner seeing," as Canadian artist Lawren S. Harris (1885–1970) might have said. Certainly, the Arctic paintings by both Harris and A.Y. Jackson from their travels in the summer of 1930 were somewhere on Bornstein's mind as he set out for Ellesmere Island. Indeed, only a few days after his arrival, he threw down the competitive gauntlet to his Group of Seven predecessors, convinced that his Structurist methods could more authentically embody northern nature than the representational paintings of Harris and Jackson.[34] But, compare Harris's *Icebergs, Davis Strait*, 1930, to Bornstein's *Multiplane Structurist Relief IV, No. 1* (Arctic Series), 1986–87: even though the two artists interpreted the Arctic in stylistically different ways, they saw their icy landscapes with shared eyes. The cold palette of Harris's painting registers the same iridescence, the same brittleness, the same clarity, and the same silence that will characterize Bornstein's Structurist reliefs, with their Plexiglas components. There is true kinship here.[35]

In 1987, Bornstein showed his watercolour studies from the Arctic at the Art Placement Gallery in Saskatoon, and in 1990, again at Art Placement, his studies from a 1988 trip to Newfoundland, along with his 1989 *Riverbank Studies* watercolours executed in his own South Saskatchewan River backyard.

Major Exhibitions and a Life in Art

At the time of this book's publication, Bornstein continues, in the twenty-first century, to expand on the potentials of the Structurist Relief, initiating a new body of work he titles *Tripart Hexaplane Constructions*. Like sculptures, they are walk-around, built out of three 320-degree Double-Plane reliefs backed up against one another and raised on a slim aluminum pedestal. But unlike sculptures-in-the-round, they reveal themselves only part by part as we circle them. It is with the long horizontal Multiplanes, however, whether seen individually, or as the tour de force River-Screen Series triptych, 1989–96, that the reliefs reach states of transcendent sublimity.

Installation view (*left to right*) of *Structurist Relief No. 6*, 1999–2000, *Structurist Relief No. 7*, 2000–2001, and *Structurist Relief No. 8*, 2000–2002, by Eli Bornstein, at the Mendel Art Gallery, Saskatoon, 2013, photograph by Troy Mamer.

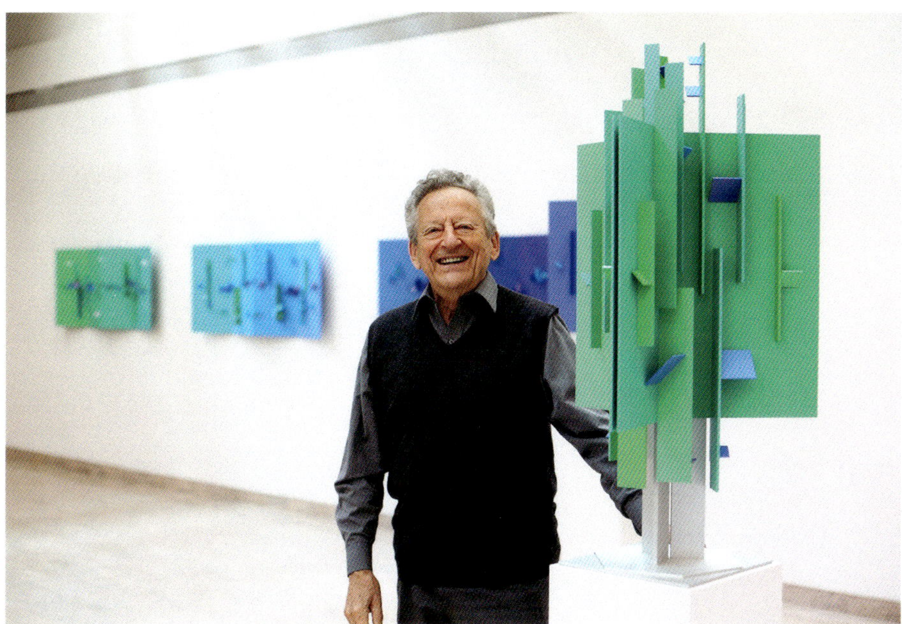

Alongside many group exhibitions, north and south of the border, that have celebrated Bornstein's contributions to modern art, the Mendel Art Gallery gave Bornstein a second retrospective in 1996, *Eli Bornstein: Art Toward Nature*, curated by the Dutch art historian Jonneke Fritz-Jobse, and in 2013, a third large-scale show, *An Art at the Mercy of Light: Recent Works by Eli Bornstein*, curated by Winnipeg art historian and frequent insightful writer on Bornstein, Oliver A.I. Botar. The installation took full advantage of the Mendel's skylit galleries, the experience well captured in the catalogue by Troy Mamer's photographs of the installation.[36] In 2019, the Remai Modern in Saskatoon staged a mini-retrospective, *Artist in Focus: Eli Bornstein*, with works drawn from its own collection and from the artist's home and studio.

On the private gallery scene, there were exhibitions at the Forum Gallery in New York (2007) and in galleries in Saskatoon, Vancouver, and Victoria. As well, since the *Tree of Knowledge*, Bornstein has completed important public commissions in Winnipeg, Regina, and Saskatoon, including his monumental *Four Part Vertical Double Plane Structurist Relief* (Winter Sky Series), 1980–83, for Regina's Wascana Centre. His major awards since 1956 include the Allied Arts Medal, Royal Architectural Institute of Canada (1968); D.Litt., University of Saskatchewan (1990); and the Saskatchewan Order of Merit (2008). As a culminating honour, in 2019 he was inducted as a Member of the Order of Canada in recognition of his "boundless creativity," and for how "his approach sheds light on current environmental issues."[37]

But finally, even as we evaluate Bornstein's Structurist reliefs—their stylistic evolution, their industrial precision, their luminous palette, their obeisance to nature, their grand historical resonances—we must remember that they are also, as the critic Steven Cochrane observed, reviewing *An Art at the Mercy of Light* in the *Winnipeg Free Press*, "emphatically, unapologetically beautiful."[38]

Eli Bornstein with one of his Structurist reliefs in *An Art at the Mercy of Light: Recent Works by Eli Bornstein* at the Mendel Art Gallery, Saskatoon, 2013, photograph by Michelle Berg.

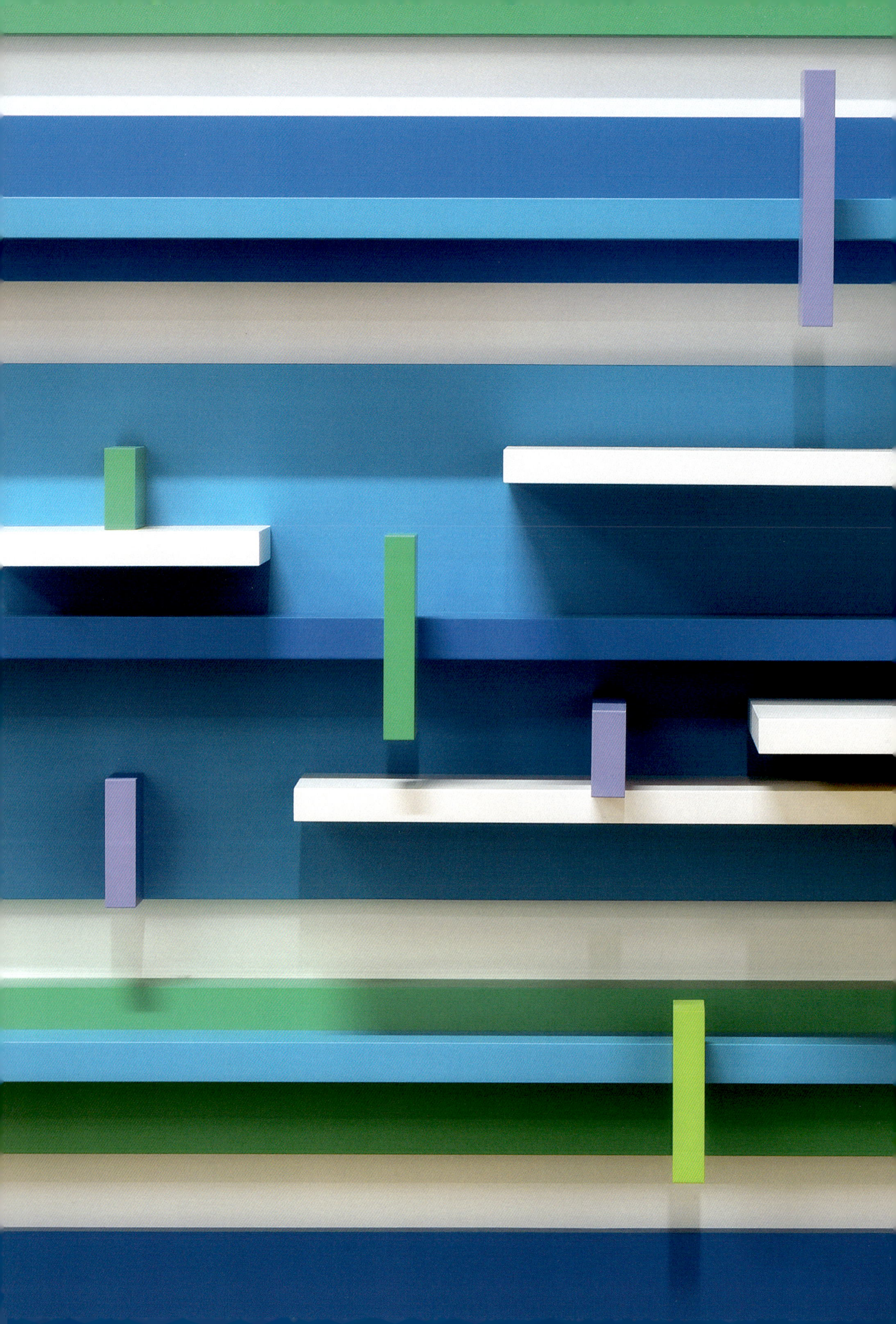

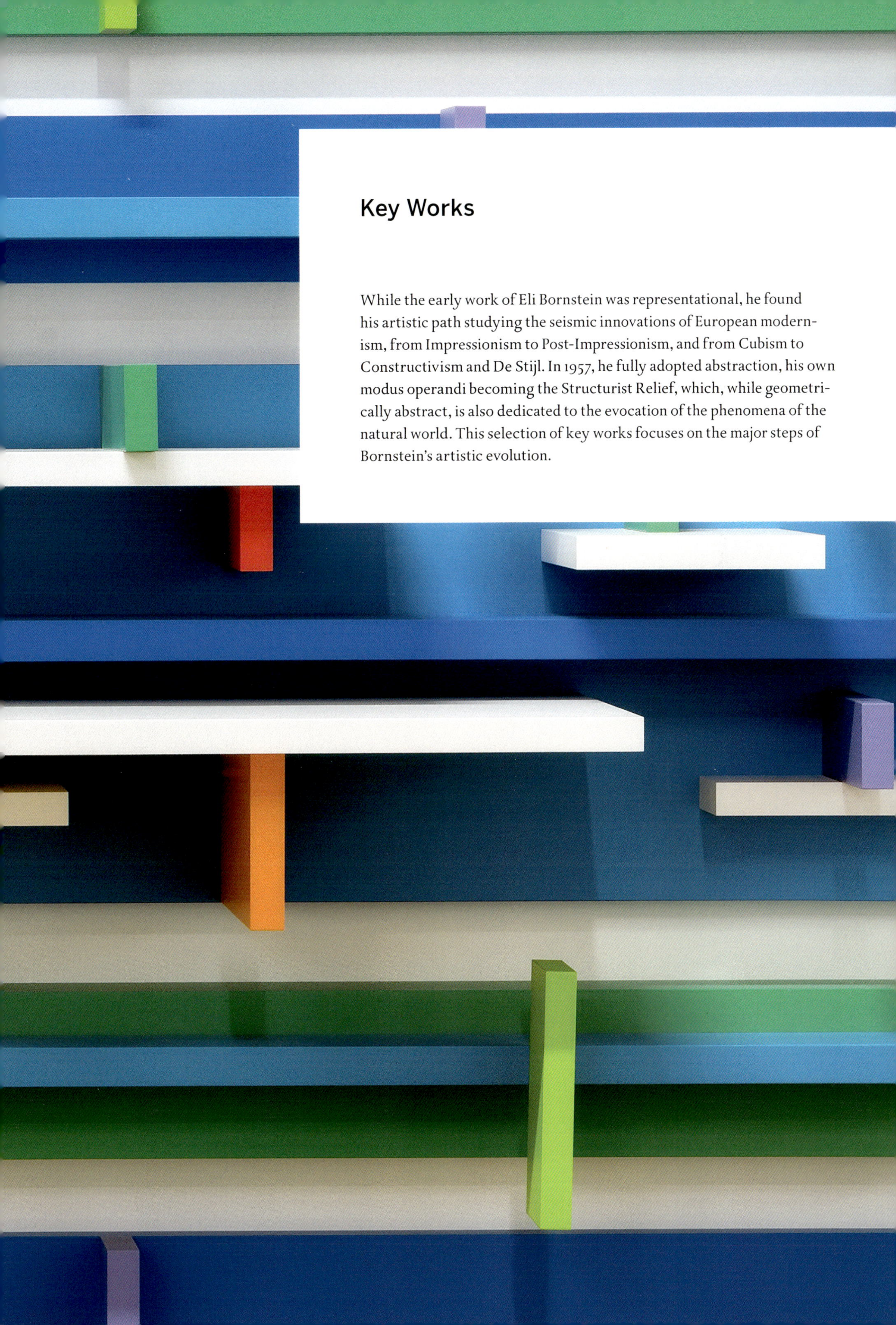

Key Works

While the early work of Eli Bornstein was representational, he found his artistic path studying the seismic innovations of European modernism, from Impressionism to Post-Impressionism, and from Cubism to Constructivism and De Stijl. In 1957, he fully adopted abstraction, his own modus operandi becoming the Structurist Relief, which, while geometrically abstract, is also dedicated to the evocation of the phenomena of the natural world. This selection of key works focuses on the major steps of Bornstein's artistic evolution.

Saskatoon
1954

Gouache on gesso panel, 58.5 x 74 cm
Private collection

At the start of his career in art, Bornstein created representational works. This jaunty gouache painting depicts the Bessborough, one of Canada's grand Château-style railway hotels, which opened in Saskatoon in 1935. Its composition is dynamic, unstable, and even dance-like. It reminds us that a young Bornstein had played percussion in jazz bands. In journal entries, he has recalled how jazz improvisation stimulated his early path into abstraction and was an important factor in how he would come to compose his Structurist reliefs.

Saskatoon may be a composition of tilted geometries and Cubistic fragmentation, but it is no imaginary rendering. It is more or less topologically correct. We are set down in the middle of Twenty-First Street, Saskatoon's major business thoroughfare, looking toward the hotel with the Canadian National Rail station behind us. In 1954, the Bessborough was still the city's tallest building. In the centre foreground, at the intersection of Twenty-First Street and Second Avenue, stands the 1929 war memorial cenotaph showing the west side of its four-faced clock (for traffic reasons, the cenotaph was relocated in 1957). The hotel reigns over a nearly symmetrical composition reminiscent of images by the German American artist Lyonel Feininger (1871–1956), especially his Cubist-inspired exultant Gothic church in *The Market Church at Halle*, 1930. Like Feininger, Bornstein peoples his streetscape with little stick-like figures (and some cars), and he even, in Feininger's spirit, crowns his edifice with a radiant aureole. But where Feininger's voice is a touch stentorian—loud, powerful, and authoritative—Bornstein's is light and scintillating.

When by 1954 Bornstein found his way to Cubism, it was a near inevitable consequence of what had become his step-by-step study of the development of modernist art from Impressionism and forward. His challenge was to master its evolutionary progression, to find his place within it, and eventually to further it. Successively, Bornstein

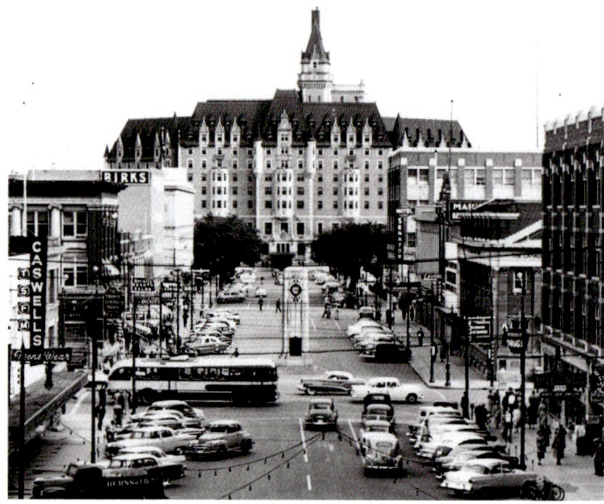

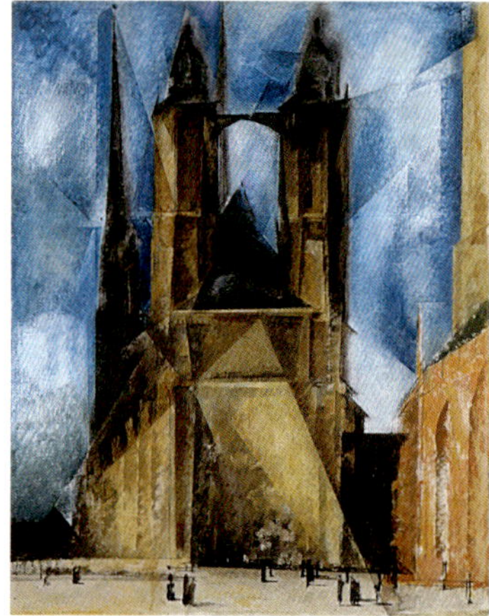

Previous spread: Eli Bornstein, *Structurist Relief No. 4-11* (Sea Series) (detail), 1965, acrylic enamel, Plexiglas on aluminum, 86.5 x 61.1 cm, Remai Modern, Saskatoon. Left: Bird's-eye view of 21st Street East, Saskatoon, 1955, photographer unknown, Saskatoon Public Library. Right: Lyonel Feininger, *The Market Church at Halle*, 1930, oil on canvas, 38 x 29 cm, Pinakothek der Moderne, Munich. © Estate of Lyonel Feininger / Bild-Kunst, Bonn / CARCC Ottawa 2025.

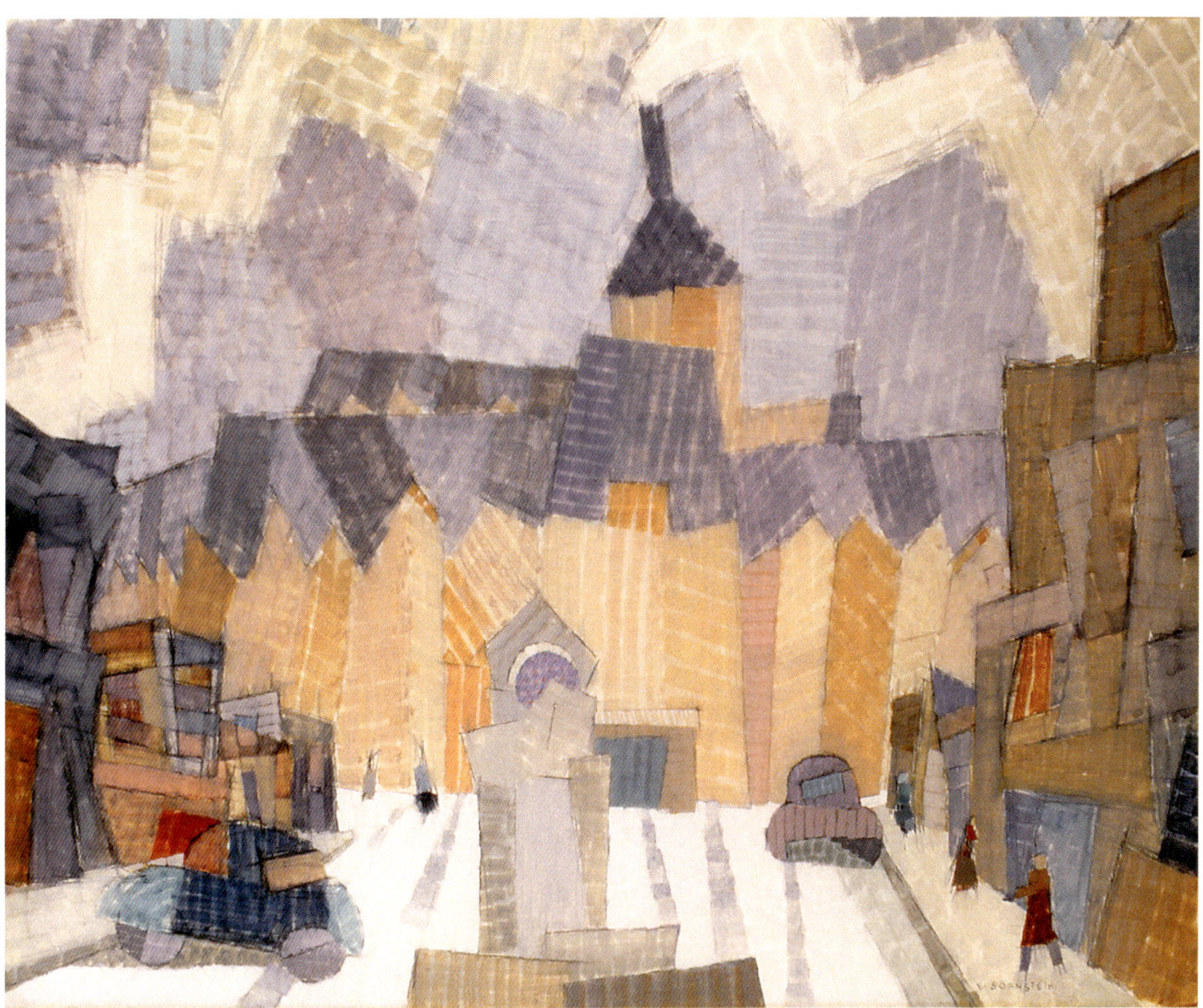

had painted with the broken brush strokes of the Impressionist; had learned from Post-Impressionist master Paul Cézanne (1839–1906) how to give Impressionism form and structure; and had gone on to master the style known as Analytic Cubism, which confounded traditional ways of representing depth, instead fragmenting its subject matter into quasi-abstract shallow webs of interpenetrating planes.

Feininger's city views also influenced Bornstein's Parisian drawings, like *Porte St. Denis*, 1954 (which was also issued as a lithograph). Moreover, the fractured scaffolding on the building's facade is a premonition of Bornstein's monumental constructed sculpture *Aluminum Construction (Tree of Knowledge)*, 1956.

The Island
1956

Watercolour on paper, 53.5 x 74 cm
Collection of the artist

The Island was the last representational watercolour painting that Bornstein made before he started to construct purely abstract reliefs. Working on the coast of Maine, he crafted a landscape of trees, rocks, and water using a vocabulary of similarly sized and semi-transparent rectangular swatches. The variations of green, brown, and blue-grey lines define the natural elements, but otherwise matter dissolves into shimmering light, the island like a mirage emerging from mist.

The Island incorporates the succession of the lessons that Bornstein had been learning over the past half decade from major movements in European modernism: Impressionism, Post-Impressionism, and Cubism. The latter, as he applies it in *Saskatoon*, 1954, organizes his pastel colours into a dynamic, tightly knit decorative pattern work. But something else is afoot in *The Island*, where Bornstein unknits all of that so that instead he can evenly spread his planar components—now individualized and similarly sized—across the whole expanse of his white paper ground and into its very corners.

It may not be self-evident at first glance, but Bornstein has taken on a new challenge here, namely that of the Dutch artist Piet Mondrian (1872–1944), who himself was in transition from representation to abstraction at the end of the 1910s. Bornstein's model for *The Island*'s dispersals was no doubt a series of Mondrian paintings from 1917 entitled Compositions with Color Planes. It is fair to suppose so because in a 1958 article published in the periodical *Structure*, he juxtaposes Mondrian's *Composition with Color Planes* 2,1917, to one of his own first reliefs, underscoring its importance to this moment of his own artistic development.[1] Mondrian, in his series, deploys an assembly of small rectangles of muted reds, yellows, and blues, evenly distributing them across a white ground. They are not absolute rectangles, and their irregularity, much like those of *The Island*, causes them to waver ever so slightly, as if still existing in what may be Mondrian's last faint acknowledgement of illusionistic space.

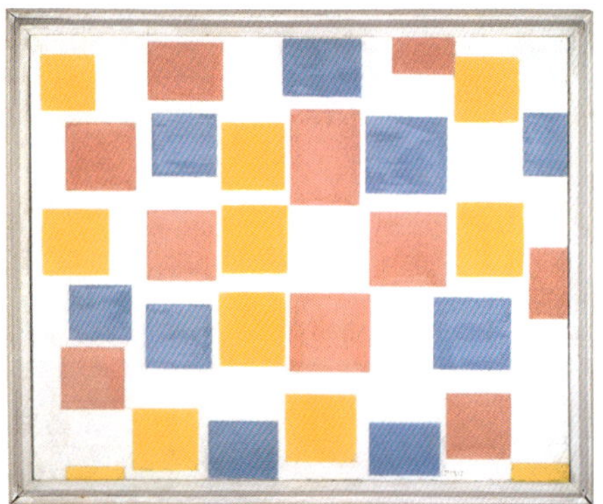

Piet Mondrian, *Composition with Color Planes 2*, 1917, oil on canvas, 48 x 61.5 cm, Museum Boijmans van Beuningen, Rotterdam.

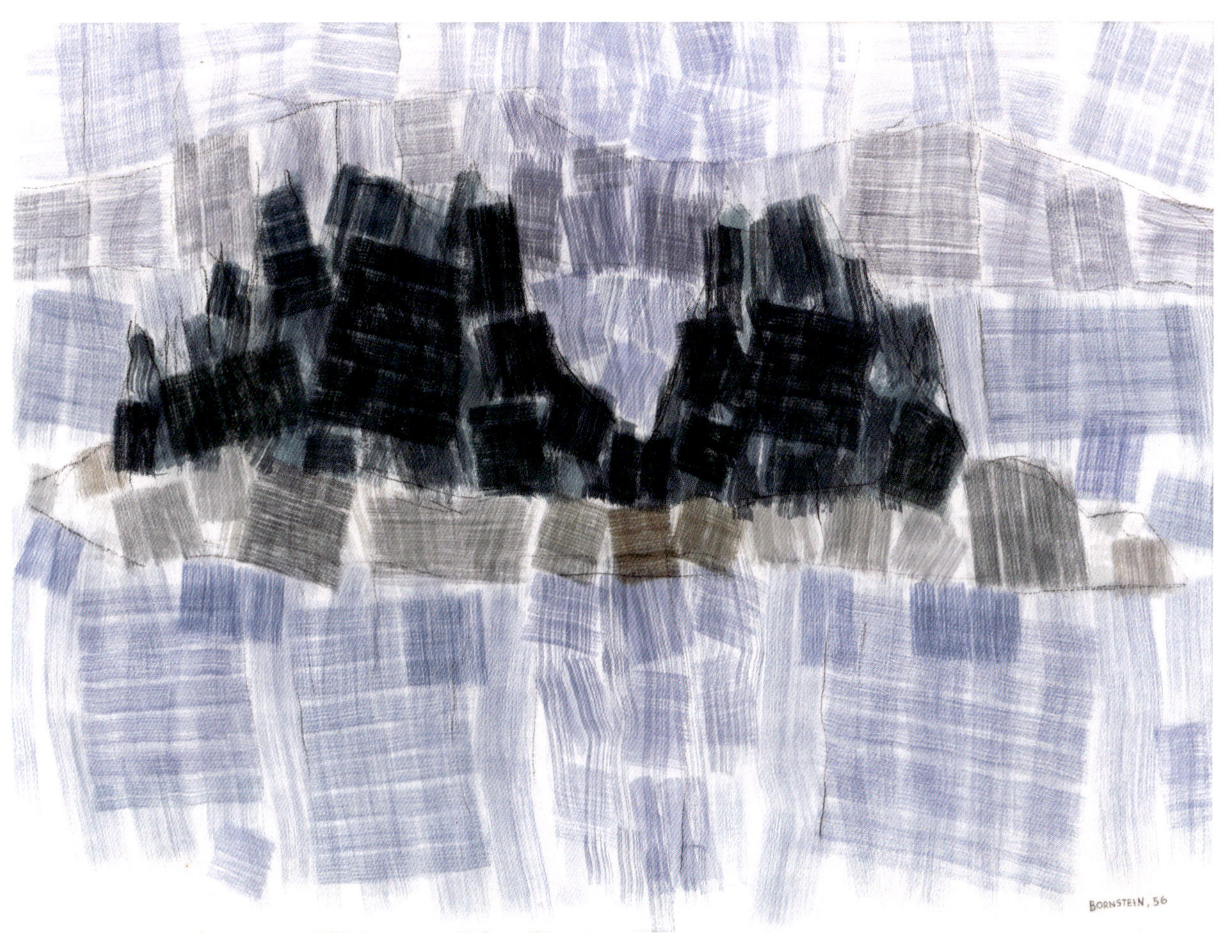
BORNSTEIN, 56

Aluminum Construction (Tree of Knowledge) 1956

Welded aluminum on stone base, 458 cm (height)
Saskatchewan Teachers' Federation Building, Saskatoon

In 1956, *Aluminum Construction (Tree of Knowledge)* was the first abstract public work to be installed in Saskatoon.[1] The initial public responses, as expressed in letters to the daily newspaper, the *Star-Phoenix*, ranged from anger to outrage and hostility. Perhaps they did not like, want, or understand abstract art. Many called for its removal and demanded that the artist be dismissed by the University of Saskatchewan. Bornstein himself was on sabbatical leave in Europe at the time, but the one person who in his absence came to his defence publicly was the musician and composer Murray Adaskin (1906–2002). As Bornstein recounts, he "as valiantly championed the validity of abstract art as he had championed new music."[2] In 1963, the American critic Clement Greenberg (1909–1994), touring the prairies for the magazine *Canadian Art*, despite some reservations, called the "overall conception" of *Tree of Knowledge* "magnificent," concluding that "the artist responsible for it stands or falls as a major artist and nothing else."[3]

Tree of Knowledge was commissioned for the new Saskatchewan Teachers' Federation Building at 902 Spadina Crescent East, designed by Saskatoon architect Tinos Kortes (1926–2014), who had also recommended Bornstein for the project. The sculpture was manufactured in Regina, where the necessary equipment for welding aluminum was available, and then shipped to Saskatoon. In 1969, the work was moved to the new Saskatchewan Teachers' Federation Building at 2317 Arlington Avenue.

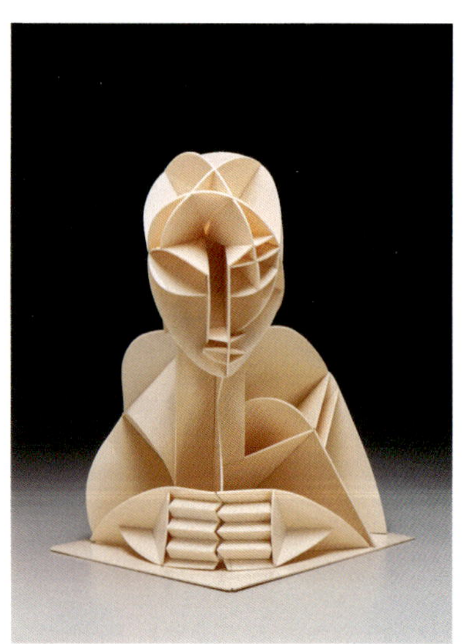

Naum Gabo, *Constructed Head No. 2*, 1923–34, ivory rhodoid, 41.9 x 42.5 x 30.5 cm, Dallas Museum of Art.

As a sculptor, Bornstein had heretofore primarily been a carver of wood and stone, often working with an eye to Constantin Brâncuși (1876–1957), and attentive to the Romanian artist's formal simplifications and his sensitivity to materials. In contrast, *Tree of Knowledge*, with its intricate internal scaffolding and its out-thrust reflective aluminum plates, shows the influence of Russian Constructivism. Constructivist sculpture, such as *Constructed Head No. 2*, 1923–34, by Naum Gabo (1890–1977), is assembled or built, usually with non-traditional industrial materials like metal and plastics.

Bornstein began to transition from working with mass to openwork metallic constructing during a stay in New York while he was envisioning how *Tree of Knowledge* should look. In his earliest models for the sculpture, he pushes light-reflective rectangular metal planes outward into space from a heftier inner core in a configuration suggesting something like pollen grains releasing from a giant flower stamen. The materials are brass and bronze, metals he was familiar with from jewellery-making classes at college. In subsequent models, he dissolved the heavy central core into an airy structure that then evolved into the final monumental 4.58-metre-tall welded aluminum construction.

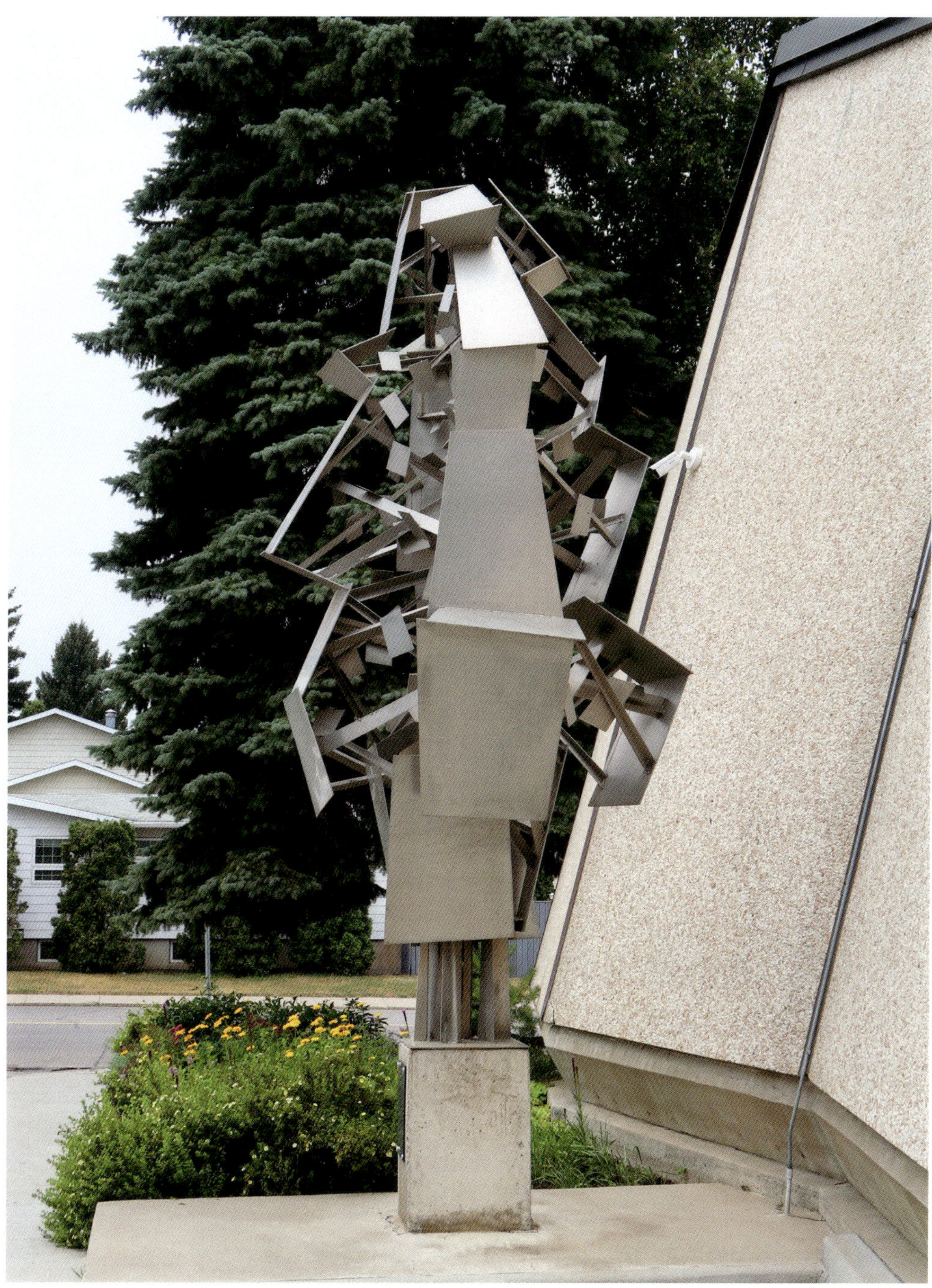

Tree of Knowledge belongs to the tradition of Cubistic abstraction, its configurations derived from the deconstruction of the appearances of the visual world; it is not to be understood as a pure abstract sculpture. Its formal components had already been predicted in drawings from a couple of years before—including *Porte St. Denis*, 1954—influenced by German American artist Lyonel Feininger (1871–1956). But now the subject matter is the natural rather than the urban world: the free-floating atmospheric rectangles of the contemporary watercolour *The Island*, 1956, here extrude as shimmering aluminum plates energized by real light. The structural whole is a geometric redesign of the anatomy of a coniferous tree, with its network of branches, tiered and drooping, and its natural growth re-experienced in the rhythmic bustle of light and shadow.

Structurist Relief No. 18-II
1958–60

Birchwood blocks on aluminum panel over wood panel, painted with acrylic urethane enamel, 259 x 259 x 22.9 cm
University of Saskatchewan, Saskatoon

In 1957, within a year of completing *Aluminum Construction (Tree of Knowledge)*, Bornstein, who in the meantime had established contact with the American relief artist Charles Biederman (1906–2004), abandoned abstracting from nature to begin to construct reliefs using pure rectilinear geometric forms and primary colours. *Structurist Relief No. 18-II* is the most monumental of his early Structurist reliefs, as he would call them. The work was originally designed for the lobby of the Arts and Science Building, University of Saskatchewan, in Saskatoon, and subsequently moved to the entrance of the Murray Library.

At this point in his career, Bornstein chose to work in three dimensions as opposed to flat painting. While the latter is fixed and viewed from a frontal position, the appearance of the relief, its individual parts, shifts as the viewer's eye and body change position. Rather than being static pictures, Bornstein's reliefs exist as real objects, like chairs or tables, for example, inhabiting with us the same physical space and environment.

Structurist Relief No. 18-II heftily embodies the principles of Dutch painter Piet Mondrian (1872–1944), including his decision to limit his palette to primary colours, but Bornstein significantly repurposes them to relief construction. He first revealed his interest in Mondrian in the free-floating rectangles of colour in *The Island*, 1956.

Another influence that informs this work came during Bornstein's 1957 to 1958 sabbatical leave when he travelled in Europe and the U.K., where his main purpose was to study the work of the Russian Constructivists in addition to Mondrian and the De Stijl movement. During the trip, he also made his own first modest and austere relief works, like *Structurist Relief No. 4*, 1957, from which the grander *Structurist Relief No. 18-II* would soon evolve. *Structurist Relief No. 4* is constructed of several squarish white rectangles on a white ground, with the exception of one dazzlingly blue one. The squares have slightly different depths, as we can tell by the shadows they cast, and they are distributed so that they animate the entire ground.

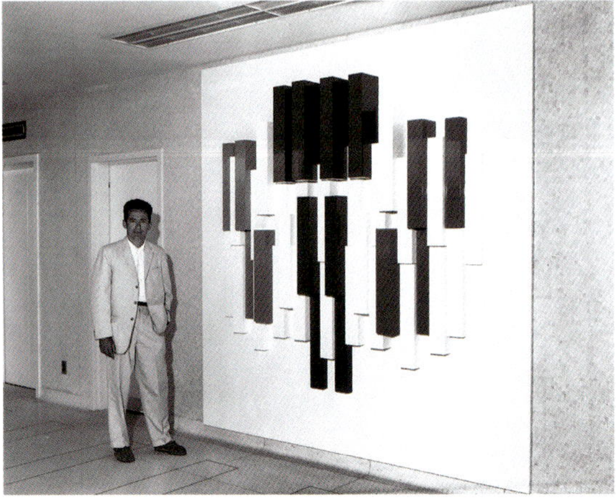

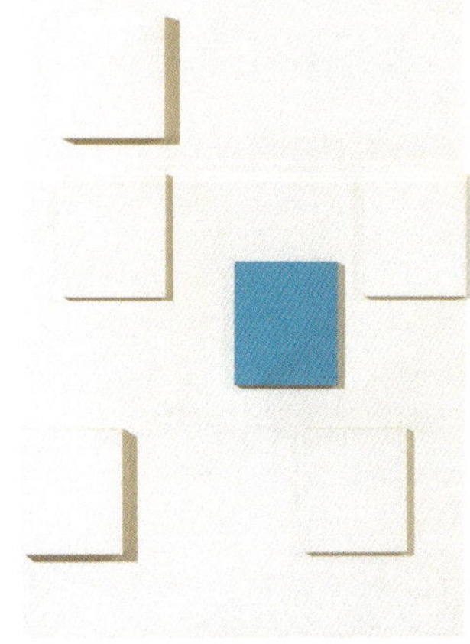

Left: Eli Bornstein with *Structurist Relief No. 18-II* in the Arts and Science Building at the University of Saskatchewan, Saskatoon, 1961, photographer unknown, University of Saskatchewan, University Archives and Special Collections. Right: Eli Bornstein, *Structurist Relief No. 4*, 1957, oil on wood, 72.4 x 49.5 x 3.8 cm, private collection.

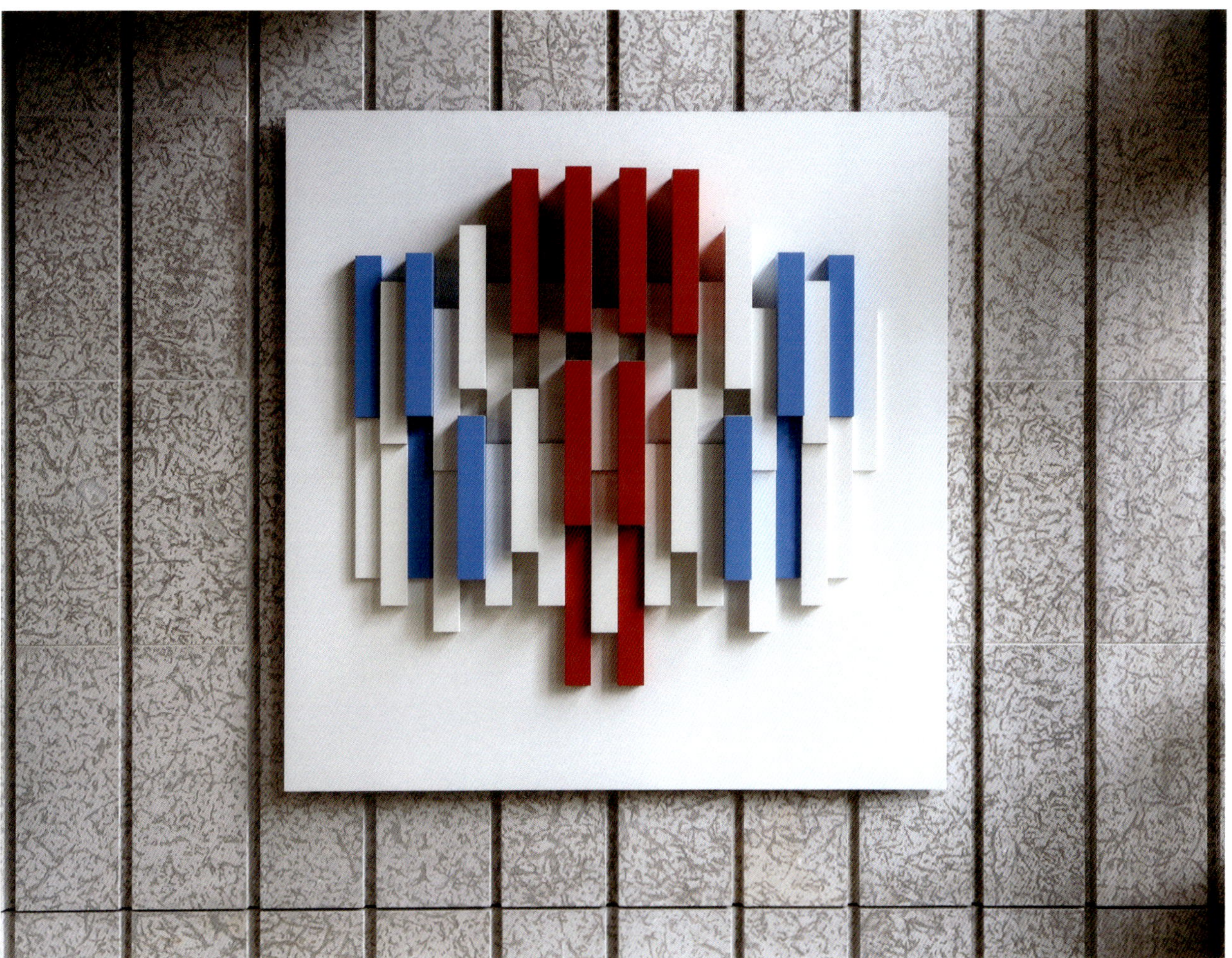

Bornstein's earliest reliefs, like *Structurist Relief No. 4*, were relatively simple, but, as his experience developed, the reliefs became more elaborate. Thus *Structurist Relief No. 18-II* is invasive: it is crisp and elegant, with the scale and presence to hold a public space. Its composition is centred and symmetrical, its relief elements deep and weighty, its colours, in addition to white, confined to two primaries: blue and red. Again, it is in its way austere, but its varied relief masses and its dispersal of bright colours perform with muscular jazzy rhythms.

Structurist Relief No. 3-1 (Canoe Lake Series) 1964

Oil on wood relief, 68.6 x 61 x 15.2 cm
Private collection

Structurist Relief No. 3-1 (Canoe Lake Series), as per its subtitle, dates to Bornstein's 1964 summer stay in Group of Seven stomping grounds, in Algonquin Park, in a cottage on Canoe Lake owned by a friend of the composer Murray Adaskin (1906–2002). The relief embodies important developments in Bornstein's use of both colour and form. He has, first of all, in response to what he was seeing, multiplied his colour choices considerably beyond simple primary hues, orchestrating an evocative play of mauve, green, yellow, and orange horizontal and vertical blocks and staves. At the same time, Bornstein has organized his relief components, not just side by side, but on top of one another, in a square-shouldered construction that brings mysterious shadows and obscure depths into being. The result is, not surprisingly, suggestive of the lakes and shorelines and deep woods of the wilderness setting in which he was working. It seems fitting that he should meet up with the Group of Seven artist A.Y. Jackson (1882–1974), who that summer made a short visit to Algonquin Park, the two of them photographed together in Adaskin's own cabin also located on Canoe Lake.

By definition, the Structurist Relief is engaged with nature, and for Bornstein's first reliefs, this meant that they inhabited not an illusionistic pictorial space, but the literal space that they shared with their viewers. They are in the world, so to speak.

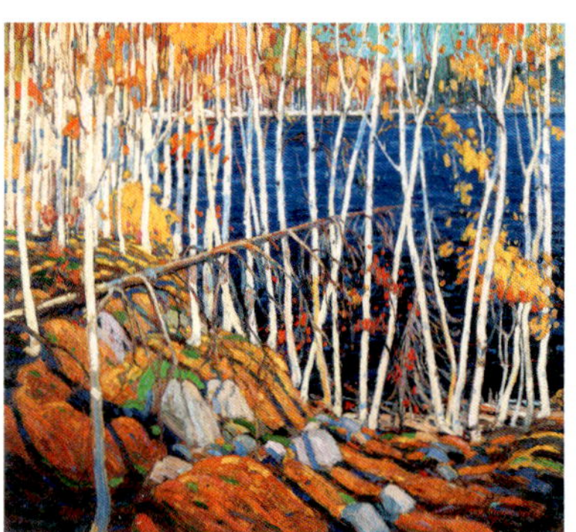

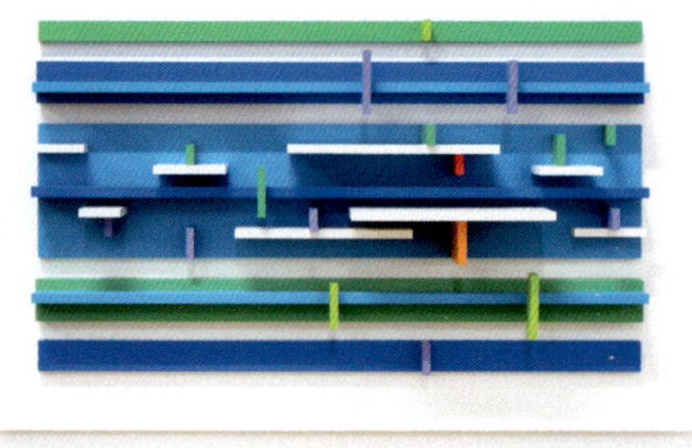

With this work, however, nature has more specifically become "Nature" (as Bornstein often capitalizes it), his subject matter now commensurate with those unpeopled natural landscapes that had earlier in the twentieth century captivated Tom Thomson (1877–1917) and the Group of Seven, such as Thomson's *In the Northland*, 1915.

Indeed, what we witness in *Structurist Relief No. 3-1* is pure non-referential abstraction giving way to the evocation of natural events. The Dutch painter Piet Mondrian (1872–1944) may have been the progenitor of Bornstein's abstraction, but *Structurist Relief No. 3-1* breaks ideologically with his De Stijl parent. Around 1918, Mondrian set out to distill a formal abstract language that, as simply as possible, could embody his aspiration for absolute ideal beauty, a realm of pure order divorced from the weather of everyday

Left: Tom Thomson, *In the Northland*, 1915, oil on canvas, 101.7 x 114.5 cm, Montreal Museum of Fine Arts.
Right: Eli Bornstein, *Structurist Relief No. 4-11* (Sea Series), 1965, acrylic enamel, Plexiglas on aluminum, 86.5 x 61.1 cm, Remai Modern, Saskatoon.

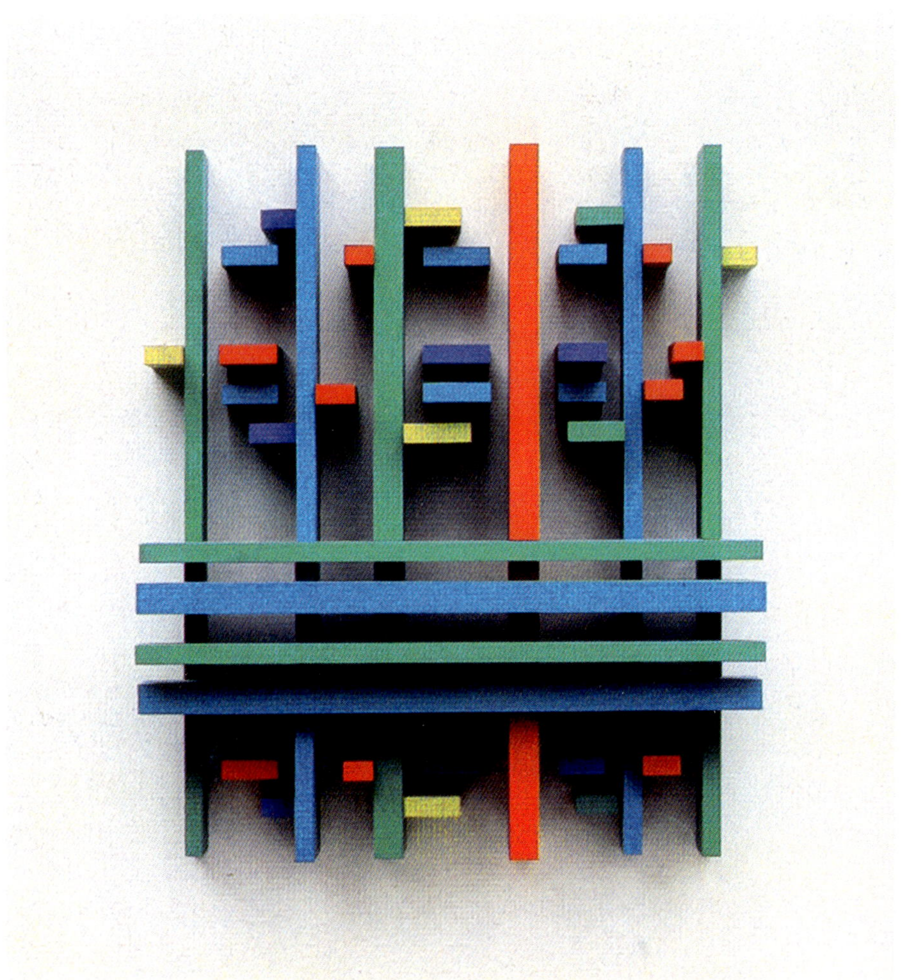

reality. But at that art historical moment, where Mondrian separated his art from nature's capriciousness, Bornstein recognized a fork in the modernist road, one that pointed him in an alternative direction. Perhaps modern art could no longer "imitate" nature, but nor could it turn its back on the world or abandon nature's diversity.

For Bornstein, therefore, if abstract art were to find a new creative direction, it should build its principles on the study of the operations of nature in all its plenitude. His challenge became to hone his capacities of observation by looking intensely at nature's life and form, its colour, space, and light—whether in the woods, by the seaside (as in *Structurist Relief No. 4-11* [Sea Series], 1965) or on prairie riverbanks—and to translate his findings into the ever-enriching formal language of his three-dimensional reliefs.

Structurist Relief No. 2
1966

Enamel on wood and Plexiglas, 86.4 x 61 x 15.6 cm
Private collection

Most Structurist reliefs, whether by Bornstein or his colleagues, had tended to project their 3-D relief compositions out in front of an otherwise impassive neutral background plane. Bornstein began to question the limitations of this way of working in a new series of reliefs, the Sea Series, which he originally conceived in 1964 during a summer stay on the coast of Southern California, and then continued to develop for several years. His objective was to set up a tighter interrelationship between figure and ground. This happens when, as in his sprightly summer-day *Structurist Relief No. 2*, the artist inserts into his composition two broad planes of blue—one above the other—one lighter, and another darker (intimations of sea and sky?), splayed out flatly behind the Technicolor interplay of the thin relief elements that jut out sharply in front of them.

These two planes remain co-extensive with the white ground, but they are now both formally and chromatically activated and integrated with the relief components in front of them. At the same time, they play an expressive role of their own. If back and front merge compositionally, the two flat blue planes nevertheless move at their own pace. They are broad and spread out, measured and slow, their quiet a marked contrast to all the foreground near-at-hand bustle. It is as if—and this will be important in the future Multiplanes—Bornstein wants to create a faceoff between two different tempos of perceptual experience, two independent dimensions of time and place: far against near, meditative reflection as a foil to immediate rapture.

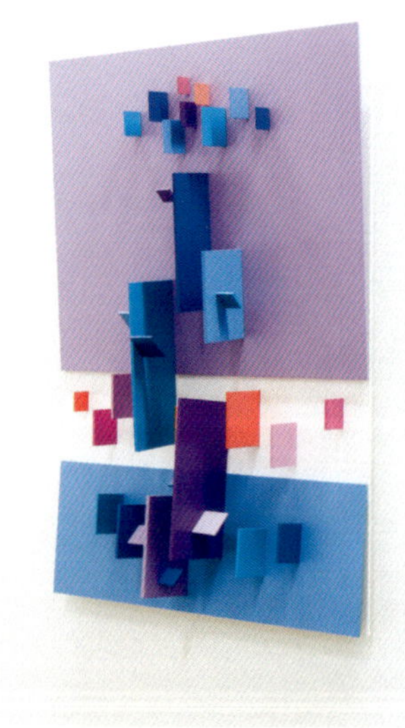

The angled view of the accompanying image of *Structurist Relief No. 2*—and that of the later *Multiplane Structurist Relief V, No. 1*, 1993, in which the mauve and blue planes slant slightly outward from the white ground plane—both illustrate the importance of moving around and looking at a Structurist relief from different angles. The advancing planes, which from the front look thin and sharp, from side views, unavailable to painting, strut their colours. There is no one ideal place at which to stand. As with sculpture, new visual information is revealed as we change position. As fellow Structurist—and former student of Bornstein—Elizabeth Willmott (b.1928) puts it, "As in life, no view is best."[1]

Eli Bornstein, *Multiplane Structurist Relief V, No. 1*, 1993, acrylic enamel, Plexiglas on aluminum, 86.5 x 61.1 x 3.1 cm, Remai Modern, Saskatoon.

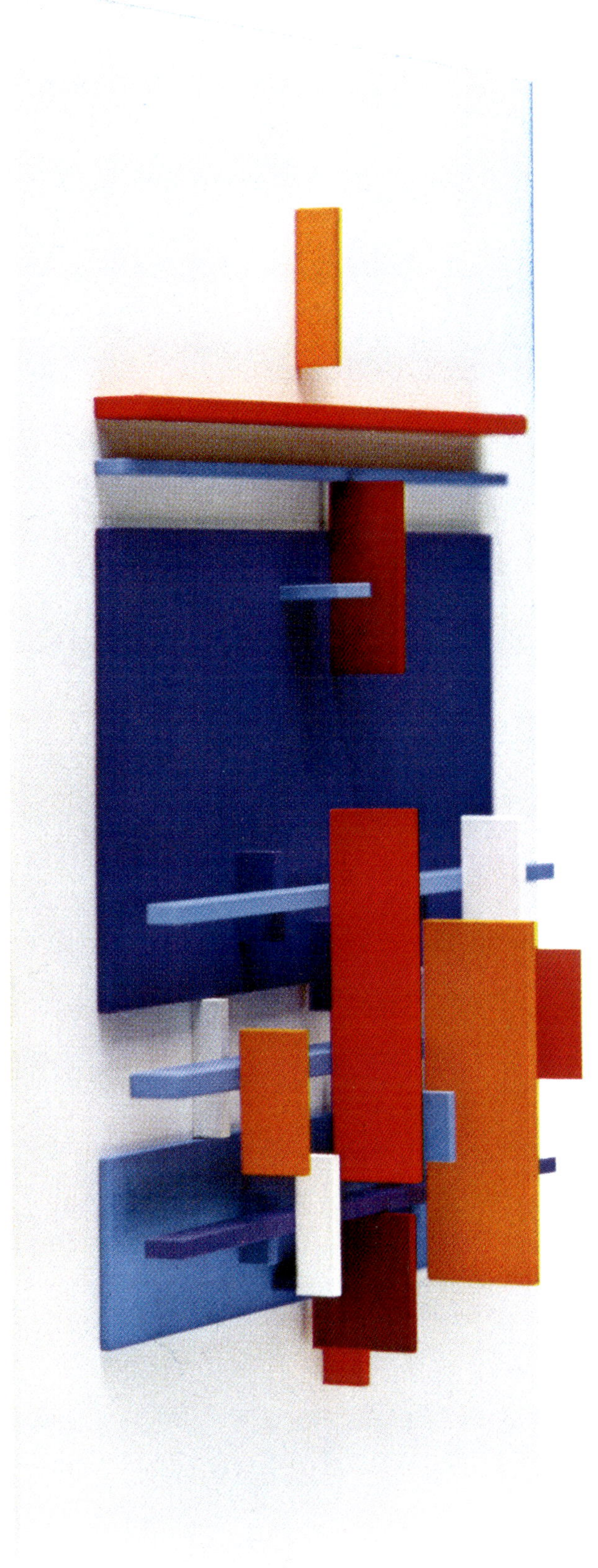

Double Plane Structurist Relief No. 3
1967–69

Enamel on Plexiglas and aluminum, 66.7 x 66.7 x 34.3 cm
University of Saskatchewan, Saskatoon

Bornstein began working on *Double Plane Structurist Relief No. 3* in 1966 while on sabbatical near Big Sur, California. As he recounts in a journal entry from 2013, "My vision opened daily to an immense sky above and the Great Pacific Ocean below that could as well have been the great prairie plane of Saskatchewan."[1] He produced *Double Plane Structurist Relief No. 3* in response to this observation and the fact that the visual ways of the natural world are infinitely variable.

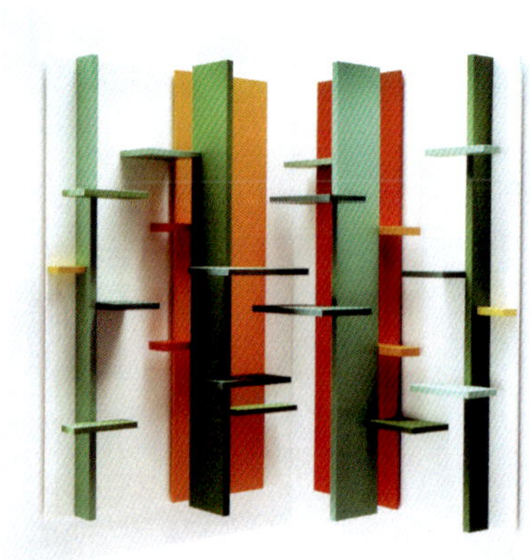

In this work, Bornstein folds his ground plane in half, at a 90-degree angle, and then installs it horizontally. It performs like a half-opened book, its spine flat to the wall. Nested in its crevices are brightly coloured, often intricate relief elements, their chromatic interactions animated by the play of light and shadow.

In *Double Plane Structurist Relief No. 2-1*, 1966–71, Bornstein flipped the axis to the vertical. This was prompted, as he writes in an article from 1969, by watching "the wild orange-red flowers that grew around our house." As he continues: when the relief's angled planes unfold, it is as if it "reaches out and draws the spectator into it, like the flower inviting the bee!"[2] Another of Bornstein's journal entries, "The First Lily," underscores the intensity of his observations of the natural world outside his door:

> Today I was startled by the appearance of the first lily. What a surprise to suddenly see the bright orange trumpet-like flower appear so strikingly, so triumphantly amidst the tall prairie grass and in the most unexpected places on the riverbank. How very different the character and gesture of the lily are from the crocus and the rose. Its form and color are more precisely articulated with its single stem and arrangement of leaves. It appears far more singularly, and in isolation, being far less gregarious than the rose. Like the solo sound of a high-pitched horn, or soprano trumpet resonant and clear, it is unmistakable for anything else but itself.[3]

Despite his deep engagement with the natural world, Bornstein reminds his viewers that when he builds his abstract constructions, they do not mirror or copy nature, preferring to describe them as "parallel creations" that "grow toward nature."[4]

Eli Bornstein, *Double Plane Structurist Relief No. 2-1*, 1966–71, enamel on Plexiglas and aluminum, 43.2 x 43.2 x 23.5 cm, private collection.

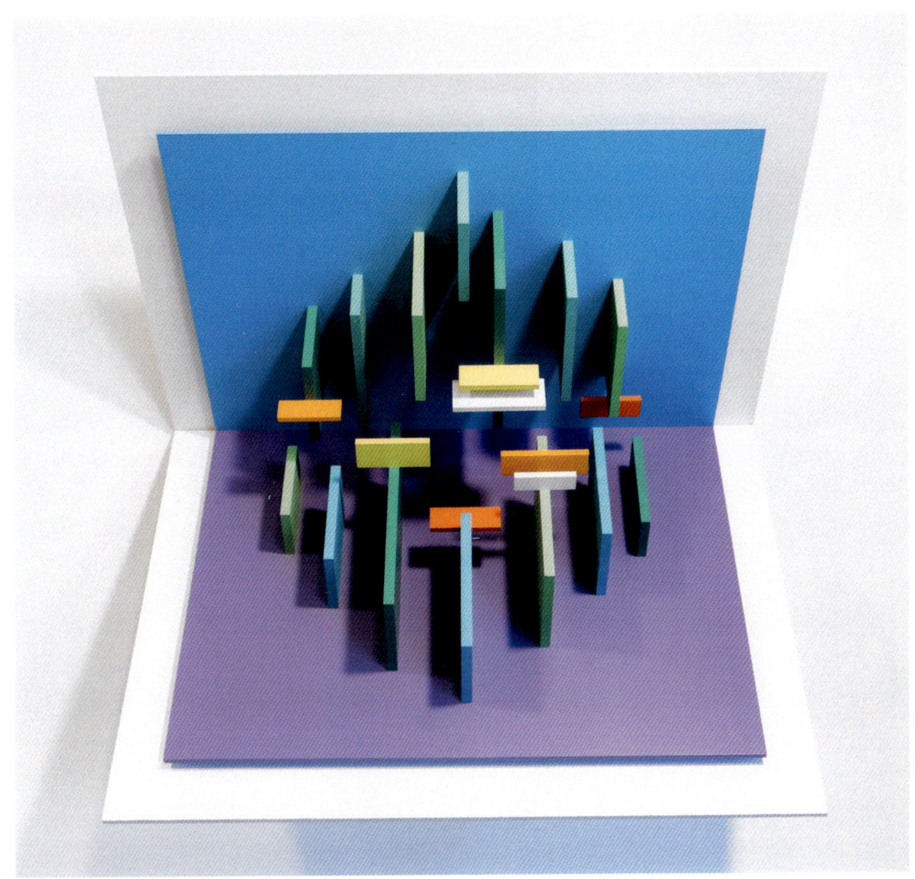

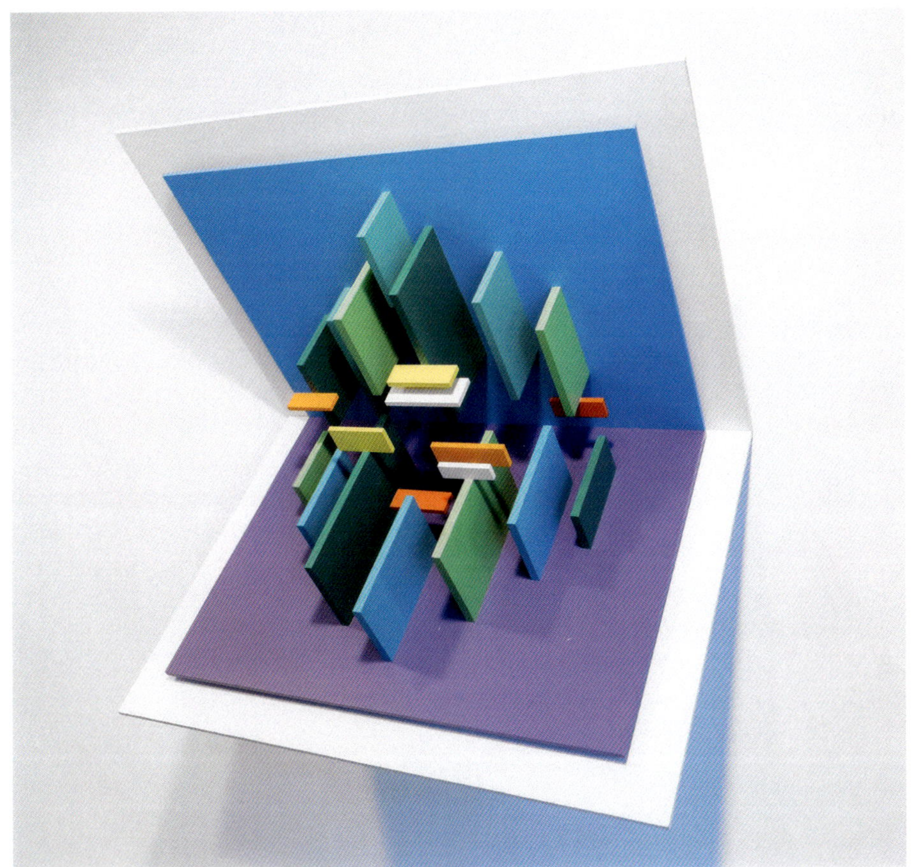

Four Part Vertical Double Plane Structurist Relief (Winter Sky Series) 1980–83

Acrylic lacquer on aluminum and Plexiglas on welded steel, 640.1 x 342 cm (diameter)
Wascana Centre Authority, Regina

The monumental *Four Part Vertical Double Plane Structurist Relief* (Winter Sky Series) was commissioned by the Wascana Centre Authority Board for the Wascana Centre, a 930-hectare urban park in Regina. Bornstein's challenge was to find a way to remain faithful to the principles of his Structurist reliefs—which, after all, were made to be hung against a wall—while fully engaging the lofty four-storey space of the Wascana Place administrative building. Bornstein's simple and efficient solution was to redeploy the structure of his Double Plane reliefs by backing four of them up against one another. The resulting 6.4-metre-tall "four-part" construction was then suspended, as if it were a giant chandelier, from the building's skylight.

Its theme—as suggested by the sculpture's subtitle, Winter Sky Series—is the metaphorical celebration of Saskatchewan's winter skies. Each of its tall, narrow, folded ground planes is coloured a different shade of blue, registering various moments and moods of the heavens overhead. In front of them hover relief formations that allude to nocturnal events in the sky, or on the horizon, from dawn to dusk.

Due to the work's size and complexity, constructing it was beyond the scope of what Bornstein could do in his studio. As had become his practice since starting using aluminum, he worked with professional machinists who cut both the aluminum and Plexiglas parts—the larger background planes and smaller relief elements—to his specifications. Once the manufactured pieces were brought back to his studio, he worked out the structure and colours with models, mixing and matching until a desired composition emerged. Bornstein would typically select the enamel colours from those commercially available; however, when subtler hues were called for, he meticulously mixed his own. The models would then be scaled up, the parts spray-painted in an auto-body shop, and the full-size work assembled by machinists.

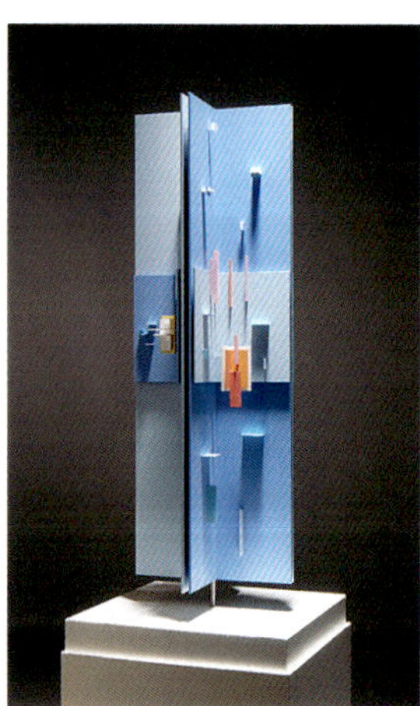

Bornstein gifted the model for *Four Part Vertical Double Plane Structurist Relief* (Winter Sky Series) to the Canadian Centre for Architecture in Montreal. Some twenty years in the future, just after the turn of the millennium, Bornstein would revisit the concept for his Wascana Place work—again backing Double-Plane reliefs up against one another—in a group of free-standing works that he would call Tripart Hexaplane Constructions.

Four Part Vertical Double Plane Structurist Relief (Winter Sky Series) is one of a succession of major public commissions that Bornstein received over the years, including *Aluminum Construction (Tree of Knowledge)* in 1956, and *Structurist Relief in Fifteen Parts*, for the new International Style airport in Winnipeg in 1962.

View A of Eli Bornstein, *Four Part Vertical Double Plane Structurist Relief Nos. 14–17* (Winter Sky Series), 1980–83, enamel on aluminum and Plexiglas on steel frame, 104.1 x 38.1 x 38.1 cm, Canadian Centre for Architecture, Montreal. Model of the commission for the Wascana Centre Authority in Regina.

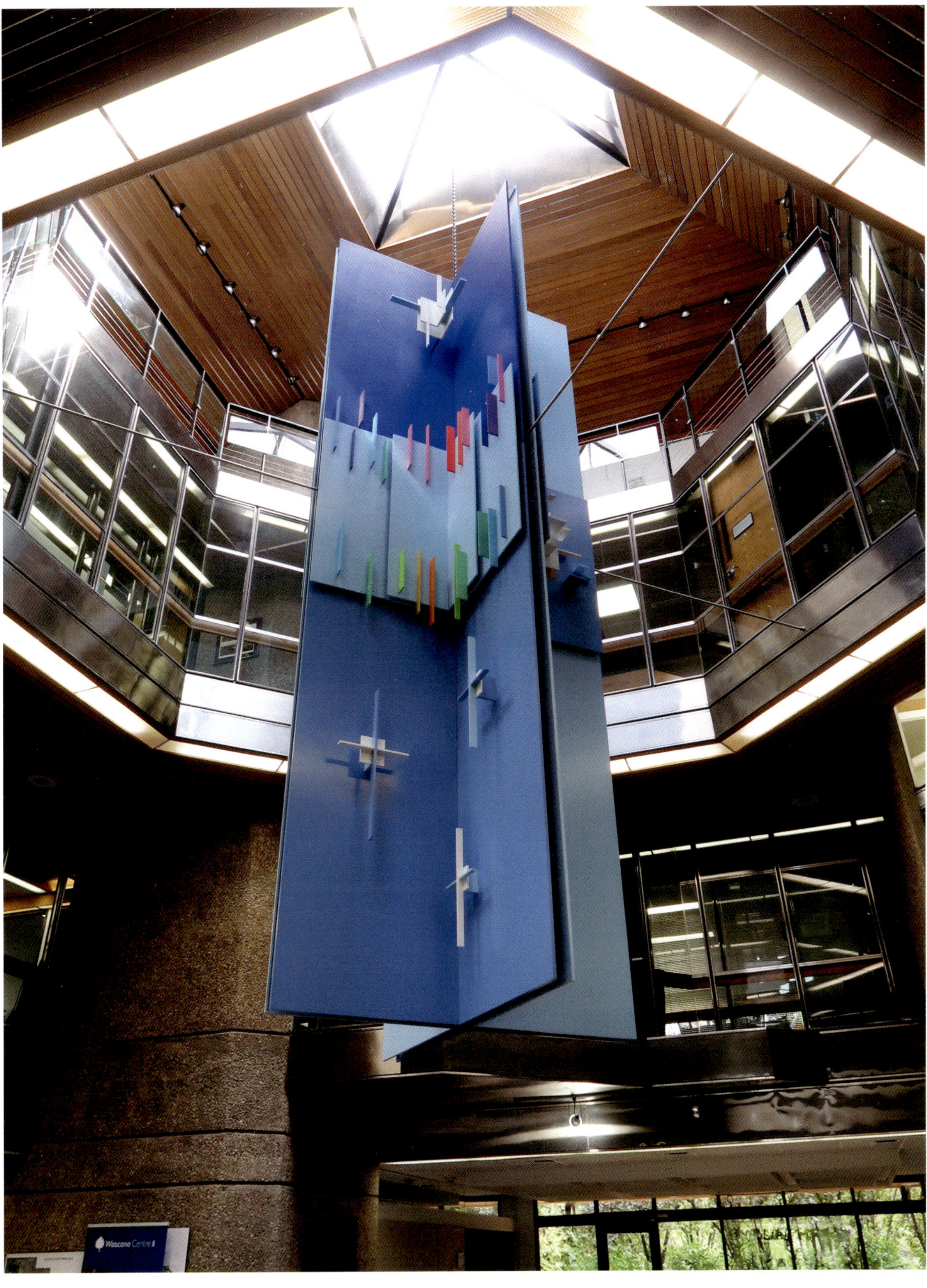
Wascana Centre

Arctic Study No. 38
1987

Watercolour on mat board, 41 x 33.9 cm
Collection of the artist

Arctic Study No. 38 is emblematic of an innovative body of watercolour paintings that emerged out of Bornstein's two journeys to Ellesmere Island in the Canadian Arctic during the summers of 1986 and 1987, travelling in the company of the photographer Hans Dommasch (1926–2017), his colleague from the University of Saskatchewan. In these watercolours, Bornstein devised for flat painting an abstract transcription of his sensations of nature. These paintings ran parallel to the innovations that he was exploring in a new group of Structurist reliefs titled the Arctic Series, which also came out of those summer experiences.[1]

To understand the painting's formal vocabulary, we need a little backstory. During the preceding three decades, Bornstein had worked almost exclusively in relief, even when travelling. But the exigencies of working out of a tent on the tundra required him, alongside drawing, to take up watercolour again. It was a medium he had not practised for some thirty years since he painted *The Island* on the coast of Maine in 1956.

The challenge again was how to put the colours of the Arctic down "in a uniquely abstract way,"[2] Bornstein writes in his journal, so as to evoke his sensory experiences of nature "without imitating [its] appearances."[3] In the watercolours from his first summer in the Arctic, he essentially picked up from where he had left off in Maine. His swatches of colour are similarly striated and loosely rectangular, quick and spontaneous when he looks to the ground, larger and elongated when they refer to bigger subjects like icebergs and vast skies, as in *Arctic Study No. 12*, 1986. In either case, however, Bornstein's compo-

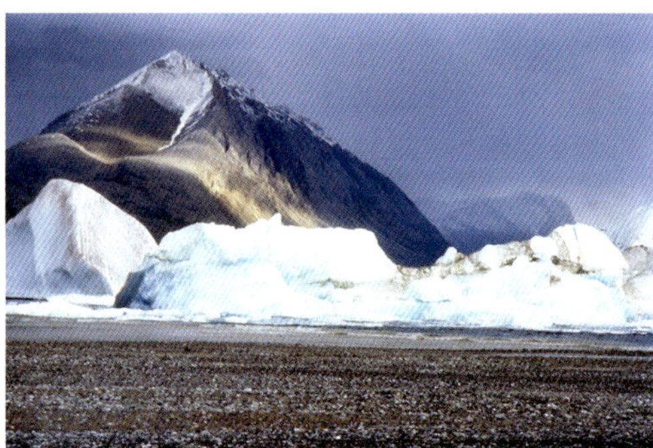

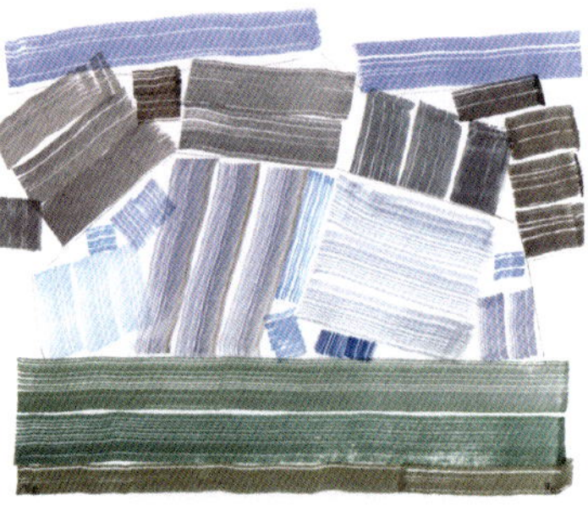

sitions still largely echo the general shapes of the landscape in front of him: the horizontal shoreline, the middle-ground icebergs, the darker mountains behind, and even clouds in the sky, much in the way that Dommasch's photograph, *Ellesmere Island—Otto Fjord*, 1986, captured a similar scene.

However, with *Arctic Study No. 38*, Bornstein has moved into new territory, thoroughly learning to abstract his vision. The striated paint swatches are now planar, some flat, others folded, some chunky and solid. They are dispersed flat on the white paper, held in place by mutual attractions or repulsions and indifferent to gravity. Their colours are luminous, fresh, and immediate. Sometimes they dance with the lightness of snowflakes. Nature is evoked, not by representation or literal allusion, but by analogy, an abstract choreography of colour.[4]

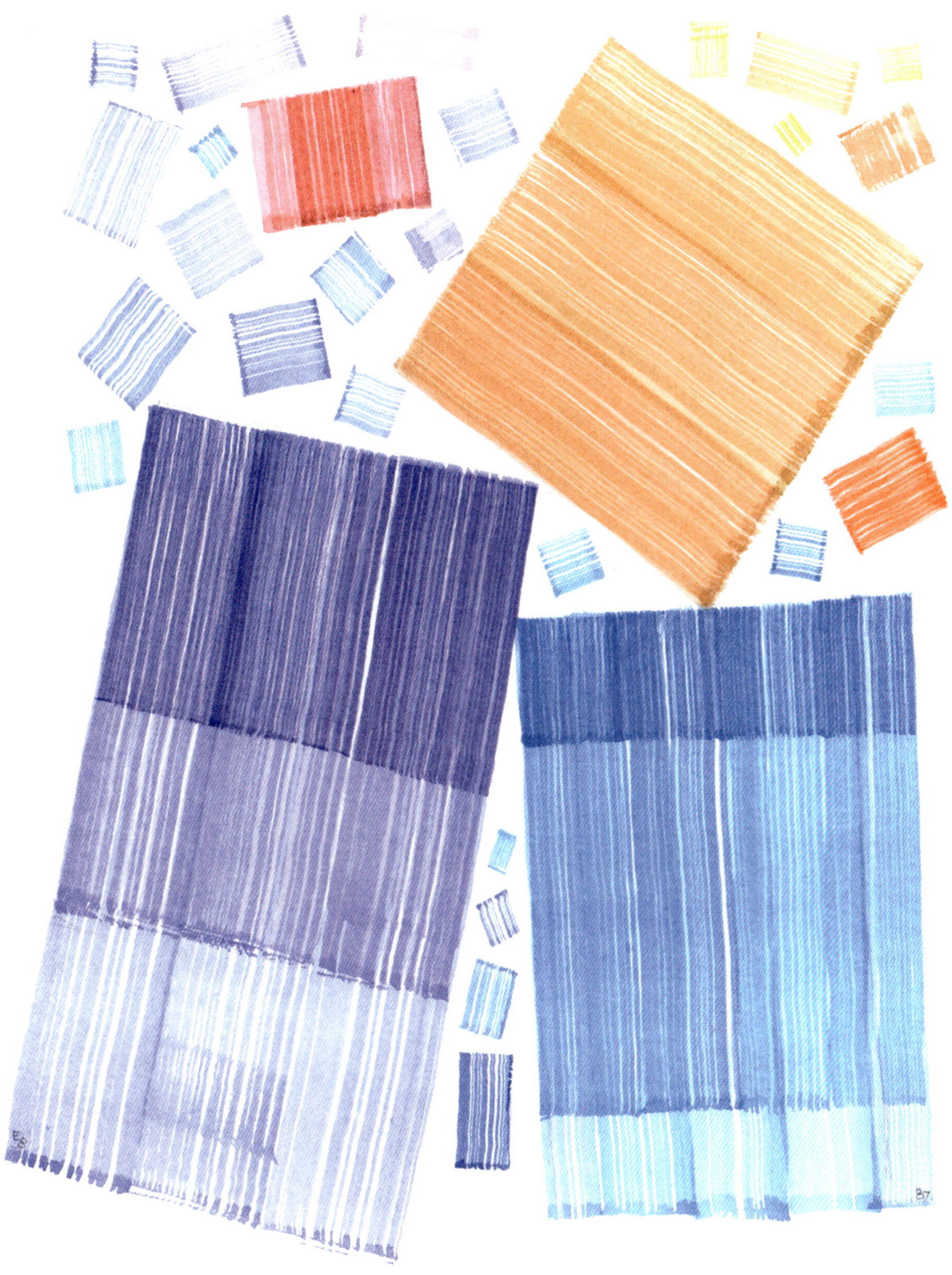

Opposite left: Hans Dommasch, *Ellesmere Island—Otto Fjord*, 1986, colour slide, 35mm, University of Saskatchewan, Saskatoon. Opposite right: Eli Bornstein, *Arctic Study No. 12*, 1986, watercolour on mat board, 20.6 x 25.4 cm, collection of the artist.

Hexaplane Structurist Relief No. 2 (Arctic Series) 1995–98

Acrylic enamel on aluminum and Plexiglas, 67.2 x 182.2 x 15.9 cm
University of Saskatchewan, Saskatoon

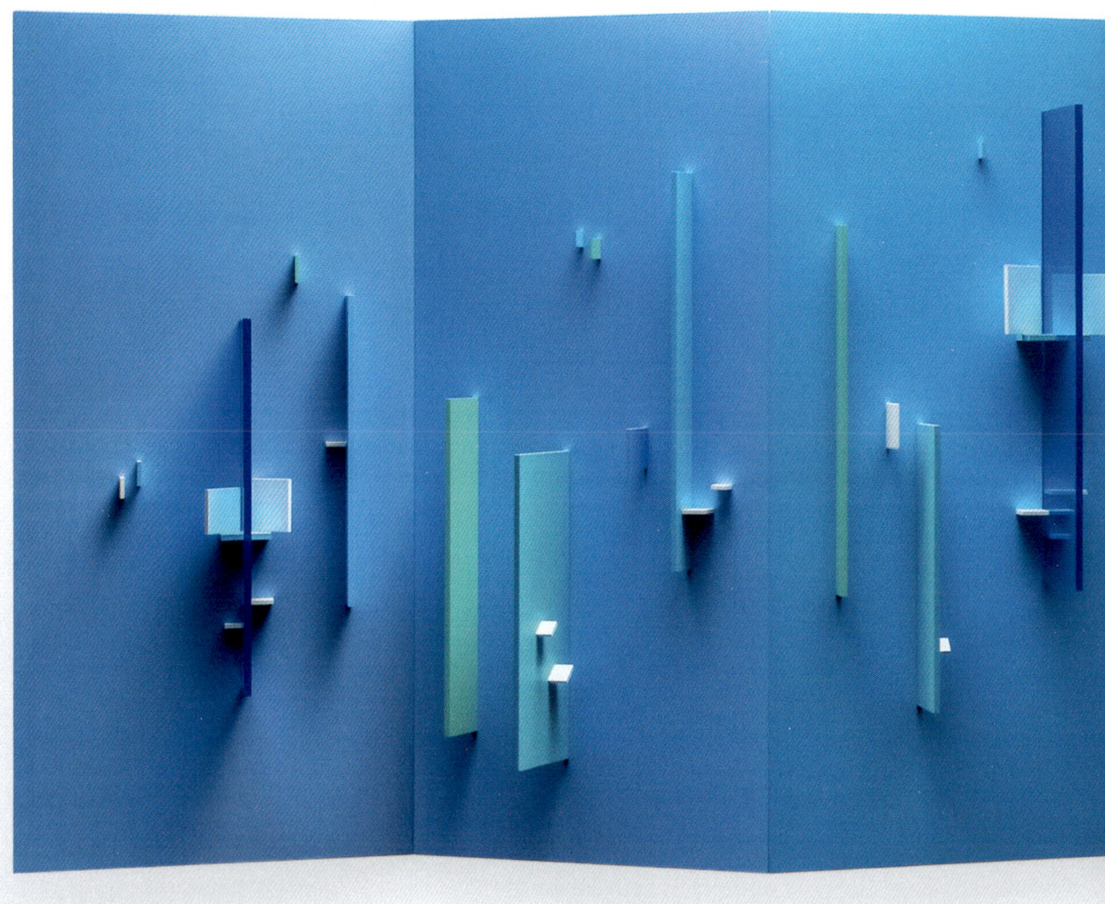

The iconic *Icebergs, Davis Strait*, 1930, by Lawren S. Harris (1885–1970) dates to when he and A.Y. Jackson (1882–1974) travelled the Arctic in the summer of 1930. Yet it is as if Harris and Bornstein—even though they were separated by over half a century—saw their northern visions with shared eyes. There is kinship here, a spiritual resonance between the two artists' respective interpretations of the icy landscape, although they came from different moments in twentieth-century modernist art history. The cold palette of both registers the same iridescence, brittleness, limpidity, and silence that is true to their northern subject matter.

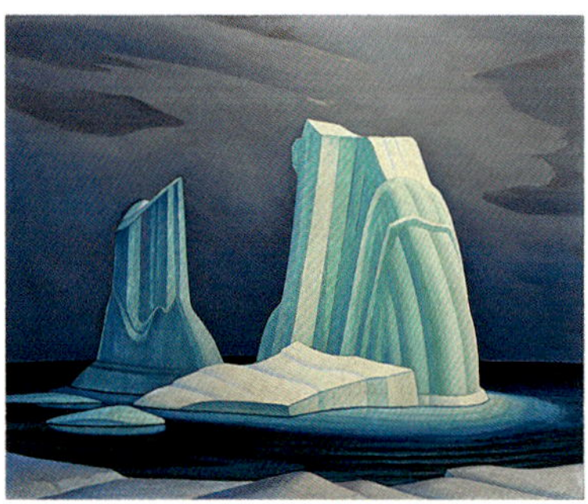

The Arctic Series reliefs were developed by Bornstein between 1986 and 1998 as a response to his profound experiences in the Arctic. *Hexaplane Structurist Relief No.* 2 (Arctic Series), with its expressive use of transparent blue Plexiglas, is the grandest of Bornstein's Arctic

Lawren S. Harris, *Icebergs, Davis Strait*, 1930, oil on canvas, 121.9 x 152.4 cm, McMichael Canadian Art Collection, Kleinburg.

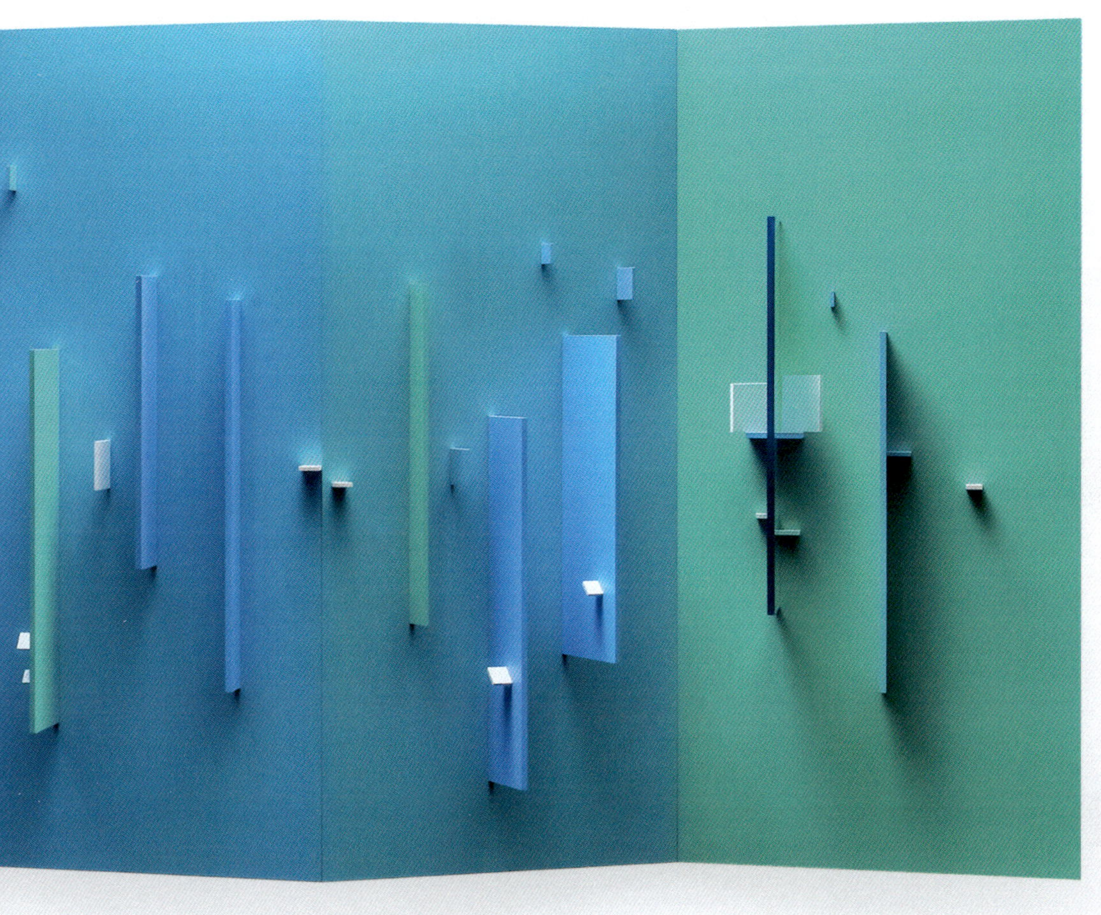

Series reliefs. The idea to use translucent coloured Plexiglas had occurred to him already on his second day in Ellesmere Island, July 26, 1986. As he explained, the thought came to him when he was struck by the sight of how icebergs reflected in water produced mirror images. The effect of inserting transparent coloured Plexiglas in the midst of the enamel-painted relief parts would not only add an additional quality of colour to the latter's space and forms but would also reflect them with a new depth. Blue Plexiglas intensified the sensation of iciness in the relief's already cold palette.

Though the Northern work of Harris and Bornstein has much in common, there are also differences. The objective of Harris's *Icebergs, Davis Strait* was to convey spiritual illumination, as the artist phrased it, the soul's "simple vision of high things."[1] Harris was a keen observer of nature, but his goal was to transcend mere appearances, marshalling Art Deco–influenced stylizations to distill nature into archetypal icons. Where Harris idealizes, in awe of nature's eternities, Bornstein moves up close, like a naturalist, to root his work in an intimate study of nature's ever-changing processes. His six zigzagging background planes in *Hexaplane Structurist Relief No. 2* may intimate something enormous and timeless, but simultaneously he recreates for the viewer a sense of close scrutiny: the feeling of being there on the ground as if at the first moment of discovery.[2]

Quadriplane Structurist Relief Nos. 1–3 (River-Screen Series) 1989–96

Acrylic enamel on aluminum and Plexiglas, 60.4 x 137.8 x 14.6 cm each
Collection of the artist

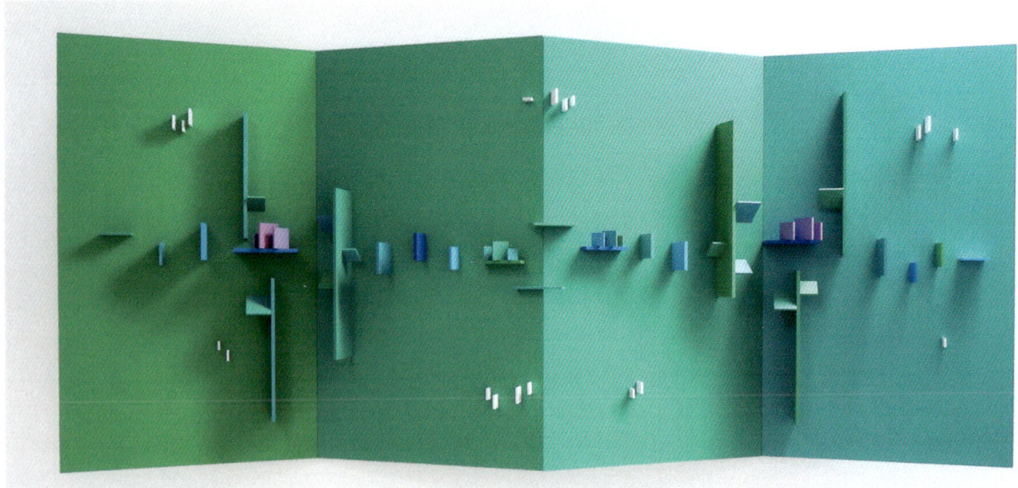

In the late 1980s, subsequent to his Arctic experiences, Bornstein began a new series of horizontally oriented Quadriplane and Hexaplane reliefs, which, with their expansiveness and their resonant intonations, stand as one of the culminating achievements of his long and creative career.

In the three-part *Quadriplane Structurist Relief Nos. 1–3* (River-Screen Series), a sequence of colour planes, one by one, advance from left to right through daylight greens into blues and late-dusk purples. When we scan the horizon of their panoramic sweep, they zigzag in and out like little jump-cuts in the continuity of time. The foreground articulations are dispersed with rhythmic dash, causing the eye to search out their individual colours and shapes, and explore their positions, angles, and relationships as they catch the light and throw shadows. They flow in space and time like a progression of musical chords interspersed with grace notes and pauses. Behind them, the ground colours unfold their quietude and fulsomeness as if to hint at a larger existence far beyond their outer edges. Before them the transitory life of nature continues to perform its ephemeral dances while the colour planes themselves hold vision in a state of suspension within a space of timelessness.

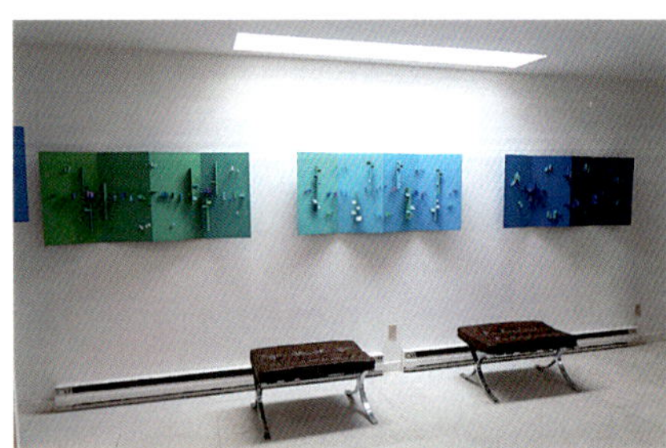

Bornstein has always been mindful about titles, preferring numbers to descriptive names in order to deter viewers from imposing representational references before exploring structural relations (what descriptions he does use—Quadriplane, Hexaplane, and Double Plane—refer to the number of planes in each relief's construction). But sometimes subtitles, such as River-Screen Series, anchor us. Let the artist himself describe the natural sources of the series' formal correlatives:

Installation view of *Quadriplane Structurist Relief Nos. 1–3* (River-Screen Series), 1989–96, by Eli Bornstein, photograph by Roald Nasgaard.

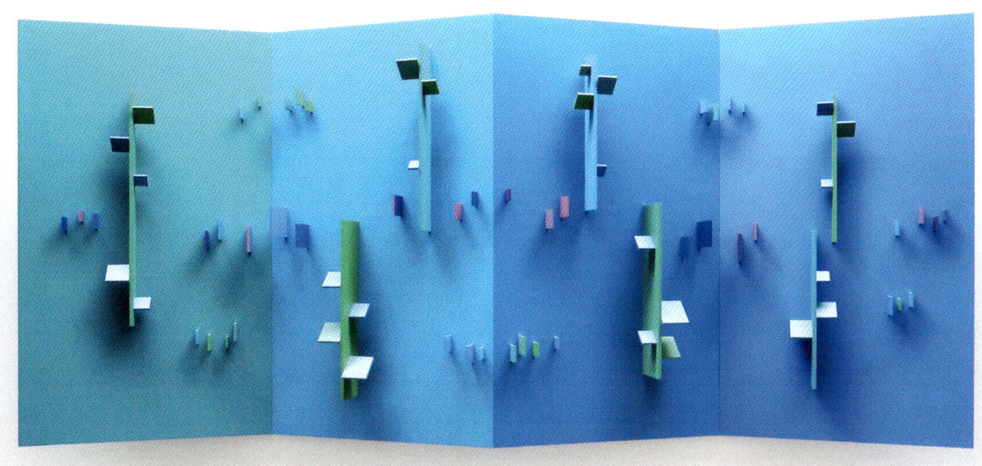

> As I walk out upon the riverbank each day.... My river is like an unfolding ribbon or screen of color that reflects the constantly changing light of the sky and position of the sun. Diurnal and nocturnal, throughout the changing seasons, there is a continuous transition of color from greens to blue-greens, green-blues, to intense blues, purple-blues and deep purples. There are ranges of intensity and value and transitions and mergings of one into another along this horizontal stretch of color. There is not a color of the entire spectrum that is not sometime to be seen here. No artist can invent a color that this strip of chromatic mirror cannot reflect.[1]

The triptych is a tour de force celebration of nature: the glory of an early morning sunrise, the greenness of spring, or the melancholy of the dying day. Scandinavians in the late nineteenth century called the latter "the blue hour," in whose twilight they could elevate their meditations into almost mystical rapture. And Bornstein's reliefs are enraptured with "Nature" (as Bornstein often capitalizes it).

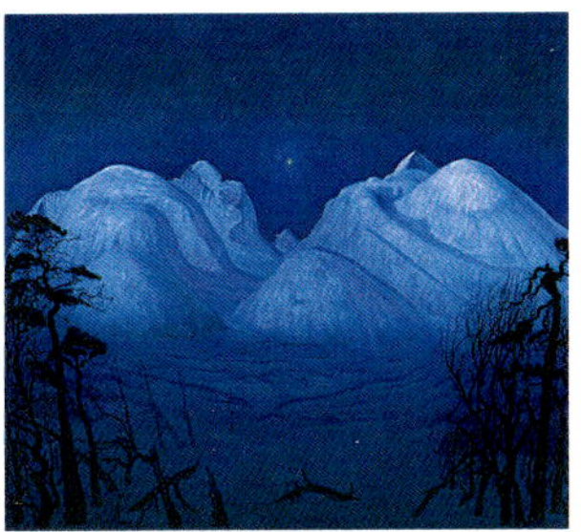

Bornstein's Multiplane reliefs are in a way unwitting descendants of the Northern Symbolist Landscape tradition, born in the 1890s from a renewed confrontation with the northern wilderness during a time of fin de siècle spiritual unease. Dissatisfied with the objective realism of Impressionist paintings, artists—like the Norwegian Harald Sohlberg (1869–1935)—began to probe behind surface appearances and meditate on nature's inner spirit. "The eternal life is sensed everywhere in the action of nature,"[2] wrote the Finnish painter Akseli Gallen-Kallela (1865–1931), as he and his Nordic-landscape colleagues abandoned realistic representation to devise new pictorial structures that would resonate, as it were, with the life of the soul.

Harald Sohlberg, *Winter Night in the Mountains*, 1914, oil on canvas, 160 x 180.5 cm, Nasjonalmuseet, Oslo.

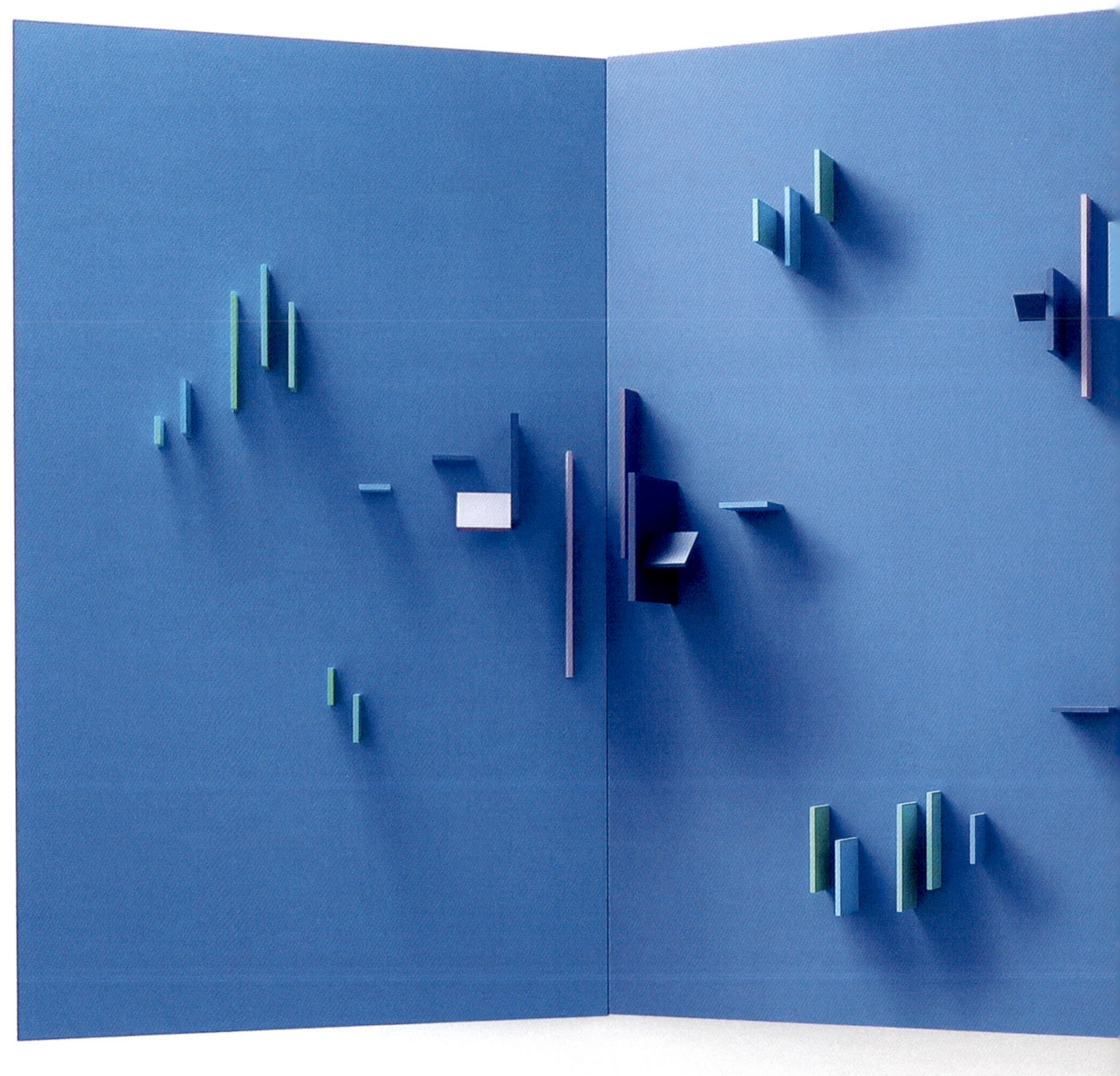

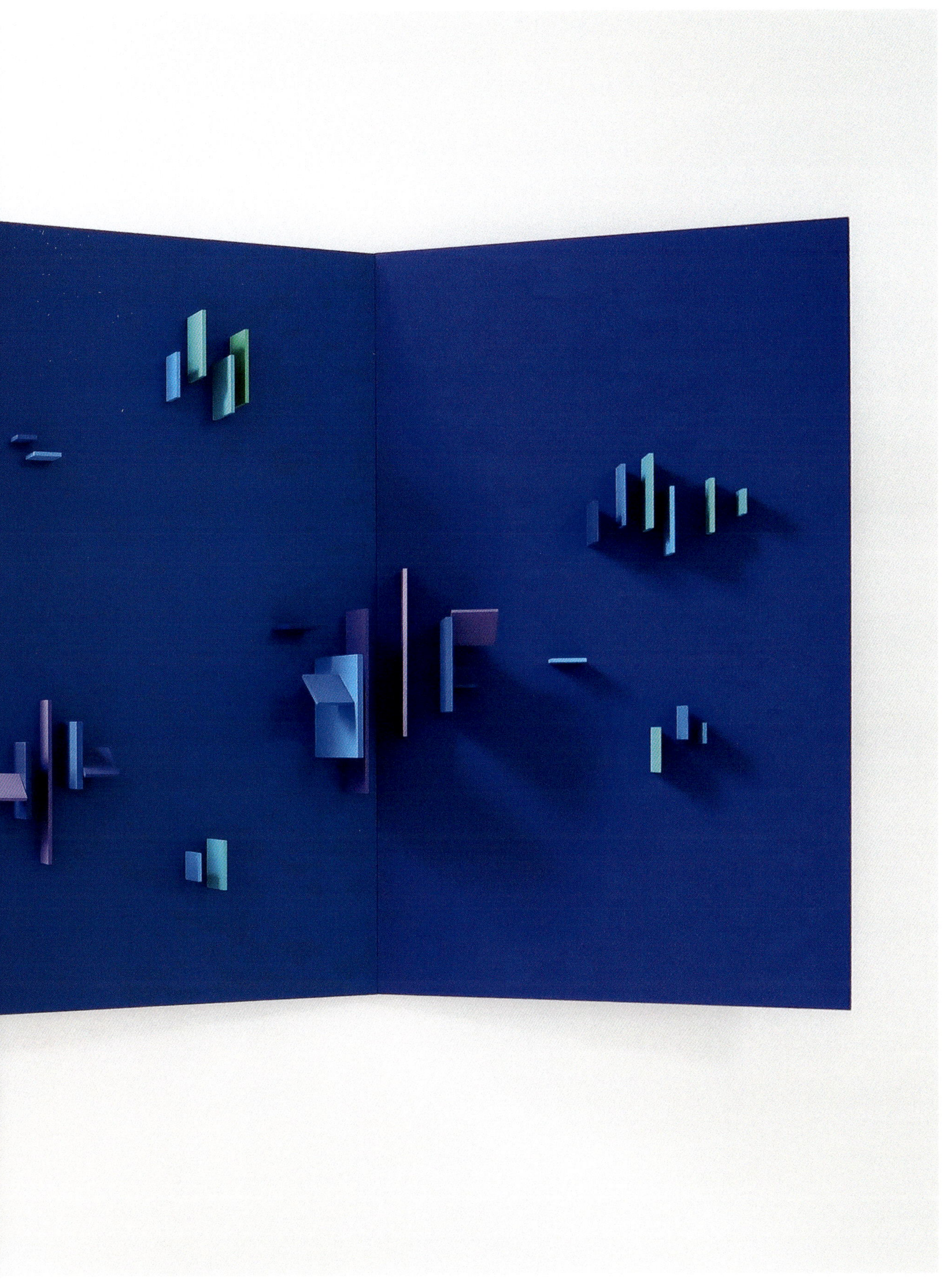

Tripart Hexaplane Construction No. 2
2002–6

Acrylic enamel on anodized aluminum and concrete base,
205.25 x 107.8 x 107.8 cm
University of Manitoba, Winnipeg

Throughout his career, Bornstein approached his work as constantly evolving, a continual search for ways to convey the vitality of nature. This approach is exemplified in a new series of free-standing works that he initiated in the early 2000s, which he would call Tripart Hexaplane Constructions. They grew out of his concept for an earlier work entitled *Four Part Vertical Double Plane Structurist Relief* (Winter Sky Series), 1980–83, which was suspended at Wascana Place in Regina. Bornstein had constructed that work by backing four 90-degree angled double-plane reliefs up against one another, and he revisited this approach around the turn of the millennium, striking a new idea for the Tripart Hexaplane Constructions that characterized his late work.

Tripart Hexaplane Construction No. 2 was installed at the University of Manitoba in Winnipeg in 2007.[1] It is assembled from three green 2-metre-high 120-degree double-plane reliefs backed onto one another and elevated from its thin pedestal by short unpainted aluminum legs. The pedestal is in turn raised on a concrete base to a height just above eye level. To view it is to walk around it, parsing and comparing its three faces, like variations on a theme. Its tall, narrow, vertical relief planes shoot upward or drop downward, defying the edges of their supportive ground planes. Smaller, obliquely angled, blue-shaded rectangular plates set at varying positions harbinger a sense of restless instability always re-enlivened by the fickle light of the work's outside setting, from sunlight to shadow, summer to winter. *Tripart Hexaplane Construction No. 1*, 2002–4, an earlier grandly scaled version of the series, had been previously unveiled on the grounds of Jacobs University, now Constructor University, in Bremen, Germany.[2]

At the time of writing, while Bornstein still has other work in progress in his studio, the Tripart Hexaplane Constructions, whether small or grand in scale, have come to stand as the culmination of his nature-infused abstract art.

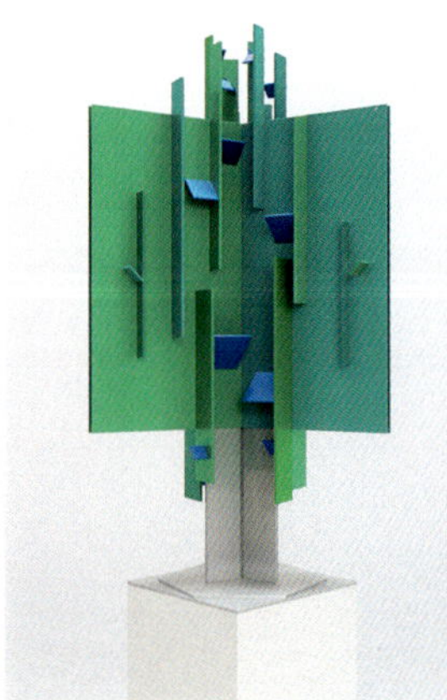
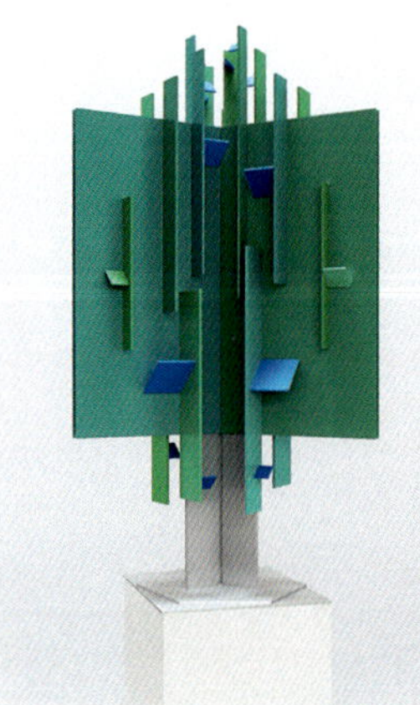
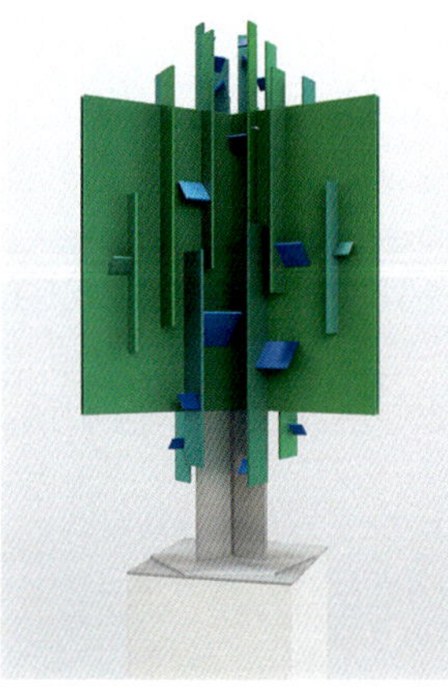

Left: View A of Eli Bornstein, *Tripart Hexaplane Construction No. 2* (model), 2002–6, acrylic enamel on aluminum and anodized aluminum, 93.4 x 47.5 cm, collection of the artist. Middle: View B of Eli Bornstein, *Tripart Hexaplane Construction No. 2* (model), 2002–6, acrylic enamel on aluminum and anodized aluminum, 93.4 x 47.5 cm, collection of the artist. Right: View C of Eli Bornstein, *Tripart Hexaplane Construction No. 2* (model), 2002–6, acrylic enamel on aluminum and anodized aluminum, 93.4 x 47.5 cm, collection of the artist.

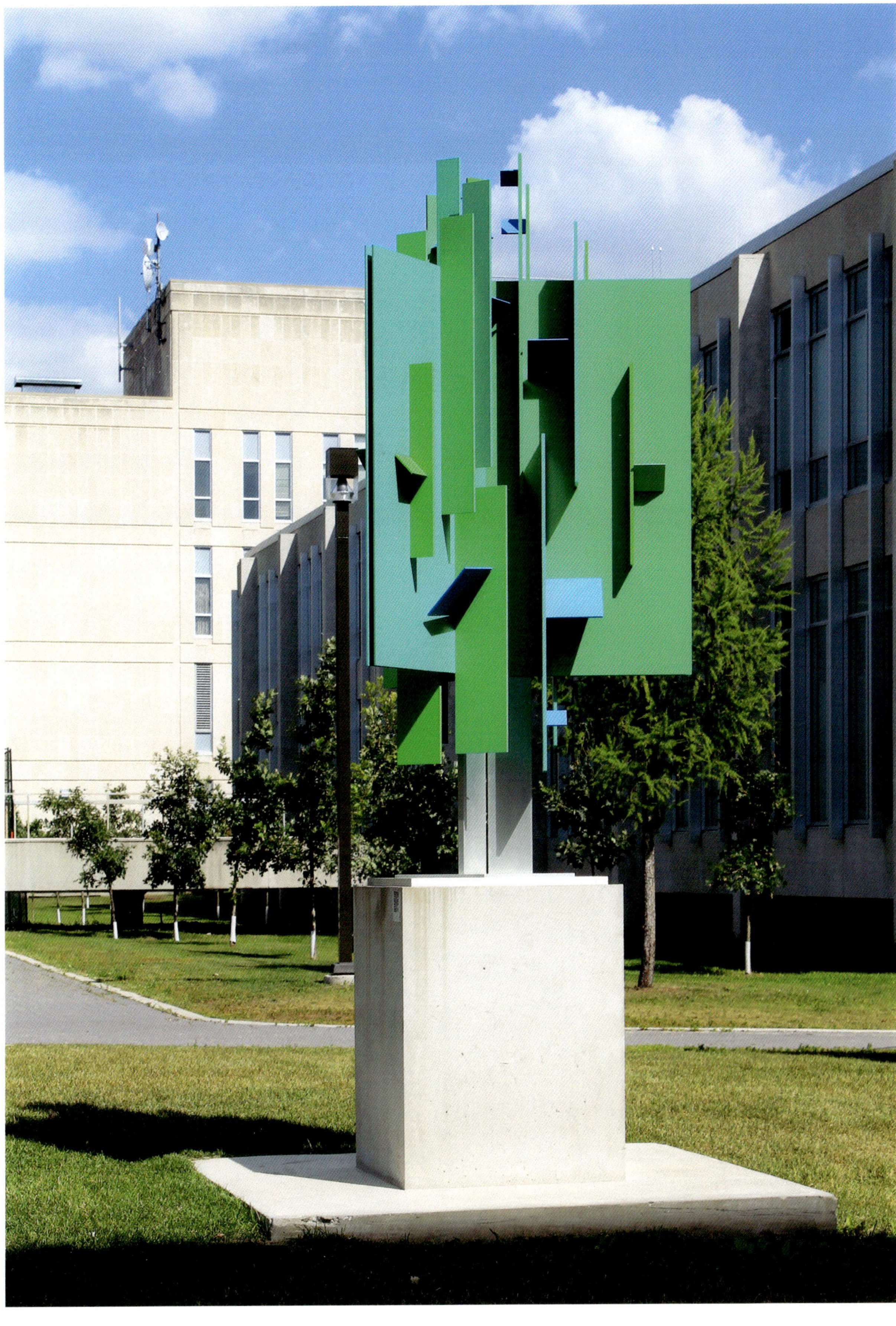

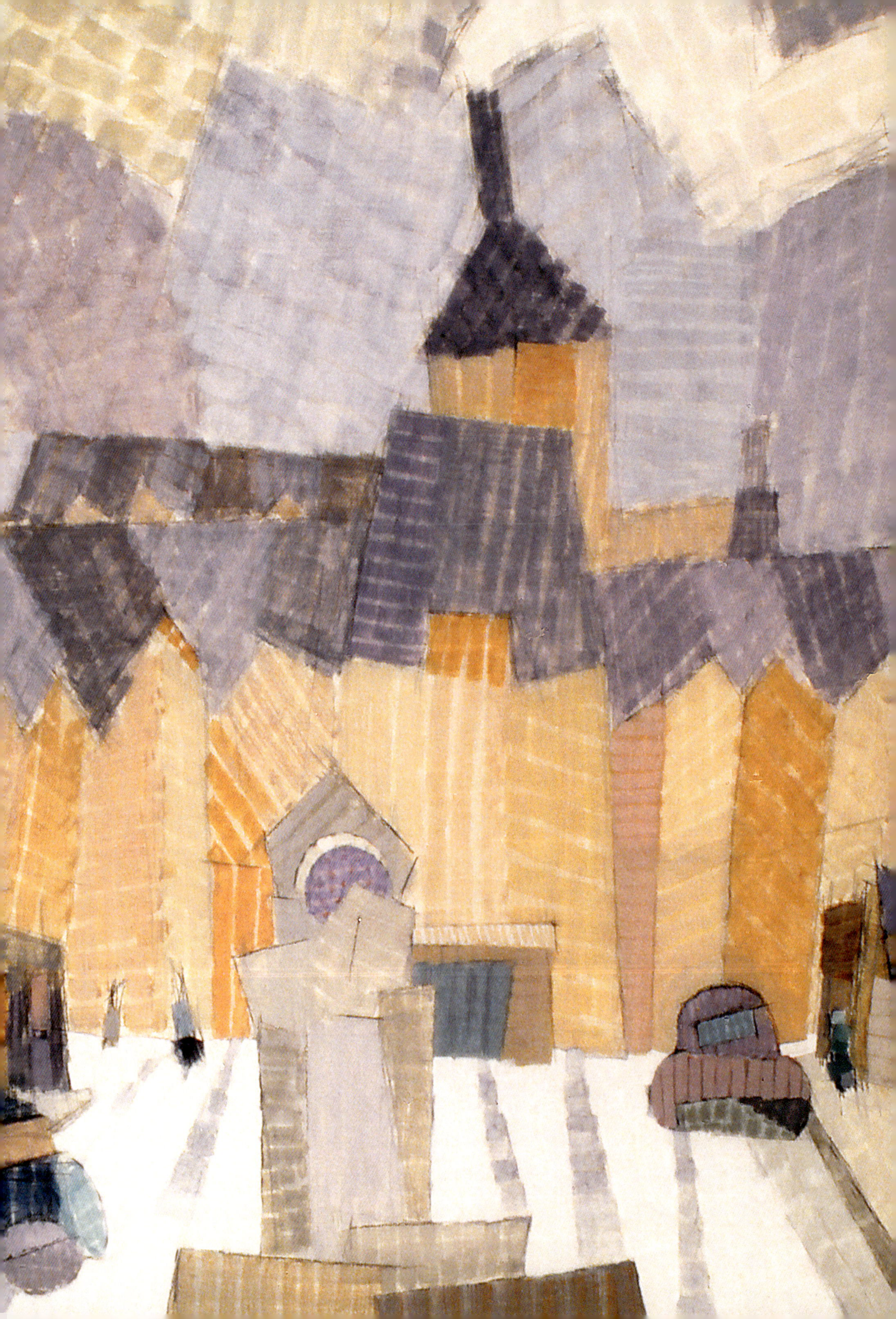

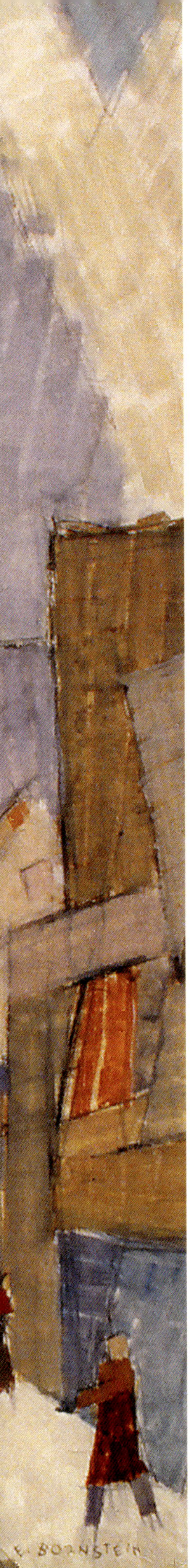

Significance & Critical Issues

Eli Bornstein's Structurist art responds to an esteemed modernist tradition that stretches from French Impressionism to the radical abstract work of Dutch De Stijl. As a devoted descendant of the American Transcendentalists, Bornstein dedicates his work to the vitality of the natural world, reinventing and re-evoking it through bold explorations of colour and geometric configuration. Bornstein was also a prolific writer and the editor of the internationally circulating periodical *The Structurist*, which he published out of the University of Saskatchewan from 1960 to 2020. Breaking new ground with the creation of his dynamic abstract reliefs, Bornstein ultimately defines his artistic self as a "builder," shedding new light on the wonders of nature in three-dimensional form.

From Representation to Abstraction

Eli Bornstein has, since the 1950s, been an exceptional contributor to abstract art in Canada. He calls his work "Structurist," a term that, per the dictionary, simply means "builder." From the start he has disallowed the label "Structurism," because, as he insists, such terminology would limit the work to a particular school or style, like Cubism or Minimalism.

As a young artist, Bornstein likely did not know that he was heading for abstraction. Yet from early on he developed an acute sense of his place within the unfolding history of modernist art from the Impressionists and onward. When in the mid-1950s he adopted the Structurist model, there was nothing gratuitous about it because he had already worked himself up to it, advancing step by step to the same stage of artistic evolution.

He would have gleaned his knowledge first from his museum visits in Milwaukee and Chicago, but more specifically he learned to hone his conception of art as an evolutionary practice from American relief artist Charles Biederman (1906–2004), whose *Art as the Evolution of Visual Knowledge* (1948) he first read in 1954. In his manifesto-like seminal essay, "Transition toward the New Art," and in subsequent writings, Bornstein would argue that a knowledge of history was crucial. "How else is the artist able to secure identity and meaning in his activity but through consciousness of his origins and the accomplishments of his ancestors?"[1] How else, to paraphrase Bornstein, can one advance and grow, except by building on one's predecessors' explorations and achievements?[2]

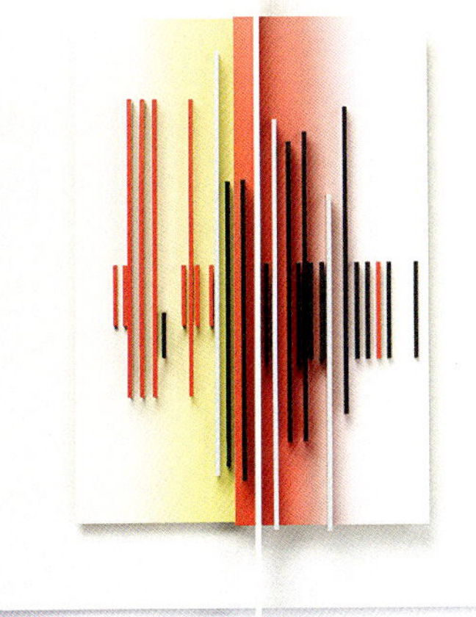

Opposite: Eli Bornstein, *Saskatoon*, 1954 (detail), gouache on gesso panel, 58.5 x 74 cm, private collection. Above: Charles Biederman, *#36-1950*, 1950, painted aluminum construction, 96.5 x 76.2 x 15.2 cm, Minneapolis Institute of Art.

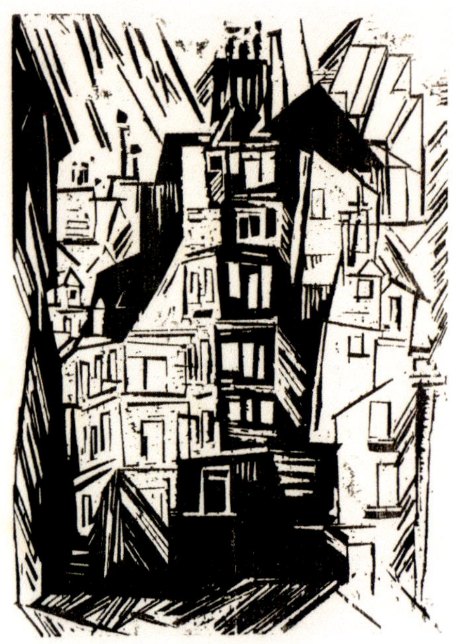

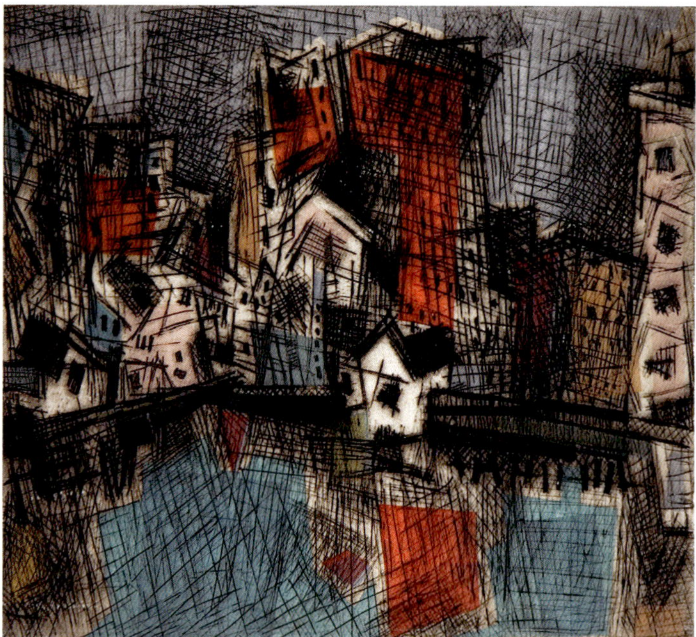

For Bornstein, who, from his earliest realist paintings of the 1940s was enthralled by the play of light, the real start was with Impressionism: its evocation of light, its broken brush strokes, its dots and dabs of colour. *Boats at Concarneau*, 1952, illustrates how he went on to learn from the Post-Impressionists, especially Paul Cézanne (1839–1906), to impose a more formal structure on Impressionism. By 1953 and 1954, he was wholeheartedly exploring the possible applications of Analytic Cubism, with the fractured cityscapes of the German American painter Lyonel Feininger (1871–1956) quite specifically standing behind his own splintered city views of Paris and Saskatoon.

Bornstein's sculpture simultaneously followed a comparable route from carving in-the-round to the open Cubist construction of his *Aluminum Construction (Tree of Knowledge)*. It, and the watercolour painting *The Island*, both from 1956, stand as the culminating works of Bornstein's representational phase. By 1957, like Jack Bush (1909–1977) in Toronto and Lionel LeMoine FitzGerald (1890–1956) in Winnipeg, he had come to share the opinion prevailing in advanced art circles of the time: that representational art no longer offered interesting options, and so, with no turning back, he adopted the abstract relief.

The catalyst for Bornstein was the work of Dutch painter Piet Mondrian (1872–1944), who was perhaps the most significant of the artists that he studied during his 1956 to 1957 sabbatical travels in Europe. In his 1958 article, "Transition toward the New Art," in *Structure* (the "New Art" soon to be dubbed the Structurist Relief), Bornstein reproduces Mondrian's *Composition with Color Planes 2*, 1917, juxtaposing it with one of his own first reliefs, as if to underscore the artist's impact at that very moment when he abandoned representation for abstraction. The year 1917 had also been a transitional one for Mondrian, who within the next year or so took the decisive step to suppress any residual naturalism, soon to lock his primary-colour planes into taut, flat, rectilinear grids. (See, for example, his *Composition with Large Red Plane, Yellow, Black, Gray and Blue*, 1921.) His intent was to distill his formal vocabulary into an abstract language that, as simply and purely as possible, could inscribe his quest for "absolute ideal beauty," a concept that

Left: Lyonel Feininger, *Paris Houses*, 1920, woodcut, 37.5 x 27 cm, RISD Museum, Providence. © Estate of Lyonel Feininger / Bild-Kunst, Bonn / CARCC Ottawa 2025. Right: Eli Bornstein, *Downtown Bridge #4*, 1954, etching and serigraph, 33.5 x 41.7 cm, Remai Modern, Saskatoon.

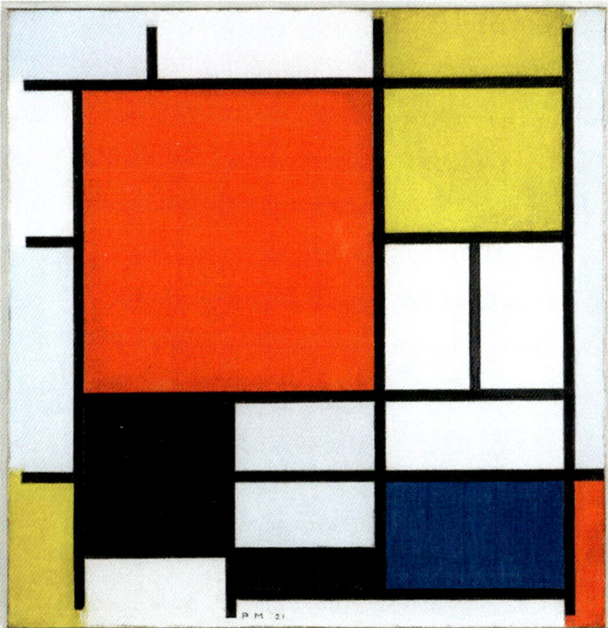

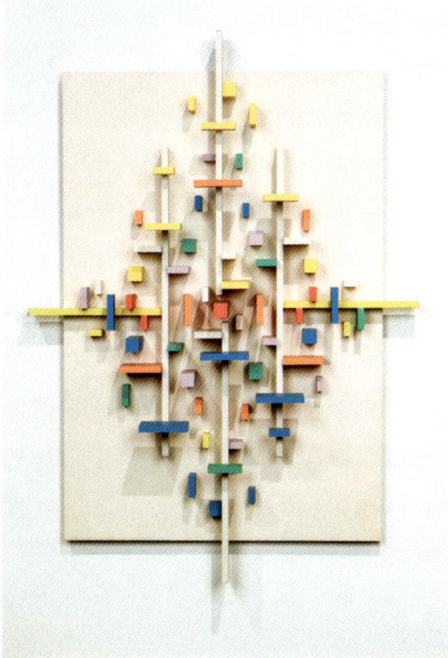

would utterly expel from his painting all that capricious weather of nature that Bornstein for his last time represents in the shimmering mists of *The Island*.[3]

Bornstein was ready to follow Mondrian, shedding representational devices and adopting his rectilinear compositions and use of primary colours, such as in *Structurist Relief No. 1* from 1966. But he could not endorse the Dutch modernist's retreat from everyday reality. Maybe advanced painting could no longer "imitate" nature, but, to Bornstein's mind, its path went astray when Mondrian decided to turn his back on the real world.[4] But how to honour the co-founder of De Stijl's formidable formal contributions to abstract art without abandoning the belief that art must encompass the life of nature? How to reject representational painting and still keep nature as your subject matter? Bornstein's solution would be the Structurist Relief. Working within its rules, he could, on the one hand, stay faithful to Mondrian's advanced abstraction. On the other hand, the relief provided him a way to re-purpose Mondrian's vocabulary, releasing it from painting's flat planes and redeploying it in terms of solid three-dimensional colour structures subject to the laws of gravity, light, and time.

Toward Nature

From the start, for Bornstein, it was a given that the Structurist Relief, even if abstract, was to be based in nature. But it could not imitate nature. Bornstein's strategy was not to copy, but to reinvent, using colour blocks of various shapes and hues to build visual metaphors for nature's own colours and events. Bornstein builds his reliefs from the ground up, so to speak, or, rather, from the wall out. The reliefs coexist with us in real space. They are experienced as much viscerally as visually. In plain-speak, we might say that we interact with Structurist reliefs just as we do with other objects, like tables and chairs, except that the function of furniture is practical, and that of the Structurist Relief is aesthetic.[5] And as nature is mutable, the reliefs are never fixed objects. They shift appearance when we change viewpoint, and in response to the light that hits them and the shadows they cast.

Left: Piet Mondrian, *Composition with Large Red Plane, Yellow, Black, Gray, and Blue*, 1921, oil on canvas, 59.5 x 59.5 cm, Kunstmuseum Den Haag. Right: Eli Bornstein, *Structurist Relief No. 1*, 1966, acrylic and wood on a wood support, 86.5 x 61 cm, Nickle Galleries, University of Calgary.

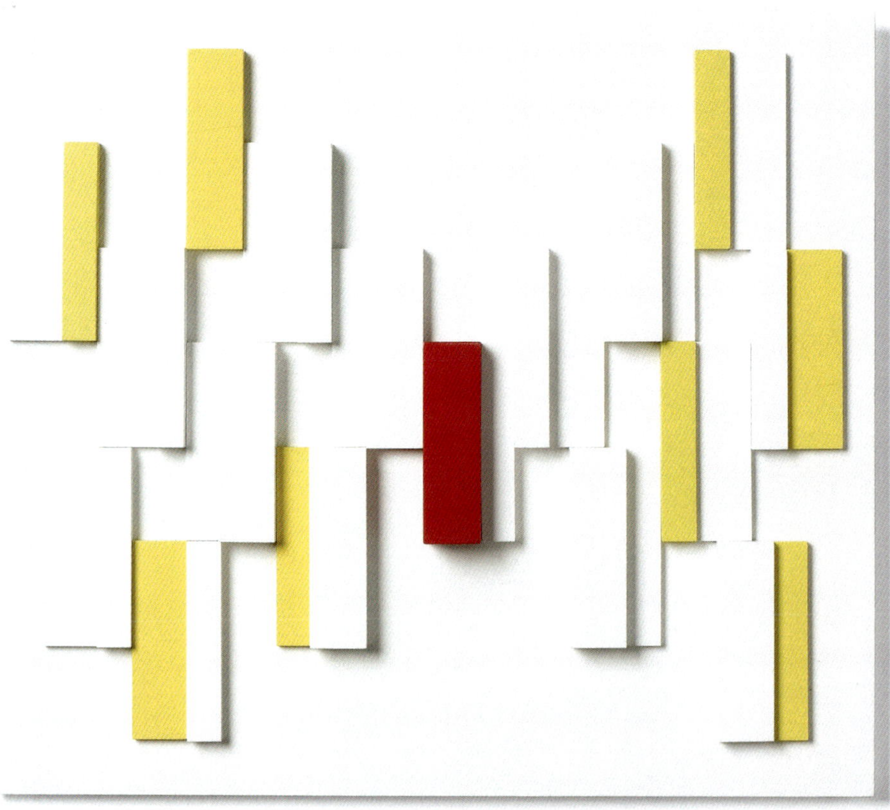

In the beginning, in the mid-1950s, Bornstein's reliefs were colour-shy—whites and one or two primaries, like in *Structurist Relief No. 14*, 1957. He had to learn his way. But already they insist on engaging us in real-world existence. *Structurist Relief No. 4*, 1957, shows us how this works. We see, first of all, the up-front compositional interplay among the six planes of slightly different sizes and thicknesses, five white ones and a blue one. Then we notice how the work has been sharply lit from the left, causing its planes to play a capricious little game of cast shadows.

These are variously weighty or slight so that the planes seem to hover differently. On the far right, one of the planes has been pushed so precipitously to the very edge of the ground, that it, along with its shadow, quite literally wants to escape into the outside world. But this is only one viewpoint, one position. Change the angle of light—or the time of day if the relief is naturally lit—and a new visual game begins. The world is in constant flux.

Then, as Bornstein's observations of the natural world become more intimate, he learns to embrace the colours of the landscapes in front of him. *Structurist Relief No. 3-1*, 1964, dates to a summer stay in Algonquin Park. Imagine him tromping through the woods or sitting lakeside, in his mind's eye inventorying the colours of sky and water, the pine needles and birch leaves, the undergrowth of fern fronds and mosses, flowers, and, perhaps, his stumbling on some prematurely dying growth already turning orange.

He would single out all these chromatic experiences individually, and focus them and transform them into what he called his "colour molecules"[6] —the blocks and strips and planes of colour that are the notes that make up his final relief composition. Structurist reliefs then, although immersive in nature, are not its mirrors. Instead, they

Eli Bornstein, *Structurist Relief No. 14*, 1957, enamel on panel, 44 x 51 x 6 cm, private collection.

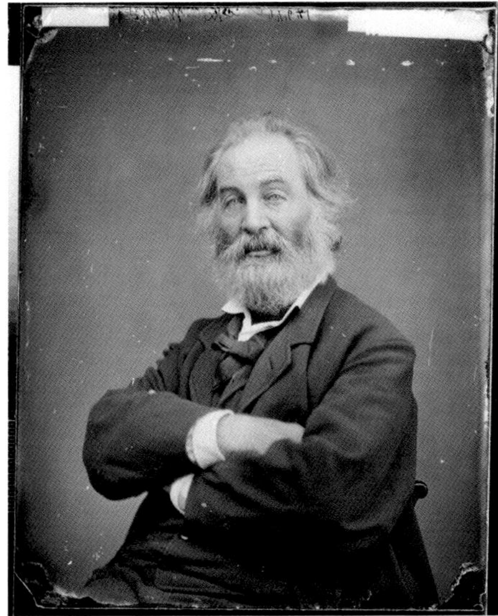

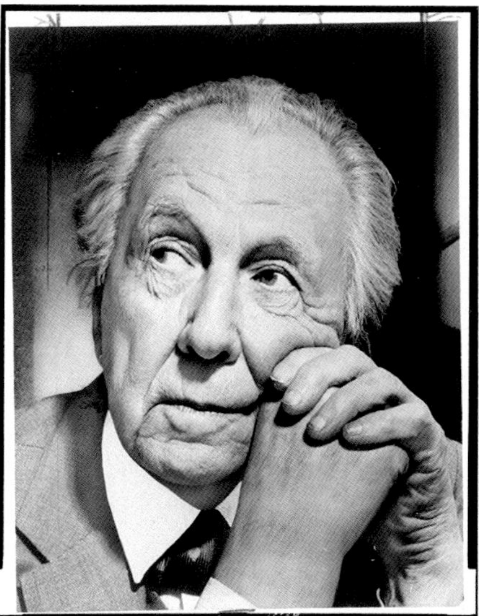

are new objects interjected into the viewer's perceptive field within whose compass nature's processes—here in the northerly forests of Ontario—are re-enacted.

This metamorphosis, the Structurist building process that brings this about, Bornstein has described metaphorically as "organic." "Through the 'organic' development of color in space and light," he argues, "the otherwise mechanical, technological aspect of the constructed relief can be transcended," and transformed, "into the warmth of human expression."[7]

Embracing the Transcendental

Formally, Bornstein's Structurist work evolves out of early twentieth-century European modernism. In subject matter, however, his dedication to the restorative powers of the undisturbed natural world is more immediately North American, rooted in Transcendentalism, a nineteenth-century intellectual movement based in New England that held that all creation is unified, humanity is essentially good, and that intuition trumps reason.

The Structurist Relief is imbued with "the American Grain," as Bornstein expressed it in a journal entry entitled "Emersonian Continuities."[8] "There is a vital thread," he notes, that connects the writings of Ralph Waldo Emerson (1803–1882), Henry David Thoreau (1817–1862), and Walt Whitman (1819–1892), among others, along with the architecture of Louis Sullivan (1856–1924) and Frank Lloyd Wright (1867–1959), to the North American Structurist Relief. For Bornstein, the Transcendentalists are our "literary, philosophical, geographical, environmental" legacy. While the work of European modernists such as Piet Mondrian motivated Bornstein's embrace of nonrepresentational art, the North American Transcendentalists spurred on his devotion to nature and his deep involvement with colour.

Bornstein called the Transcendentalists at heart "realists" because of how they related directly to nature. And so too is the Structurist Relief "realist," as both Bornstein and Charles Biederman had argued in their articles in the 1958 issue of *Structure*. Direct observation and unmediated experience, they insisted, were essential if an artist intended to realize the "palpableness of creative nature."[9] A Structurist's work, then,

Left: Walt Whitman, c.1860–65, photograph by Matthew Brady, National Archive and Records Administration, Washington, D.C. Right: Frank Lloyd Wright, 1954, photograph by Al Ravenna, Library of Congress, Washington, D.C.

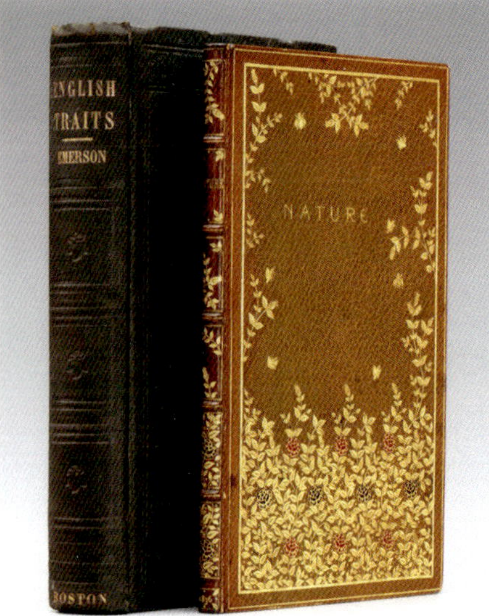

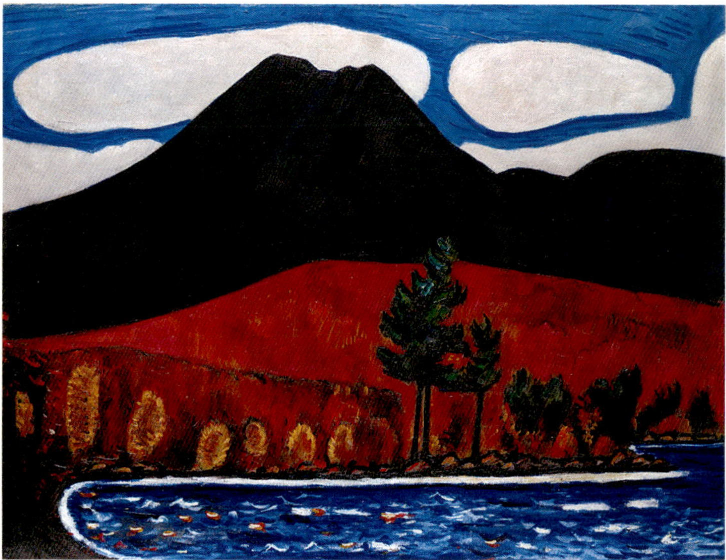

is an objective, even a scientific pursuit. It must, therefore, never be considered an "expressionist" art, lacking any emphasis on internal psychology. Art is not, Bornstein writes, about individual subjectivity or personal feelings, because "art and nature are something greater than the individual person," greater than a person's "own ego and unconscious self."[10] Bornstein considered expressionism in all its forms narcissistic, "a flight from reality" that can only lead to "confusion and lack of direction."[11]

The Structurist artist, instead, looks at the world with Emerson's much celebrated "transparent eye-ball," which banishes all egotism and understands no distinction between the self and the Universal Being.[12] Emerson did not accept any essential distinction between subjective and objective experience, instead maintaining that ideal and transcendental truth coincides with the stuff of reality and flows with it directly and inseparably. Whitman, too, held that "the greatest poet has less a marked style and is more the channel of thoughts and things without increase or diminution.... What I tell I tell for precisely what it is."[13] Whatever an artist individually may desire to represent and express, wrote the Transcendentalist-influenced Marsden Hartley (1877–1943), is itself "of no importance."[14]

In a 2009 article, Bornstein summarized the distinction between expressionist-based art and the holistic purview of his Structurist art:

> Some art may be viewed as reflecting our own image, internal nature, aspects of our human preoccupations, conflicts, and creativity. Other cultures and kinds of art have been more focused and interconnected to larger natural and cosmic processes of which humans are only a minute and transient part. The first view is anthropocentric, while the other is more ecocentric.[15]

Bornstein's Structurist art has been wholly devoted to the ecocentric position, evoking the flux of the natural world through our perception of the dynamic behaviour of his three-dimensional reliefs in light and space.

Left: Cover of *Nature* by Ralph Waldo Emerson (Boston: James Munroe and Company, 1836). First published in 1836, Emerson's *Nature* is a foundational work in the American Transcendentalist movement. Right: Marsden Hartley, *Mount Katahdin (Maine), Autumn #2*, 1939–40, oil on canvas, 76.8 x 102.2 cm, The Metropolitan Museum of Art, New York.

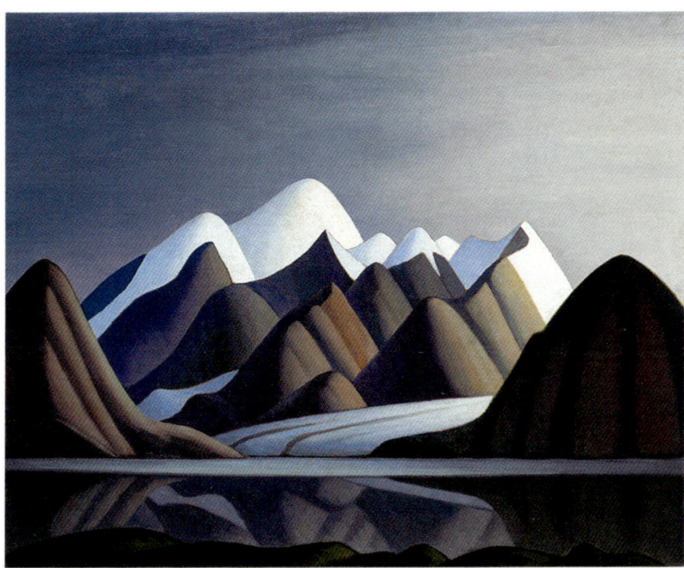
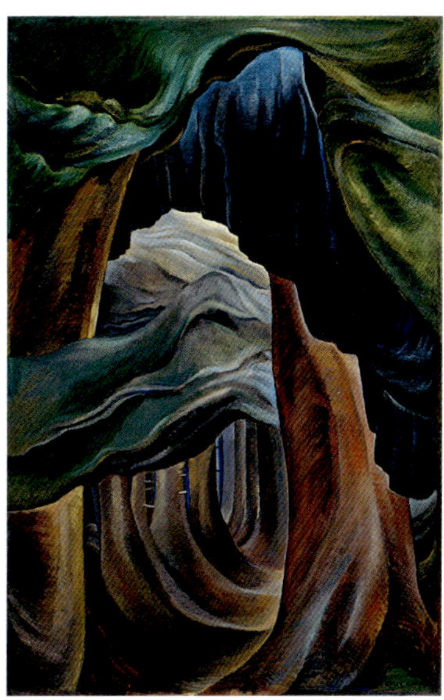

Art as an Act of Worship

Many Canadian landscape artists were influenced by the idea of nature as spiritual, either through Transcendentalism or other "spiritualist" approaches to the landscape. The consummate Canadian landscape artists Lawren S. Harris (1885–1970) and Emily Carr (1871–1945), both devotees of Transcendentalist literature, thought in comparable terms. For instance, in the 1920s and 1930s, Harris spoke from theosophical heights of nature's sublimities, and Carr used a language that was intimately Christian. A problem for Bornstein, a committed secularist, was just how to give expression to his own wonderment, so comparable to theirs: "It is the failure of written or spoken language," as he noted in a journal entry, "to find adequate words to describe the experience. 'Spiritual,' 'emotional,' 'aesthetic,' 'supreme sensory response' as well as 'religious' fail to capture or describe such experience fully or to our complete satisfaction."[16] Nevertheless, as he had already concluded, writing in *The Structurist* in 1970:

> The creation of art in its deepest sense is like an act of worship, like a prayer. As such it is a communion with Nature and with other human beings. It is at its best an act of belief in life. Transcending the ego, art expands beyond itself towards values and meanings greater than the self.... Here art is essentially a religious act, in the fullest sense of the word "religious."[17]

The passage is almost mystical and draws Bornstein's abstract relief landscapes—especially the later horizontal Multiplanes—both spiritually and formally into the tradition that I have elsewhere called Northern Symbolist Landscape Painting.[18]

One can argue that he is an unwitting descendant of that lineage, which includes Northern Europeans like Harald Sohlberg (1869–1935), Ferdinand Hodler (1853–1918), and the pre-abstract Piet Mondrian, along with North Americans like Marsden Hartley and Georgia O'Keeffe (1887–1986), Harris, and Carr. This was painting also born out of French Impressionism but, by the end of the nineteenth century, bred from a renewed confrontation with the artists' own northern wildernesses. Driven by their respective senses of a burgeoning spiritual unease, they sought to look beyond surface appearances

Left: Lawren S. Harris, *Mount Thule, Bylot Island*, 1930, oil on canvas, 82 x 102.3 cm, Vancouver Art Gallery. Right: Emily Carr, *Forest, British Columbia*, 1931–32, oil on canvas, 130 x 86.8 cm, Vancouver Art Gallery.

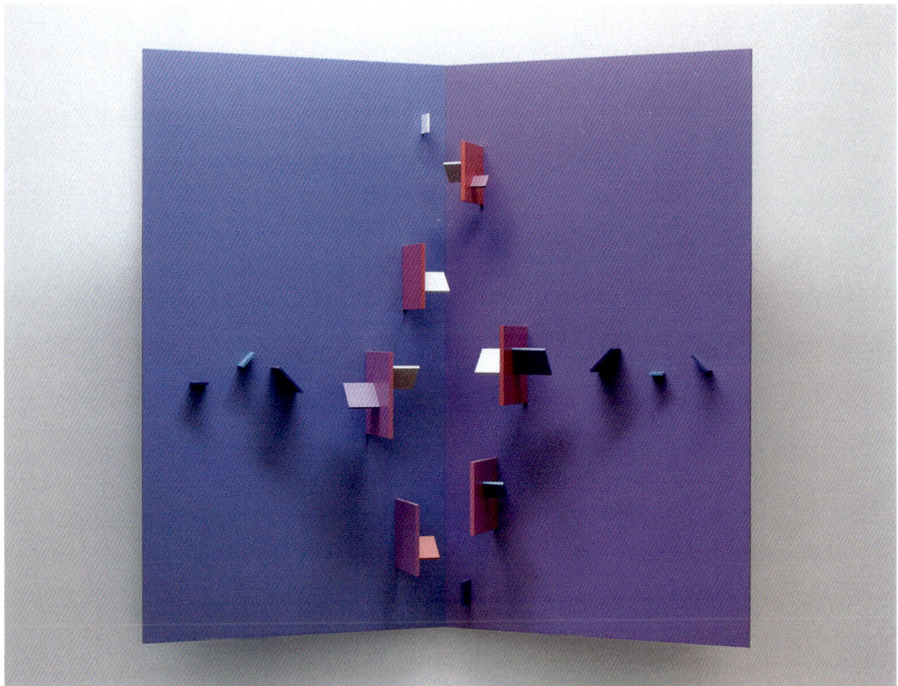

and to discover something of nature's inner spirit. "The eternal life is sensed everywhere in the action of nature,"[19] wrote the Finnish painter Akseli Gallen-Kallela (1865–1931), as he and his Nordic landscape colleagues abandoned realistic representation to devise new pictorial structures that would resonate, as it were, with the life of the soul. Except for Mondrian, there was little occasion for Bornstein to know these artists, but their paintings shared compositional tropes that he would intuit out of analogous convictions, deconstruct, and then rethink in accordance with his personal artistic impulses and on his own three-dimensional Structurist terms.[20]

Their creators may not be relief artists, but from among the works of Bornstein's immediate contemporaries, equally dedicated to the landscape sublime, we might add the transformed Northern Manitoba helicopter views of Gershon Iskowitz (1919–1988), where landscape is present only by allusion; the Rococo-sublime skyscapes of Charles Gagnon (1934–2003); the late-career West Coast "entanglements" of Gordon Smith (1919–2020); or, most recently, the digitally generated large-scale sublime landscape images of Christian Eckart (b.1959).

Ecological and Environmental Concerns

Even as Bornstein celebrates the natural world, he nevertheless shares with early twentieth-century abstract movements a progressive, even utopian vision that art can be practically applied to contemporary life and to the improvement of the common good. As he writes in a journal entry:

> Just as green spaces of wild vegetation, like trees and grass (as well as free expanses of sky and water) are necessary to human health, perhaps even a genetic requirement to our survival in our technological man-made cityscapes, so art, like music, can or should provide the kind of inspiration, tranquility, sense of

Eli Bornstein, *Multiplane Structurist Relief VI, No. 1* (Sunset Series), 1998–99, acrylic enamel on aluminum, 85 x 71.8 x 15 cm, collection of the artist.

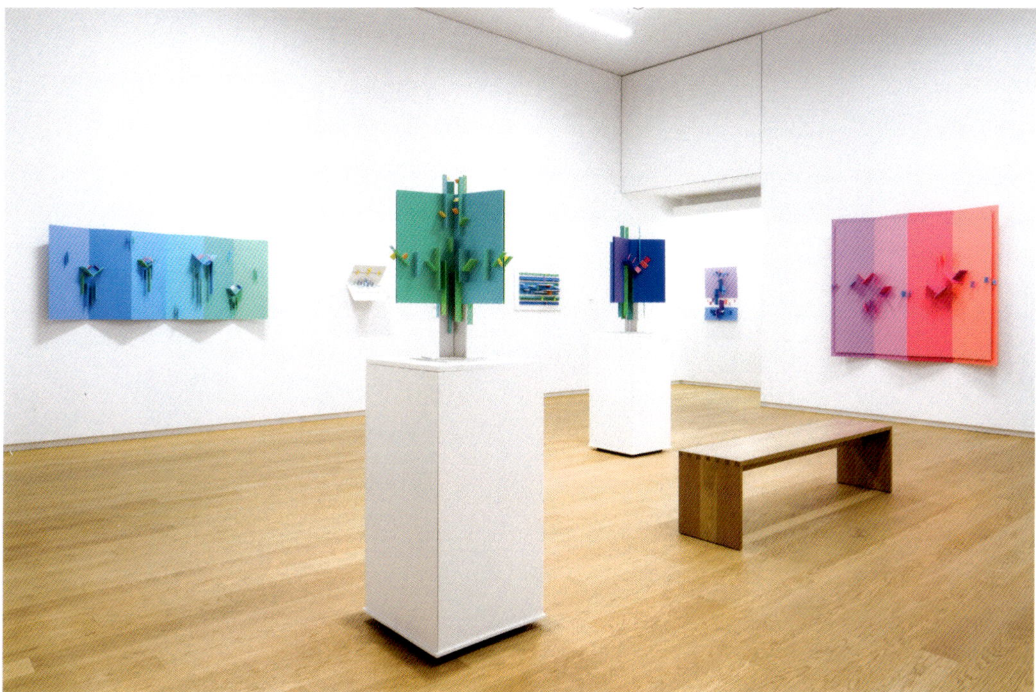

> belonging in our increasingly hostile or inhuman environments. How to live a sane, peaceful, and relatively simple life in our increasingly complex world is a primary question confronting the twenty-first century.[21]

This, for all intents and purposes, is the mission statement of *The Structurist*, the internationally circulating periodical that Bornstein founded in 1960 and produced regularly until 2010 (with an anniversary issue in 2020). Art historian Oliver A.I. Botar has called this publishing venture one of Bornstein's "most important achievements within the landscape of Canadian art and intellectual history."[22] Botar has also highlighted how Bornstein's periodical declared his ecological thinking and environmentalism "years before the rise of politically engaged art beginning in the late 1960s, and well before any other Canadian artistic periodical."[23]

Over the years, the contributors to *The Structurist* have included a host of artists, architects, and intellectual luminaries from around the world: Josef Albers (1888–1976), Naum Gabo (1890–1977), Walter Benjamin (1892–1940), Erwin Panofsky (1892–1968), Murray Adaskin (1906–2002), Marshall McLuhan (1911–1980), George Woodcock (1912–1995), Elizabeth Willmott (b.1928), Zaha Hadid (1950–2016), and Arne Næss (1912–2009). More recently, the journal has featured a long list of younger international contributors, as well as writings by Bornstein himself, with essays or interviews in every issue. The periodical has explored art and its relations to science, technology, music, architecture, literature, philosophy, religion, and environmentalism, with many of its articles not directly associated with Structurist art.

As Bornstein has explained, it was in the spirit of free inquiry that he solicited articles that were "meaningful and provocative challenges" to his own artistic position: "It seems increasingly apparent that real nourishment for art is not to be found in art writing" alone.[24] Rather, he believed, the real problems in art relate to the problems of

Installation view of *Artist in Focus: Eli Bornstein* at Remai Modern, Saskatoon, 2019, photograph by Blaine Campbell.

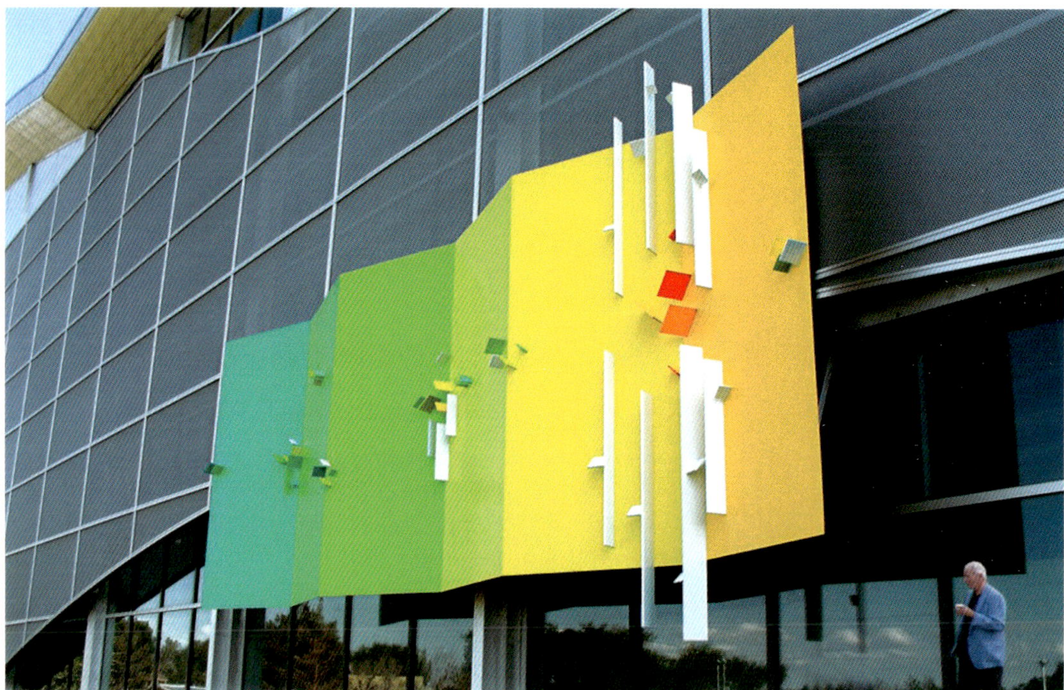

society and to humanity itself.[25] The cover of the 1971 issue of *The Structurist*, which was adorned with an iconic NASA view of the Earth from space, "was devoted in its entirety to the relationship between humanity and nature in relation to artistic production, surely the first eco-artistic publication in Canada, and one of the first anywhere."[26] Later, Bornstein declared his critical sympathy with both Earth First! (1980–), perhaps the most radical of the environmental activist groups, and *Adbusters* (1989–), the Vancouver-based anti-consumerist and environmentalist journal. The 2009–10 issue of *The Structurist* is subtitled "Toward an Earth-Centred Greening of Art and Architecture."

What Bornstein wrote in a journal entry from 2012 speaks to his sense of ecological and environmentalist urgency: "The overwhelming dysfunctionality that pervades our global culture calls for the emergence of an ethos with a need and determination for exploring a new sustainable and consilient art and architecture that will lead towards a vital rebirth and to the efflorescence of a new harmony, beauty, and enrichment for our future world."[27]

Installation view of *Untitled Hexaplane Structurist Relief*, 2004, by Eli Bornstein on the Canadian Light Source Building, University of Saskatchewan, Saskatoon, date unknown, photographer unknown.

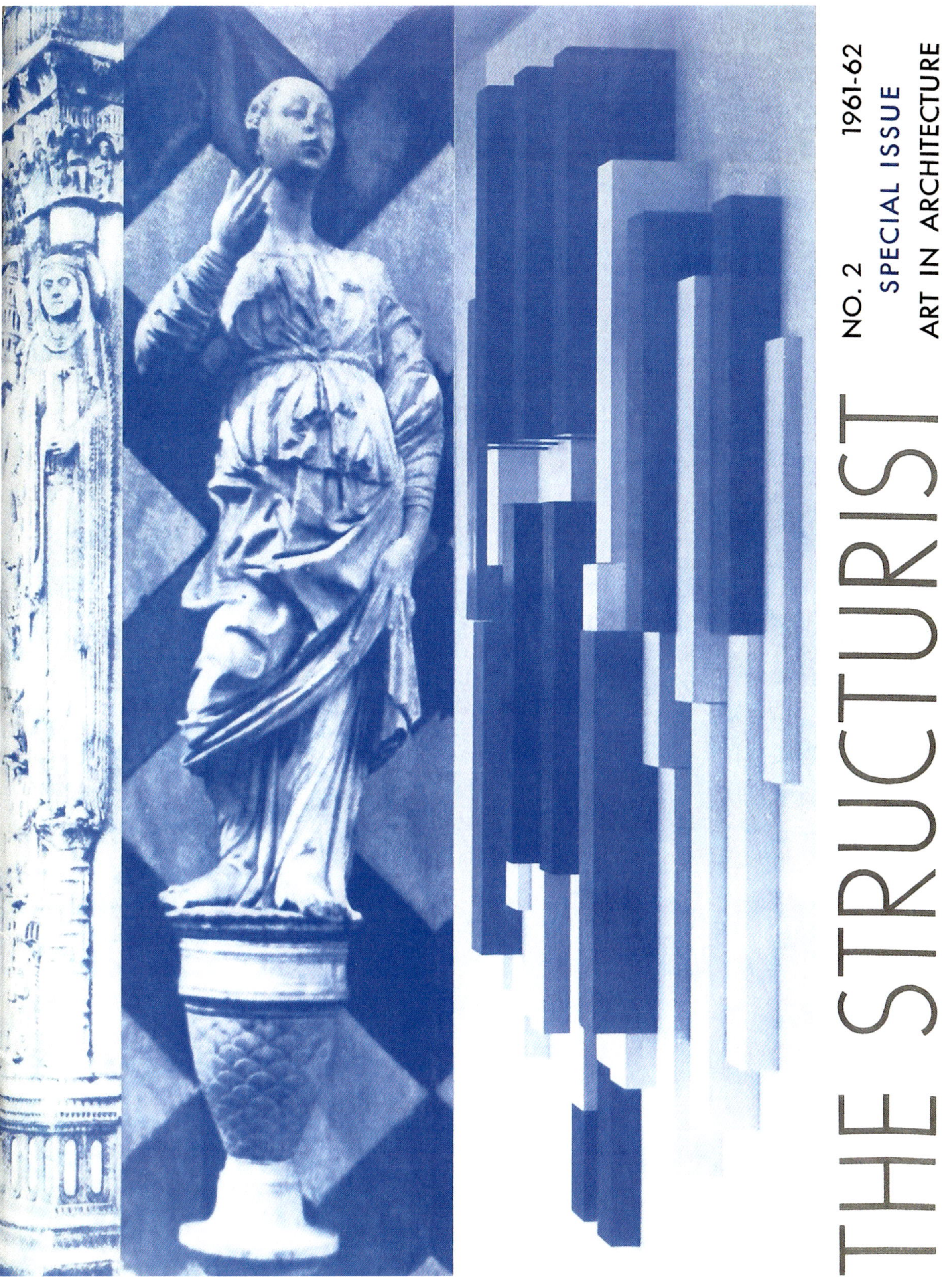

Cover of *The Structurist*, no. 2, "Art in Architecture," edited by Eli Bornstein (Saskatoon: University of Saskatchewan, 1962).

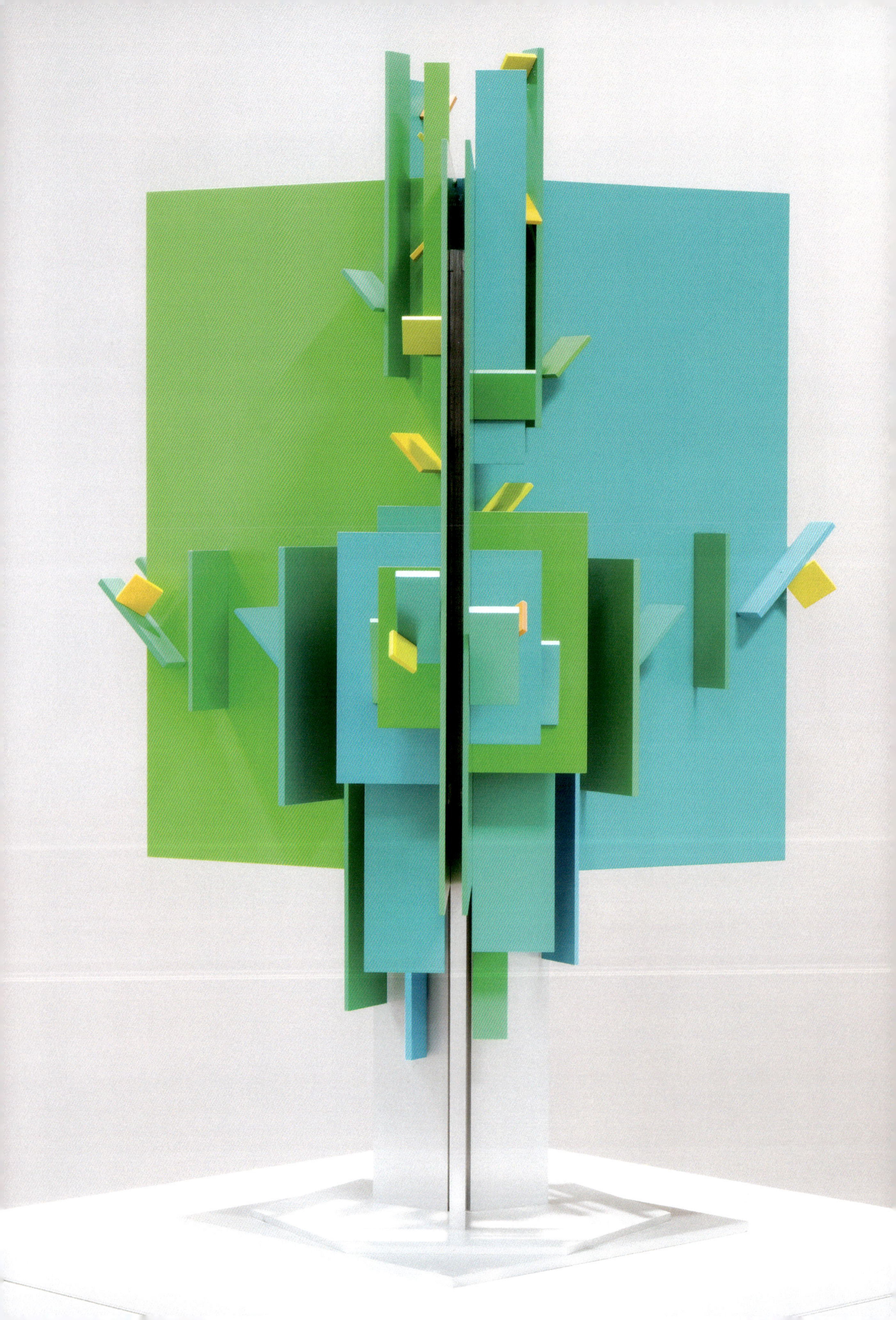

Style & Technique

The primary contribution that Eli Bornstein made to abstract art in Canada was his development of the Structurist Relief: a singular art form that draws from both painting and sculpture. The innovation lies in Bornstein's approach, freeing abstract painting from the restrictions of the flat picture plane, and advancing it into the real, three-dimensional space of sculpture. His reliefs are built using colour blocks and planes that are activated by ambient light and meticulously choreographed by the artist into a dynamic organic unity.

Painting into Relief

As a student, and during his early career, Bornstein worked in the traditional media of printmaking, drawing, painting, and sculpture. In his painting, he systematically incorporated lessons learned from early twentieth-century European modernism; from Impressionism's emphasis on the transitory effects of light; from Post-Impressionism's focus on form and structure; and from Cubism's radical deconstruction of the figure-ground relationship. Streetscapes such as *Downtown*, 1954, and *Porte St. Denis*, 1954, may be vibrant with energy, but they are also tightly ordered constructions of colour swatches and tilted planes that echo works by French Post-Impressionists like Paul Cézanne (1839–1906) and Cubists like Lyonel Feininger (1871–1956). An example of Feininger's work that may have influenced Bornstein is *Cathedral (Kathedrale)* for the Program of the *State Bauhaus in Weimar (Programm des Staatlichen Bauhauses in Weimar)*, 1919. As to landscapes, Bornstein's watercolour *The Island*, 1956, takes its cues from Piet Mondrian (1872–1944) from the moment when the Dutch painter was turning toward

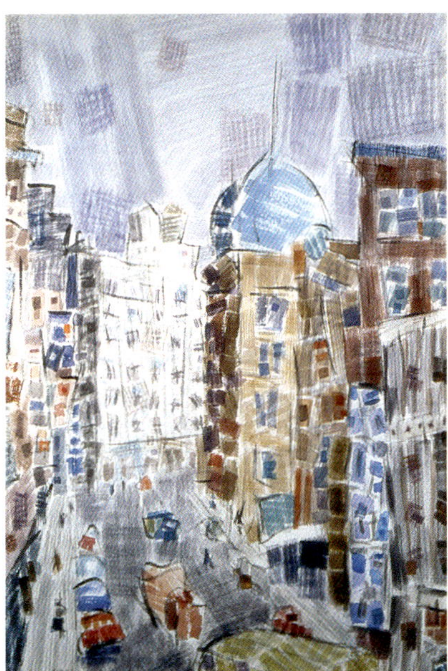

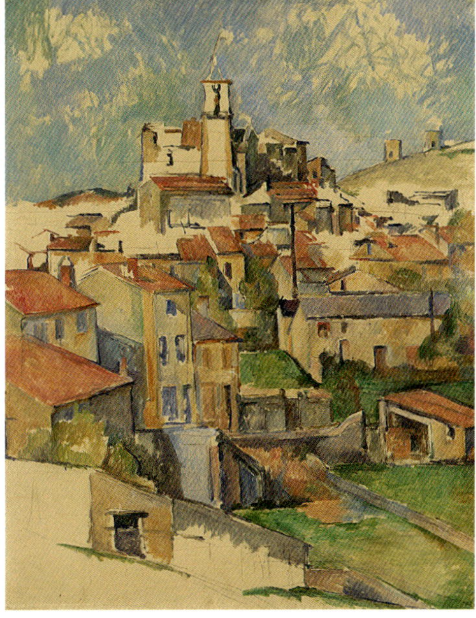

Opposite: Eli Bornstein, *Tripart Hexaplane Construction No. 3*, 2008–10, acrylic enamel on aluminum and anodized aluminum, 73.7 x 43.2 x 43.2 cm, Remai Modern, Saskatoon. Left: Eli Bornstein, *Downtown*, 1954, watercolour on paper, 50 x 70 cm, University of Saskatchewan, Saskatoon. Right: Paul Cézanne, *Gardanne*, 1885–86, oil on canvas, 80 x 64.1 cm, The Metropolitan Museum of Art, New York.

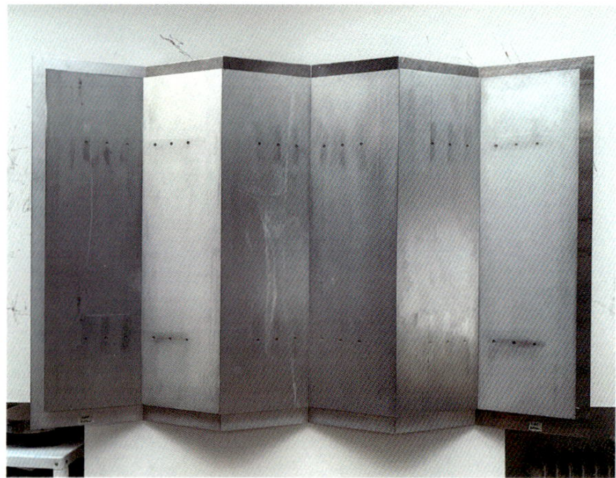

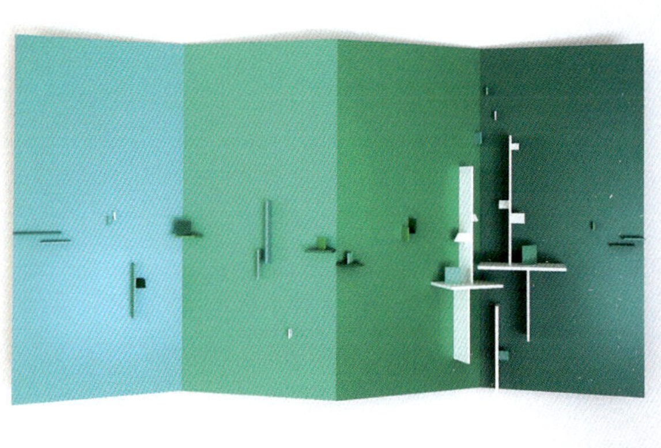

pure abstraction. Bornstein looked particularly at Mondrian's 1917 series Compositions with Color Planes, learning from them to disperse his own shimmering patches of colour flatly across the whole of a white sheet of paper.

In 1957, after a crucial meeting with American relief artist Charles Biederman (1906–2004), and after a sabbatical trip to Europe to meet a host of prominent abstract, geometric-relief artists such as Jean Gorin (1899–1981), Mary Martin (1907–1969), Victor Pasmore (1908–1998), and Georges Vantongerloo (1886–1965), among others, Bornstein largely abandoned two-dimensional media. Instead, he began to construct his first Structurist reliefs, an art form he has continued to develop throughout his career. Like Biederman, and unlike the Europeans, Bornstein insisted that art, even abstract art, should remain rooted in the close study of the phenomena of the natural world.

The Structurist Relief can thus be understood as a continuation of the tradition of landscape painting. But it does not transcribe or represent nature. Rather, it translates our experiences of the natural world into a new, parallel abstract language. In his article "Art Toward Nature" (1975–76), Bornstein spelled out the physical distinctions between traditional two-dimensional painting and the Structurist Relief. Whereas a painting hangs flat on the wall, a relief projects out from the wall into real space; that is, into the space of the viewer. Whereas the image in a painting remains unchanged regardless of where the viewer stands, the colours and structural relationships in a relief continually change in response to the viewer's movements and angles of perception. Whereas a painting remains static, a relief unfolds as an ongoing dynamic event.[1]

But, we may well ask, if "Nature" (as Bornstein often capitalized) is the subject matter, how can a reductive artistic vocabulary that is hard-edged and geometric embody nature's abundance? In a journal entry, Bornstein posed the question this way: "How can an art (the art that I practice) that so often seems and is so mistakenly regarded as almost high-tech—involving as it does drill presses, air-compressors, computerized milling machines, industrial materials like aluminum, plexiglass and acrylic enamel—relate to nature, its preservation and conservation? How does an art that looks so engineered, 'foster increasing reverence for Nature in its broadest and deepest sense?'"[2] Would it, on the contrary, he asks, be more relevant and meaningful if his medium "were mud or sand," or if it "were fabricated with fur and feathers?"[3]

But Structurist art is not about the touchy-feely or about tactile sensibility. Instead, Bornstein harnesses technology to finesse his expressive means. Industrial-type

Left: View of an unfinished Structurist relief (front) in Eli Bornstein's studio, Saskatoon, 2020, photograph by Roald Nasgaard. Right: Eli Bornstein, *Quadriplane Structurist Relief No. 8*, 2000–2002, acrylic enamel on aluminum, 76.4 x 135.8 x 16.2 cm, collection of the artist.

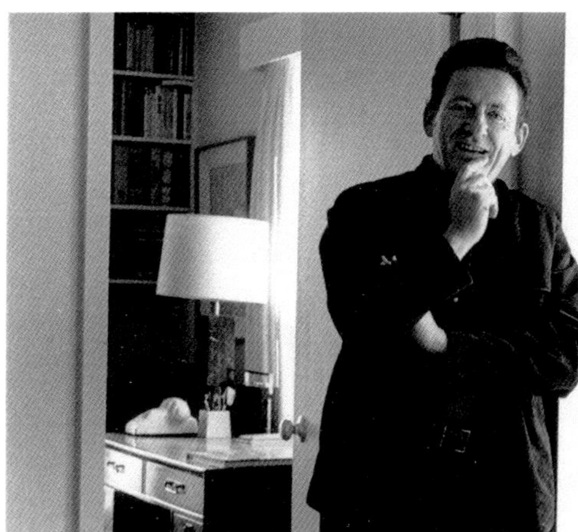
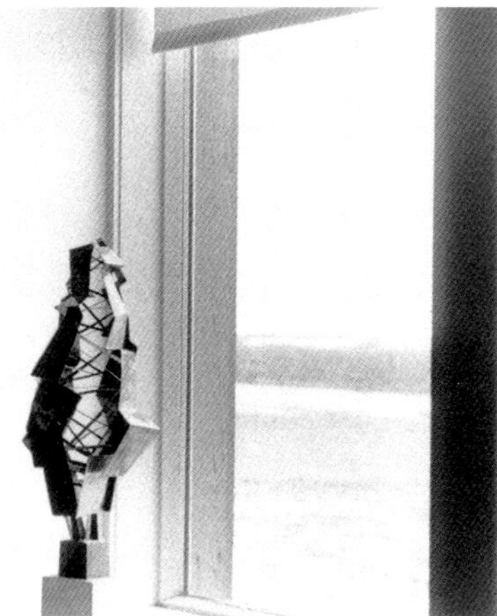

manufacture yields precision and clarity so as to purge the structural components of traces of the handmade. It allows material substance to be dissolved into colour phenomena. To compose with colour and light, and space and structure, in Bornstein's words, is like performing "a multi-spatial visual choreography of chromatic and structural counterpoint"; it is like enacting a piece of music or performing a feat of choreography.[4] The effects can be as delicate as "the winged color of birds and butterflies"[5] or dramatic like music unfolding from intimate chamber performances to the magnitudes of symphonies and operas: "great polyrhythms, collisions, silences, repetitions and variations."[6]

Toward Construction

At the beginning of his career, Bornstein, alongside drawing and painting, also made sculpture. He carved in wood and stone and made small constructions—such as *Shelomo*, 1949–56—often with an eye to the work of Romanian artist Constantin Brâncuşi (1876–1957), his formal reductions, his sensitivity to materials, and the care with which he crafted his bases.

Growth Motif Construction No. 3, 1956, is both a self-sufficient work as well as a predecessor, or an early model, for his public commission *Aluminum Construction (Tree of Knowledge)*, 1956, the monumental 4.5-metre-tall welded aluminum sculpture that had been commissioned for the new Saskatchewan Teachers' Federation Building in Saskatoon, and was completed later that year. *Growth Motif* bears witness to how Bornstein, while testing out new ideas, was evolving from a carver into an assembler, from a sculptor of mass to an openwork metal constructor, thus initiating an important stage along his journey to the Structurist Relief. *Growth Motif* was executed during a stay in New York, while Bornstein was at the Sculpture Studio in Long Island City, Queens. He was already adept at working with brass and bronze, materials he had learned how to handle in jewellery-making classes at Milwaukee State Teachers College in the 1940s, but the Sculpture Studio offered other techniques and new materials. Also while in New Jersey, he learned at a factory how to weld aluminum, a still relatively new technique for artists.

In *Growth Motif*, Bornstein thrusts his light reflective metal planes vigorously outward from a sturdy inner core. Through subsequent models, the core cedes its mass until it dissolves into an open metal construction, the configuration of which, as we will remember, he had earlier envisaged in the skeletal building structures in the lithograph *Porte St. Denis*, 1954, and which is ultimately fulfilled in *Tree of Knowledge*.

Tree of Knowledge, with its grand concatenations of reflective aluminum plates, large and small, and its intricate internal scaffolding, is a Constructivist sculpture. It is not

Eli Bornstein posing with the maquette for *Tree of Knowledge*, 1979, photograph by Sandra Semchuk.

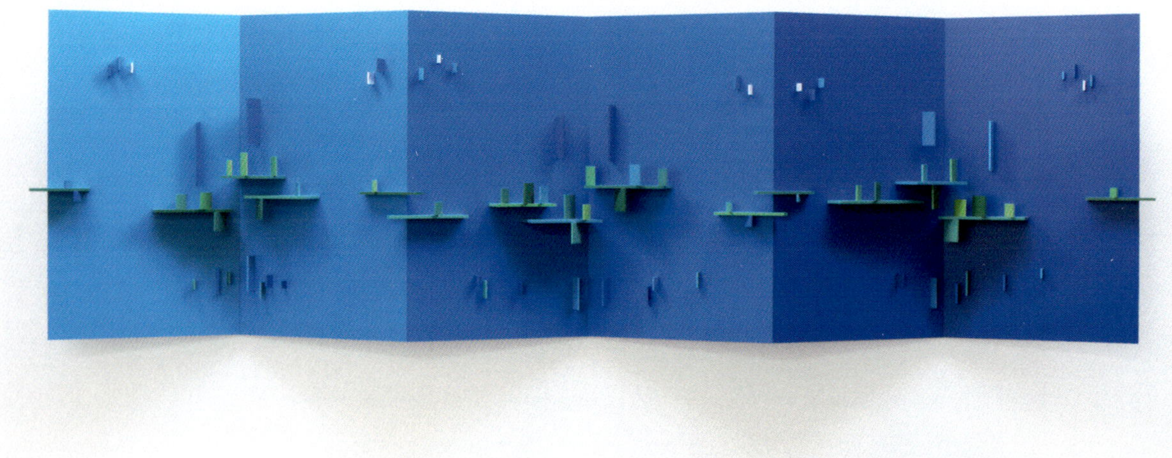

yet a Structurist one. It's a Cubistic abstraction, the free-floating shimmering planes of Bornstein's watercolour *The Island*, 1956, here extruded as aluminum plates. It is the geometric equivalent of the conical shape of a coniferous tree with its tiered and drooping branches, now formally reconceived. Even so, some of the key ingredients of Structurist reliefs are already here: how the sculpture is built by construction and energized by light. But to cross the threshold from making abstract art based in nature to inventing a new vocabulary that would act in *parallel* to nature's vital processes necessitated not another incremental move, but a restart from ground zero.

Structurist Art

In his conception of the Structurist Relief, Bornstein wanted to invent a purely abstract vocabulary that could still incorporate our immediate experiences of nature. This required him to restart from the point where Piet Mondrian had divorced his art from nature and crossed the threshold into pure abstraction. During his sabbatical leave in Europe in 1957, Bornstein set out to meet a number of artists working within the orbit of Mondrian's De Stijl traditions. Their work indeed provided foundational principles on which he could build his own "New Art" (soon to be renamed the Structurist Relief). But he also found their work too rationally self-contained, reconfirming a conviction that he shared with his American colleague Charles Biederman that art should found its operations on the evidence of our visual senses. The future of Structurist art therefore should depend on its artists ever honing their observations of the natural world and painstakingly learning how to translate nature's interdependent forms, colours, spaces, and light into abstract relief constructions.

Bornstein's early reliefs, such as *Low Form Relief No. 10*, 1957, are shallow projections and white with a few primary colours. He worked out their structure in smaller models (tempera on composition board), executing the final versions in oil on wood. The individual relief planes are quite large, often splayed out in asymmetrical compositions, engaging the full surface of their background supports, out to their very edges. Because they are mostly white, they can look a little puritanical, but there is also wit in their asymmetries and in their shadow play. By the early 1960s, the relief elements in works

Eli Bornstein, *Hexaplane Structurist Relief No. 1* (River-Screen Series), 1989–96, acrylic enamel on aluminum and Plexiglas, 54.6 x 192.2 x 17.2 cm, collection of the artist.

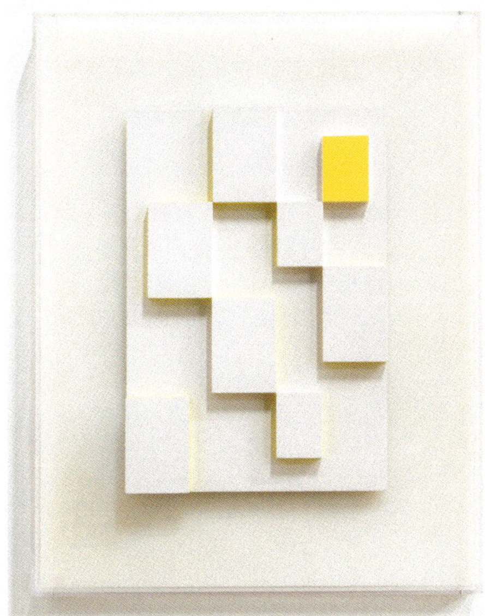

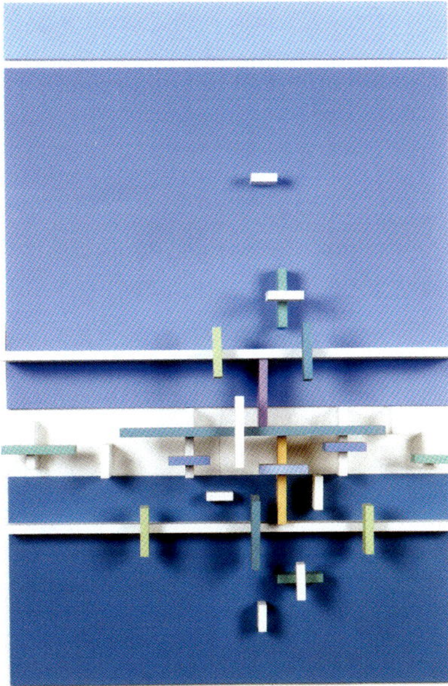

such as *Structurist Relief No. 1*, 1966, become more differentiated, thinner and deeper, their relationships more complex and their colours more active, their hues venturing beyond the primaries.

It may be simplifying a little, but something crucial happened around 1965 and 1966 in Bornstein's evolution, quickening his work toward new expressive potential. Heretofore, Bornstein had used his ground planes more like neutral backdrops against which to stage the main action of the foreground relief constructions. Concomitantly, the reliefs had also tended to shy away from the edges of their supports, leaving them centrally clustered and self-sufficient, somehow independent from their backgrounds. This was, after all, the modus operandi of most Constructivist reliefs at the time, including Biederman's own Structurist work.

When Bornstein first introduced broad, flatly applied colour planes—like those blue ones, dark and light, in the sprightly *Structurist Relief No. 1-1* (Sea Series), 1966—they were perhaps simply more relief components. But they perform differently. They sit flush to the surface of the support, reinforcing its planar spread. They are engaged formally, chromatically, and expressively with the relief components in front of them. But they also stand apart because of their expanse, and because of the outspread of their colours. They are slow and measured in contrast to the bustle of the foreground assemblages. Here it is as if Bornstein sets out to juxtapose two different zones of perceptual experience, two independent dimensions of time and place.[7]

In another way, Bornstein complicated his figure-ground relationships when, in 1966, he folded the ground planes of his reliefs to make works like *Double Plane Structurist Relief No. 8*, 1973, presenting them vertically or horizontally, like half-opened books, their spines flat to the wall, the relief events with their play of light and shadow nested in their intimate 90-degree crevices. But the real potential of the colour-ground planes would flourish with the Multiplane Structurist reliefs, the Quadriplanes and Hexaplanes (literally, four and six planes) that he began in the late 1980s, and which would become the culminating achievement of Bornstein's long and creative career, their voices increasingly spacious and resonant.

Left: Eli Bornstein, *Low Form Relief No. 10*, 1957, tempera on composition board, 24.3 x 16.8 x 1.9 cm, collection of the artist. Right: Eli Bornstein, *Structurist Relief No. 1-1* (Sea Series), 1966, enamel on aluminum and Plexiglas, 91.4 x 64.1 x 14.3 cm, Forum Gallery, New York.

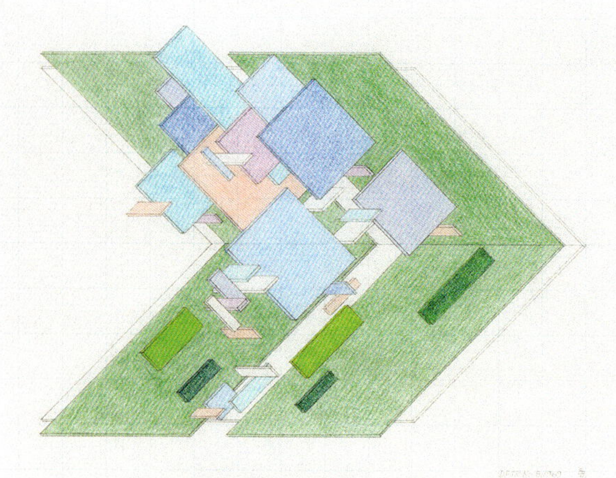

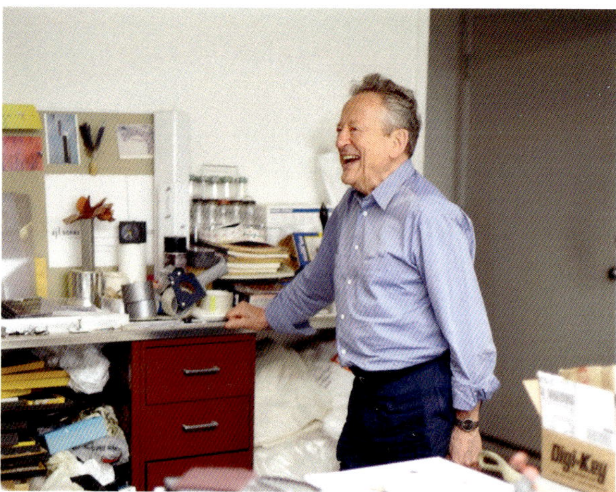

In the Multiplane reliefs, the ground planes zigzag slowly and majestically, each undulation marked by a finely tuned shift in colour gradation. In *Quadriplane Structurist Relief No. 4* (Sunset Series), 1997–99, a progression of mauves, reds, and oranges act like little jump-cuts in the continuity of time, as our eyes scan the horizon of their panoramic sweep. As the foreground relief articulations become more sparsely dispersed, their colours and shapes catching the light and throwing shadows, the ground colours deepen their stillness and widen their compass implicitly to extend far beyond their outer edges into a space of timelessness. Simultaneously, in the foreground, the ephemeral life of nature performs regardless.[8] Another development was the free-standing Tripart Hexaplane Constructions, built from three double-plane reliefs backed onto one another, and raised on a slim aluminum pedestal.

Materials and Processes

For Bornstein, a new work can emerge in any number of ways: with an idea, a gesture, or a feeling. It can start with a drawing, a painting, or some elementary construction. Colour and spatial relationships may be worked out in sketches or in three-dimensional drawings or models. The process is always one of trial and error. "Regardless of how one begins, it rarely develops as one anticipates or intends," as he reminds us in his journal.[9] There are always, from beginning to end, new and unforeseen qualities to negotiate.

The early reliefs, such as *Structurist Relief No. 22*, 1959, were oil on wood. These he constructed at home in his studio using standard tools and materials—saws, a drill press, screws, etc.—and his own carpentry skills. Wood, however, posed problems, because with time and changing temperatures it would crack (or check)[10] and show grain, compromising its intended look of technical anonymity. By the mid-1960s, Bornstein stopped using wood in favour of aluminum and Plexiglas, which both delivered smoother surfaces and were lighter and more permanent. For similar reasons, he replaced oil paint with enamel because it was shiny, clean, and reflective. The enamel is applied with a spray gun in order to obtain as immaculate a surface as possible.

It was during his Arctic travels in 1986, especially when fascinated by the crisp clarity of the reflection of icebergs in water, that Bornstein became alert to another potential of Plexiglas. Back in the studio in Saskatoon, in works that would evolve into his Arctic Series reliefs, he found he could use not only clear but also coloured Plexiglas

Left: Eli Bornstein, *Isometric Study for Double Plane Structurist Relief*, 1969, colour pencil on paper, dimensions unknown, collection of the artist. Right: Eli Bornstein in his studio, date unknown, photograph by Oliver A.I. Botar.

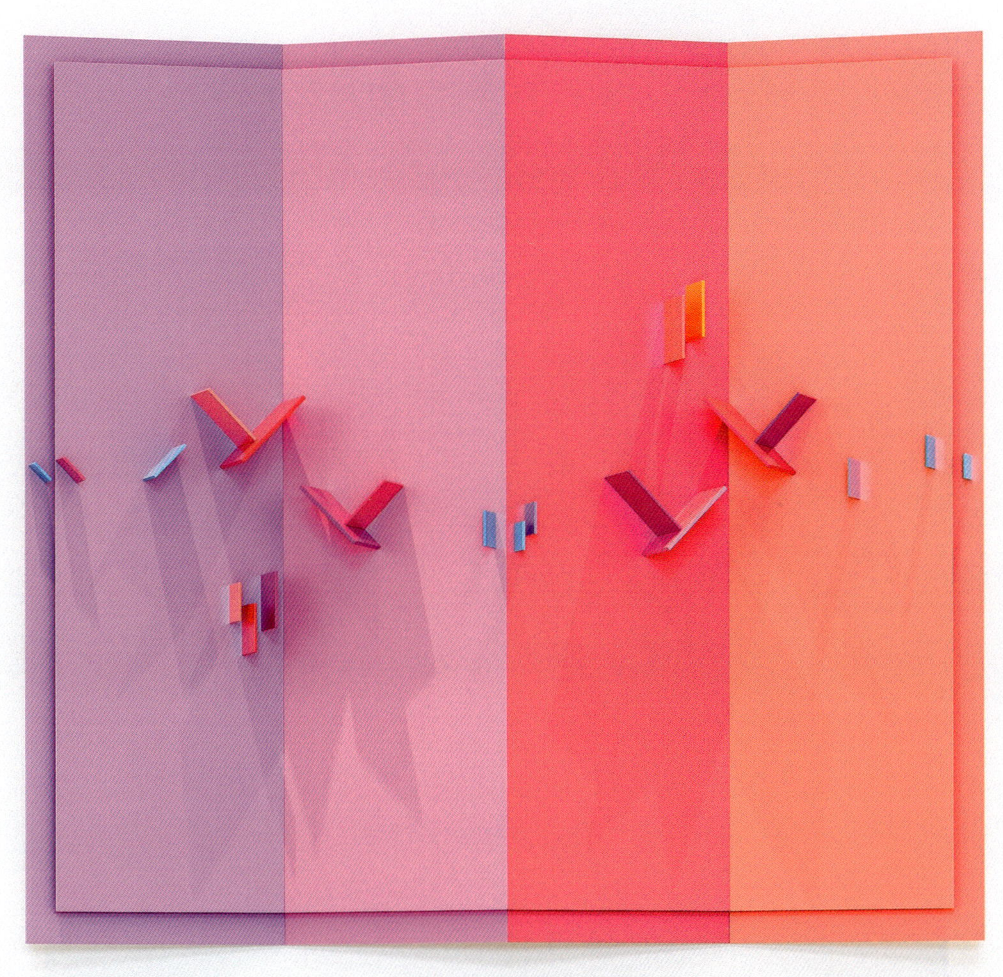

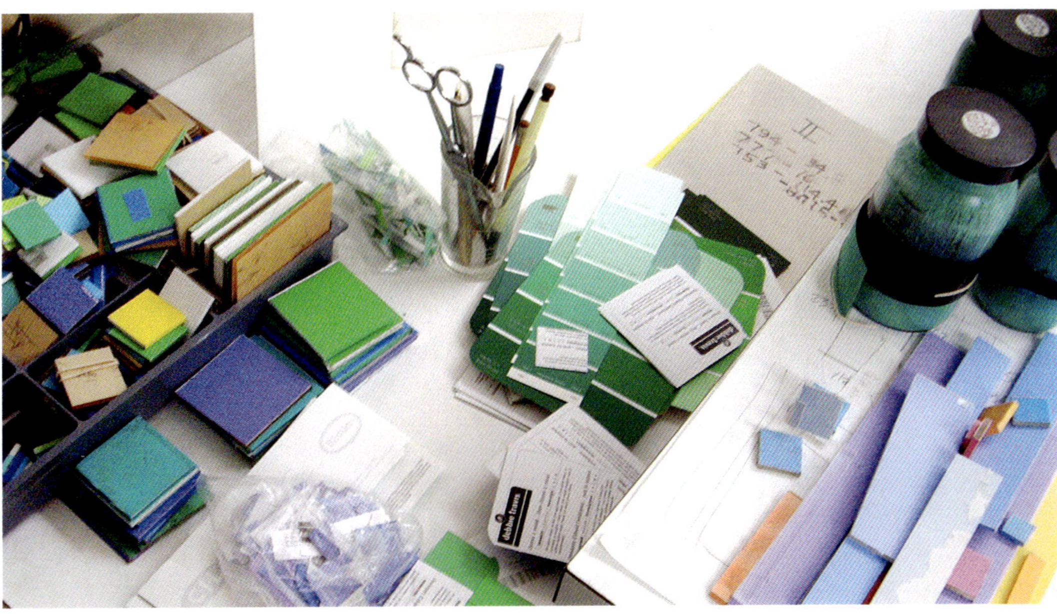

Top: Eli Bornstein, *Quadriplane Structurist Relief No. 15-II*, 2016–17, acrylic enamel on aluminum, 122 x 137 x 15.3 cm, Remai Modern, Saskatoon. Bottom: View of Eli Bornstein's studio featuring a collection of colour swatches for enamel paints, date unknown, Saskatoon, photograph by Oliver A.I. Botar.

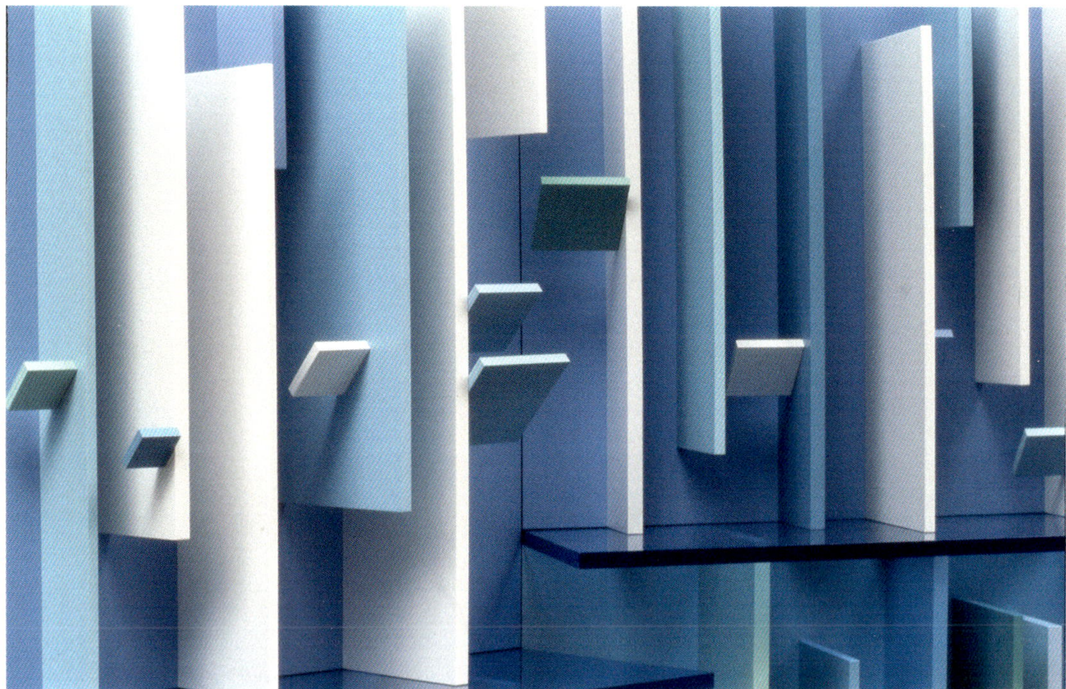

to convey his experiences of the iridescence and the brittleness of the icy Ellesmere Island landscape. Plexiglas is transparent, as he explained in 1987, so it "not only colors the space and forms around it, but reflects the structure in depth, as well as seeming to extend the work beyond its physical limits."[11] Despite its expressive virtues, however, Plexiglas also had its limitations. Unlike wood it didn't check, but it was subject to cracking from impact, especially in transport. There were also impracticalities in that the material was only available in a limited number of colours and, because it could be purchased in just one size—4-by-8-foot sheets—there was too much waste.[12]

In the end, Bornstein's materials of choice became aluminum and enamel paint. However, working with aluminum also required specialized skills and equipment, all of which he did not have, especially as his reliefs grew larger. He therefore started to work with professionals in a machine shop at the University of Saskatchewan's engineering department.

Bornstein would begin the process of working out a new idea for a relief in his home studio.[13] On a pre-ordered blank aluminum quadriplane or hexaplane support he would start to compose, using coloured papers and woodblocks. He would paste pieces of coloured paper directly onto the flat planes in order to determine his background colours, and onto individual wooden blocks, of various sizes and shapes, that he would position on top of the background plane as he experimented simultaneously with formal and colour relationships, and with the play of light and shadow. From this he would develop a plan for the relief from which the machinists would manufacture the individual relief blocks and drill the holes where they would be screwed on. The screws were countersunk to leave no visible trace of the manufacturing process.

The parts would then be sent back to Bornstein's studio, where he would paint the individual parts and assemble them. Colours would be selected from the enamel paints commercially available or be supplemented by others that Bornstein meticulously mixed himself. At this final stage—because there were only so many coloured papers to choose from—adjustments could be needed to find the perfect final colours and colour

Eli Bornstein, *Multiplane Structurist Relief IV, No. 2* (Arctic Series) (detail), 1987–88, enamel on aluminum and Plexiglas, 43 x 58.5 x 17.7 cm, collection of the artist.

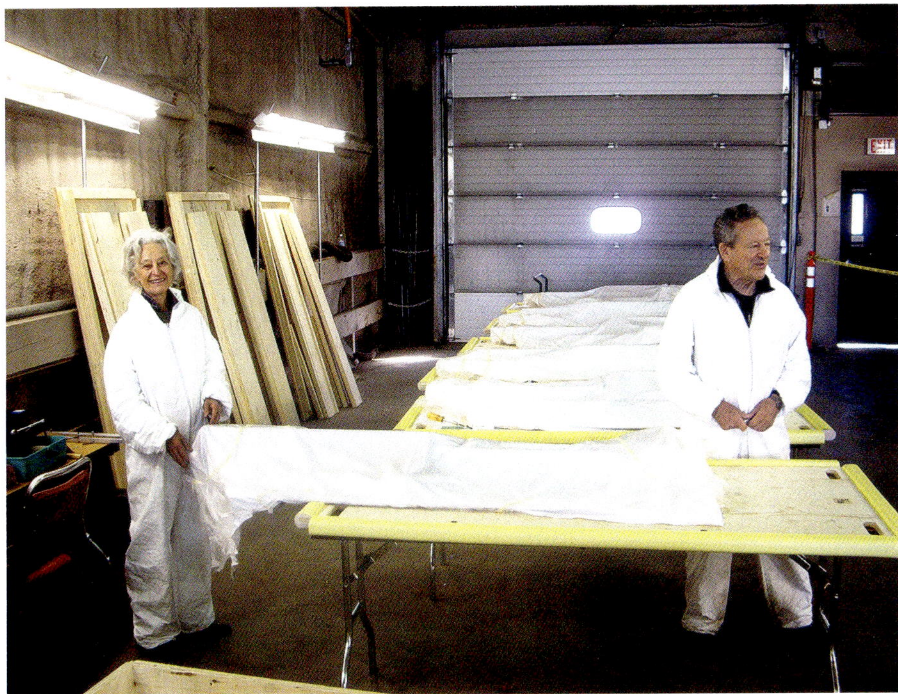

relations. At first, he applied his paint in a spray booth in the basement of his studio, and then later, in an auto-body shop. Completing a work was a lengthy and time-consuming process, reflected in how Bornstein's reliefs are often dated to a time span of several years.

But when is a work really complete? To answer, Bornstein turns to the viewer to remind us, as he does in a journal entry: "Finished works are not finalities but works-in-progress," open-ended to allow for continually new completions in the "perceptions and interpretations" of their audience.[14]

At the Mercy of Light

Light is indeed the great transformer, the bringer of light and illumination. It is the "Destroyer and Preserver," the great artificer, of form and structure. Light is the guardian of the spectrum of color and all its grandeur.[15]

An Art at the Mercy of Light was the title of a 2013 exhibition of Bornstein's recent work, curated by Oliver A.I. Botar, and held at the former Mendel Art Gallery in Saskatoon. The exhibition was installed in the gallery's skylighted spaces, the reliefs subject to the play of natural light with all its variation from dawn to dusk, an ambience seldom, if ever, achieved by more common windowless gallery and museum spaces with their rigid track lighting systems.

Bornstein's work is indeed at the mercy of light, among other factors, and he has given much thought to and written extensively on lighting his work. He has designed his own house and studio with skylights above his hanging walls in order to allow the most responsive viewing conditions, changeable with time and weather. As he describes in a journal entry, the goal of sensitive lighting is to make the work itself exist in its truest character, to display its colour in its fullest and richest reality. It's the holy grail, of which the artist is appropriately protective. It is when the reliefs enter the public world, especially for exhibition, that their "precarious existence" becomes most vulnerable, when they pose special challenges to gallerists and museum curators.[16]

Eli and Christina Bornstein in the artist's studio, date unknown, Saskatoon, photograph by Oliver A.I. Botar.

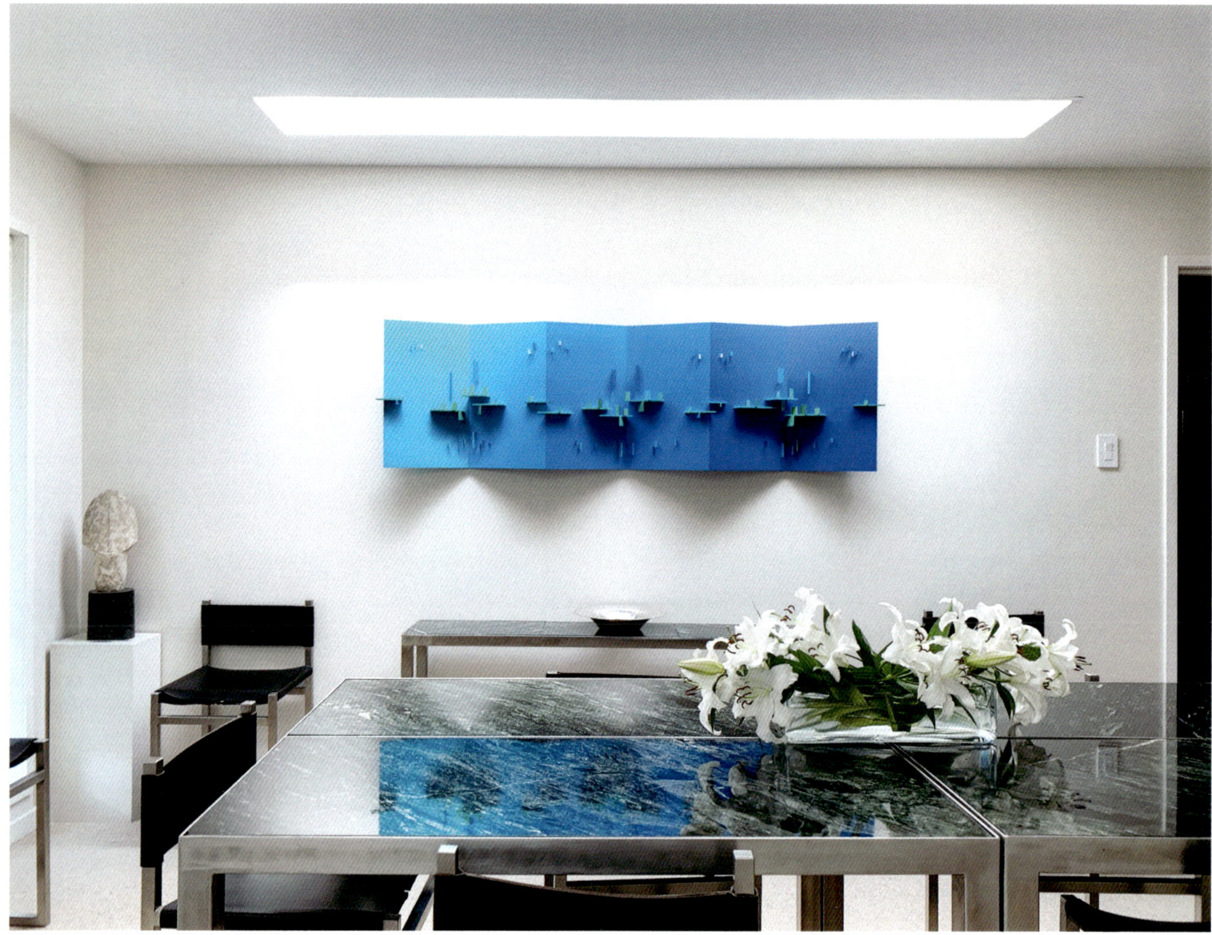

Structurist reliefs, such as *Quadriplane Structurist Relief No. 9*, 2000–2001, are not easy to display. The work perishes or is incapable of revealing its subtlety and richness without sufficient light falling down upon it from above. Nor can the desired effect of the work survive harsh, frontal lighting; directional spotlights; or floodlights that, as Bornstein writes, "dissolve the work's true and gentle character or complicate and confuse its structural relationships with multiple contradictory shadows."[17] Insufficient light, on the other hand, while not as devastating as too much illumination, also prevents colour from revealing its full intensity, its true hue and value.

Space also offers challenges. An installation must allow sufficient distance so that the viewer can see the work both en face and move about it. "Frontal, side and oblique views are intrinsic" to its viewing and "often the difference between the front and side views is as dramatic as Nature's plant and animal forms."[18] Indeed, the entire physical context in which the work is presented can either compromise or fulfill the conditions essential to its optimum realization. The Structurist Relief, to conclude with Bornstein's own words, is "a fragile medium, like a rare blossom, flower, butterfly, easily destroyed or mishandled, easily vulnerable to abuse."[19]

Eli and Christina Bornstein's dining room in Saskatoon, with skylight, 2020, photograph by Roald Nasgaard.

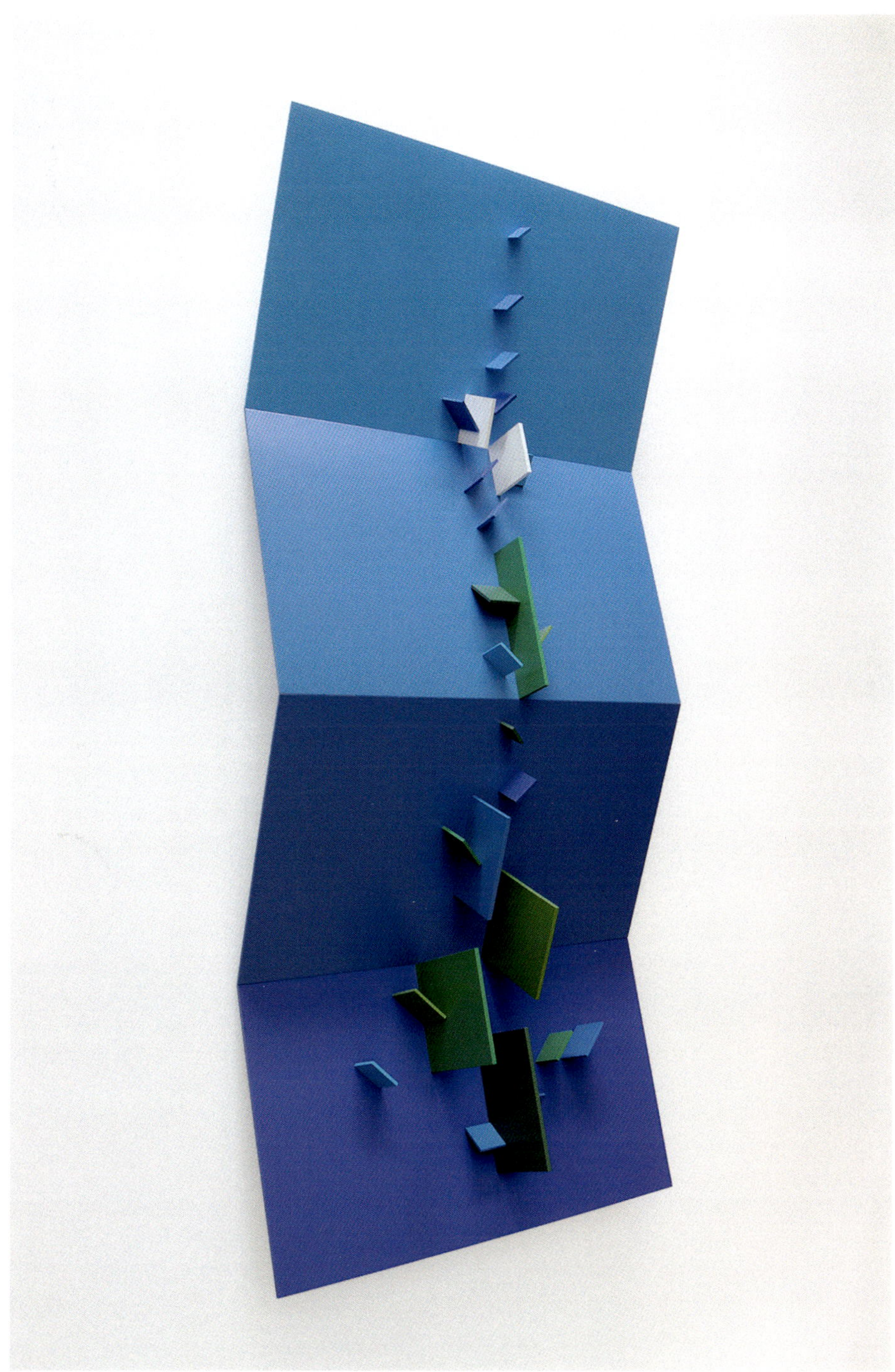

Eli Bornstein, *Quadriplane Structurist Relief No. 9*, 2000–2001, acrylic enamel on aluminum, 86.3 x 148.2 x 22.1 cm, private collection, Toronto.

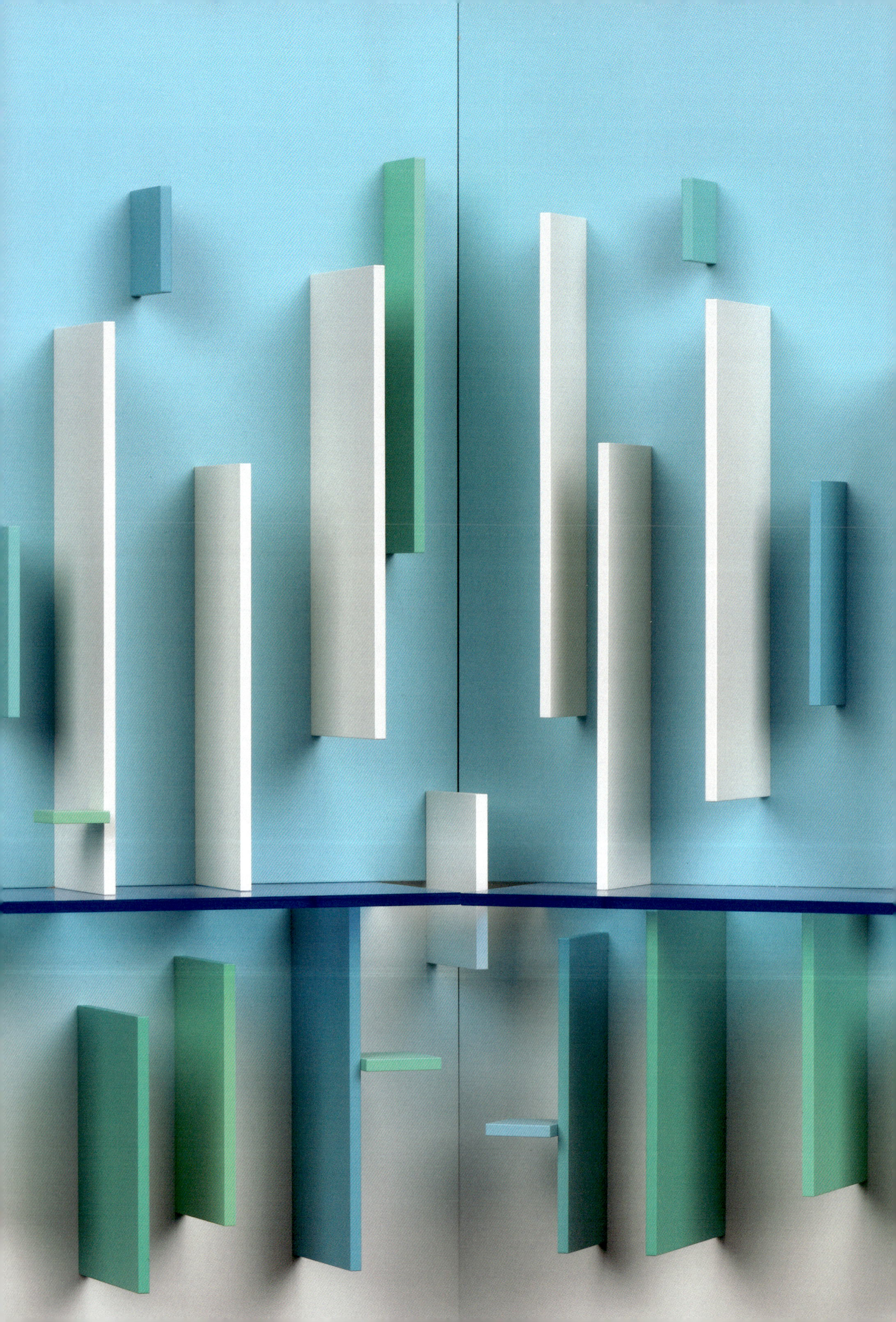

Sources & Resources

Eli Bornstein is a prolific writer whose many critical and theoretical articles have been included in national and international anthologies. Most prominently, they were included in the periodical *The Structurist*, which Bornstein published and edited out of the University of Saskatchewan, Saskatoon, annually from 1960 to 1972 and then biennially until 2000, with anniversary issues in 2010 and 2020. He is also a journal keeper. The major curators/historians to have dealt with his work are Jonneke Fritz-Jobse and Oliver A.I. Botar.

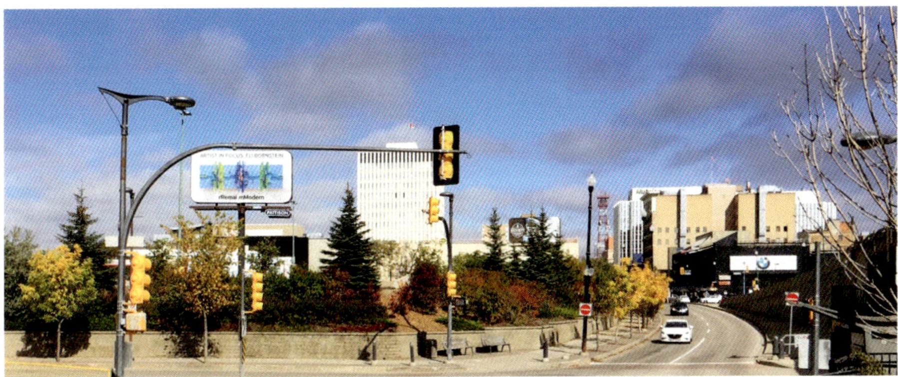

Billboard advertising the exhibition *Artist in Focus: Eli Bornstein* at Remai Modern, Saskatoon, 2019, photograph by Roald Nasgaard.

Exhibition History

Selected Solo Exhibitions

1954

Eli Bornstein: Sculpture, Paintings, Drawings and Prints. Convocation Hall, University of Saskatchewan, Saskatoon

1956

Eli Bornstein: Graphics. Hart House, University of Toronto

1957

Eli Bornstein: Paintings, Sculpture, Graphics, Drawings. Saskatoon Art Centre; Norman MacKenzie Art Gallery, Regina; Murray Memorial Library, University of Saskatchewan, Saskatoon

1965

Eli Bornstein: Structurist Reliefs. Kazimir Gallery, Chicago

Eli Bornstein: Retrospective Exhibition 1943–1964. Mendel Art Gallery, Saskatoon

1967

Structurist Reliefs by Eli Bornstein. Kazimir Gallery, Chicago

Opposite: Eli Bornstein, *Multiplane Structurist Relief IV, No. 1* (Arctic Series) (detail), 1986–87, enamel on aluminum and Plexiglas, 38.1 cm x 38.2 cm, Beaverbrook Art Gallery, Fredericton.

1975

Eli Bornstein: Structurist Reliefs 1966–1975. Saskatoon Public Library Art Gallery, Saskatoon

1976

Eli Bornstein: Structurist Reliefs 1966–1975. Centre culturel canadien, Paris

1981

Eli Bornstein: Early Works 1940 to 1956. Gordon Snelgrove Gallery, University of Saskatchewan, Saskatoon

1982–84

Eli Bornstein: Selected Works / Œuvres choisies, 1957–1982. Mendel Art Gallery, Saskatoon; Art Gallery of York University, Toronto; Confederation Centre Art Gallery and Museum, Charlottetown; Owens Art Gallery, Mount Allison University, Sackville; Fine Art Gallery of University of Wisconsin-Milwaukee

1986

Eli Bornstein: Structurist Reliefs. Momentum Fine Arts, Minneapolis

1987

Eli Bornstein: Arctic Studies. Watercolours 1986–1987. The Gallery/Art Placement, Saskatoon

1990

Eli Bornstein: Newfoundland Studies (1988) and Riverbank Studies (1989). Watercolours. The Gallery/Art Placement, Saskatoon

1996

Eli Bornstein: Art Toward Nature. Mendel Art Gallery, Saskatoon

2007

Eli Bornstein. Forum Gallery, New York

2013

An Art at the Mercy of Light: Recent Works by Eli Bornstein. Mendel Art Gallery, Saskatoon, and the School of Art Gallery, University of Manitoba, Winnipeg

2014–15

Eli Bornstein: Constructed Works, 1960 to Present. Winchester Modern, Victoria

2015

Eli Bornstein: A New Awareness of Beauty. Initial Gallery, Vancouver

2017

Eli Bornstein. Darrell Bell Gallery, Saskatoon

2019

Artist in Focus: Eli Bornstein. Remai Modern, Saskatoon

Selected Group Exhibitions

1950

Beginning in 1950 and for the next decade, Bornstein participated regularly in the annual and biennial survey exhibitions that then were staple fare for art museums in North America: Milwaukee Art Institute; Walker Art Center, Minneapolis; Art Institute of Chicago; Pennsylvania Academy of the Fine Arts, Philadelphia; National Gallery of Canada, Ottawa; Montreal Museum of Fine Arts; Winnipeg Art Gallery; Seattle Art Museum

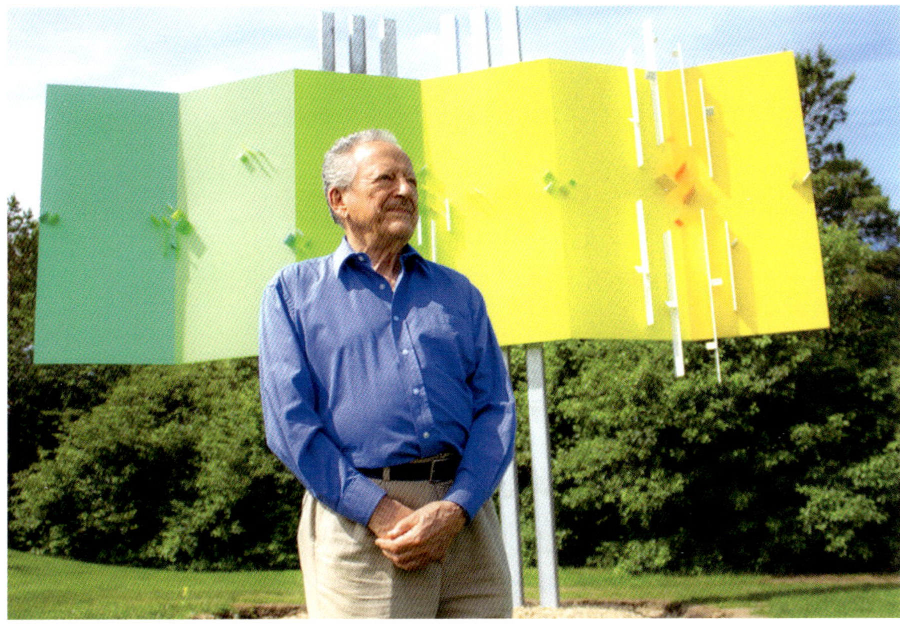

Eli Bornstein with *Untitled Hexaplane Structurist Relief*, date unknown, photographer unknown.

1967

Statements: 18 Canadian Artists. Norman MacKenzie Art Gallery, Regina

1968

Relief/Construction/Relief. Museum of Contemporary Art Chicago; Herron Museum of Art, Indianapolis; Cranbrook Academy of Art Galleries, Bloomfield Hills; High Museum of Art, Atlanta

1970

II Bienal de Arte Coltejer-Medellín. Museo de la Universidad de Antioquia, Medellín, Colombia

1973

Structure in Art. University of Saskatchewan, Saskatoon

1979–80

The Evolution of the Constructed Relief 1913–1979. Nickle Museum, University of Calgary; Mendel Art Gallery, Saskatoon; University of Manitoba Art Gallery, Winnipeg

1983–84

Winnipeg West: Painting and Sculpture in Western Canada 1946–1970. The Edmonton Art Gallery; Surrey Art Gallery; Rodman Hall Art Centre, St. Catharines; Sarnia Public Library and Art Gallery; Art Gallery of Hamilton; Art Gallery of Windsor; Glenbow Museum, Calgary

1983–85

Five from Saskatchewan. Canada House, London, England; Canadian Cultural Centre, Brussels; Centre culturel canadien, Paris; Alexander-Koenig Museum, Bonn

1984

Tribute to Eli Bornstein: European and American Relief Masters. Milwaukee Art Museum

1992–94

Achieving the Modern: Canadian Abstract Art and Design in the 1950s. Winnipeg Art Gallery; Confederation Centre Art Gallery and Museum, Charlottetown; Mendel Art Gallery, Saskatoon; the Edmonton Art Gallery; Art Gallery of Windsor

The Crisis in Abstraction in Canada: The 1950s. Musée du Québec, Quebec City; National Gallery of Canada, Ottawa; MacKenzie Art Gallery, Regina; Glenbow Museum, Calgary; Art Gallery of Hamilton

Writings by the Artist

"Abstract Art on the Prairies." *Perspectives of Saskatchewan*. Ed. Jene M. Porter. Winnipeg: University of Manitoba Press, 2009. Pages 273–88.

"The Constructed Relief as a New Medium." *Structure in Art*. Saskatoon: University of Saskatchewan, 1973). Pages 17–23.

"Continuity and Renewal: A Place for Art." *Eli Bornstein: A New Awareness of Beauty*. Vancouver: Initial Gallery, 2015. Exhibition catalogue.

Eli Bornstein: Arctic Journals 1986 and 1987. Introduction by Roald Nasgaard. Vancouver: Figure 1, 2022.

Eli Bornstein's personal journal, 1990–2017, 1,136 typewritten pages, unpublished except for excerpts in two Mendel Art Gallery exhibition catalogues: Mendel (1996), pages 38–46, and Mendel (2013), pages 32–39.

"Notes on Art-I." *Statements: 18 Canadian Artists*. Regina: Norman MacKenzie Art Gallery, 1967. Pages 24–29.

"Notes on structurist process." *DATA: Directions in Art, Theory and Aesthetics*. Ed. Anthony Hill. London: Faber and Faber, 1968. Pages 192–203.

"Notes on Structurist Vision." *Canadian Art Today*. Ed. William Townsend. London: Studio International, 1970. Pages 52–55.

"Of Time in Art and Nature." *Time as a Human Resource*. Ed. E.J. McCullough and R.L. Calder. Calgary: University of Calgary Press, 1991. Pages 257–63.

"Pioneering Abstract Art on the Prairies." *A Celebration of Canada's Arts 1930–1970*. Ed. Glen Carruthers and Gordana Lazarevich. Toronto: Canadian Scholars Press, 1996. Pages 147–52.

"Structurist Art and Creative Integration." *Art International* 11 (April 1967). Pages 31–36.

"Transitions toward the New Art." *Structure* no. 1 (1958). Pages 1, 30–46.

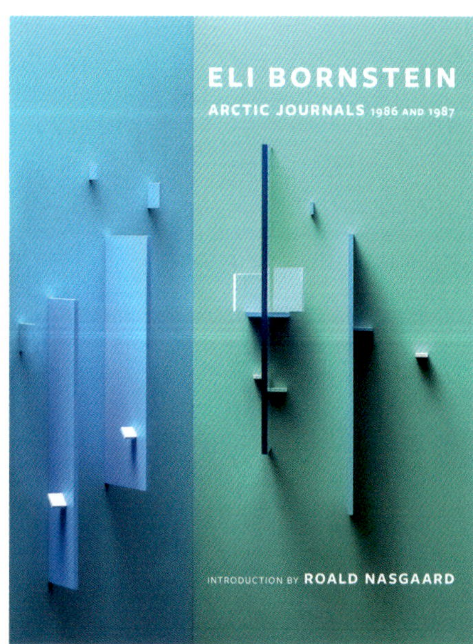

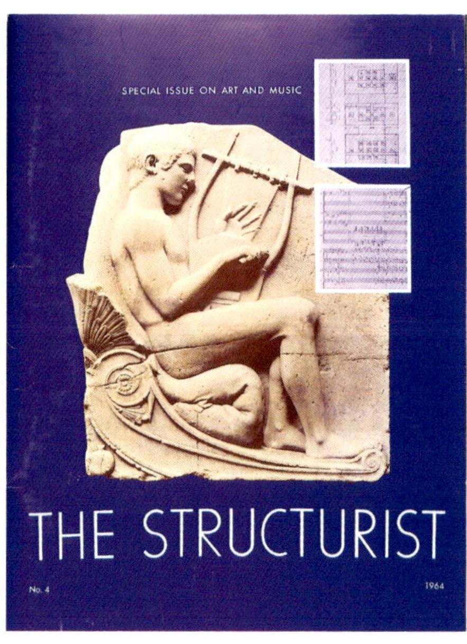

Left: Cover of *Eli Bornstein: Arctic Journals 1986 and 1987*, by Eli Bornstein, with contributions by Roald Nasgaard (Vancouver: Figure 1 Publishing, 2022). Right: Cover of *The Structurist*, no. 4, "Art and Music," edited by Eli Bornstein (Saskatoon: University of Saskatchewan, 1964).

Selected Critical Writings on the Artist's Work

Botar, Oliver A.I. "'The constructed relief is an art at the mercy of light.'" *An Art at the Mercy of Light: Recent Work by Eli Bornstein*. Saskatoon: Mendel Art Gallery, 2013. Exhibition catalogue with contributions from Eli Bornstein and Rodney La Tourelle. https://valmesta.files.wordpress.com/2014/04/soa_catalogue_anartatthemercyoflight_elibornstein.pdf.

———. "The poetics of Eli Bornstein's Art of Light, Structure and Perception." *Eli Bornstein: Constructed Works from 1960 to Present*. Victoria: Winchester Modern, 2015. Exhibition catalogue.

———. "The Importance of Eli Bornstein." *Eli Bornstein*. Saskatoon: Darrell Bell Gallery, 2017. Exhibition catalogue.

Fritz-Jobse, Jonneke. *Eli Bornstein: Art Toward Nature*. Saskatoon: Mendel Art Gallery, 1996. Exhibition catalogue with contributions by Eli Bornstein, and a detailed list of exhibitions and bibliography to 1996.

———. *De Stijl Continued: The Journal Structure (1958–1964): An Artists' Debate*. Rotterdam: 010 Publishers, 2005.

Greenberg, Clement. "Painting and Sculpture in Prairie Canada." *Canadian Art* (March–April, 1961). Reprinted in *Clement Greenberg: The Collected Essays and Criticism*, Volume 4. *Modernism with a Vengeance, 1957–1969*. Ed. John O'Brian. Chicago: University of Chicago Press, 1993. Pages 153–75.

Hayton, Harold. "The Structurist Movement." *Chicago Omnibus* (May 1967). Pages 58–62.

Karpuszko, Kazimir. *Eli Bornstein: Selected Works / Œuvres choisies, 1957–1982*. Saskatoon: Mendel Art Gallery, 1982. Exhibition catalogue including catalogue raisonné, 1957–1982.

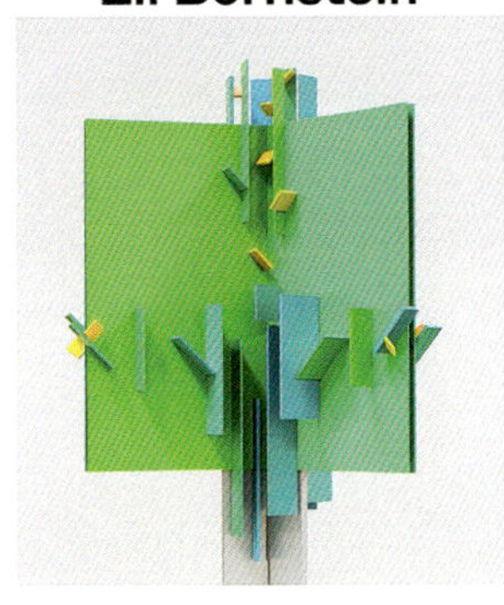

Cover of *Artist in Focus: Eli Bornstein*, with contributions by Sandra Fraser and Roald Nasgaard (Saskatoon: Remai Modern, 2019).

Leclerc, Denise. *The Crisis of Abstraction in Canada: The 1950s*. Ottawa: National Gallery of Canada, 1992. Pages 95–96.

Nasgaard, Roald. *Abstract Painting in Canada*. Vancouver: Douglas and McIntyre, 2007. Pages 292–93.

———. "To Invent the Truth" *Artist in Focus: Eli Bornstein*. Saskatoon: Remai Modern, 2019. Exhibition catalogue.

Nemiroff, Diana. "Geometric Abstraction after 1950." *The Visual Arts in Canada: The Twentieth Century*. Eds. Anne Whitelaw, Brian Foss, and Sandra Paikowsky. Don Mills, ON: Oxford University Press, 2011. Pages 218–19.

Nordland, Gerald. *Eli Bornstein*. New York: Forum Gallery, 2007. Exhibition catalogue.

Regan, Ron. "A New Awareness of Beauty." *Eli Bornstein, A New Awareness of Beauty*. Vancouver: Initial Gallery, 2015. Exhibition catalogue.

Recent Interviews: Print and Television

Enright, Robert. "Plane Talk: An Interview with Eli Bornstein." *Border Crossings* no. 128 (December 2013). https://bordercrossingsmag.com/article/plane-talk.

"galaMODERN honours Eli Bornstein. July 4, 2019." https://www.youtube.com/watch?v=-nUPqSh-JGVE.

Grebinski, Leisha. *A look at the home of artist Eli Bornstein*. CBC Saskatoon, September 11, 2019.

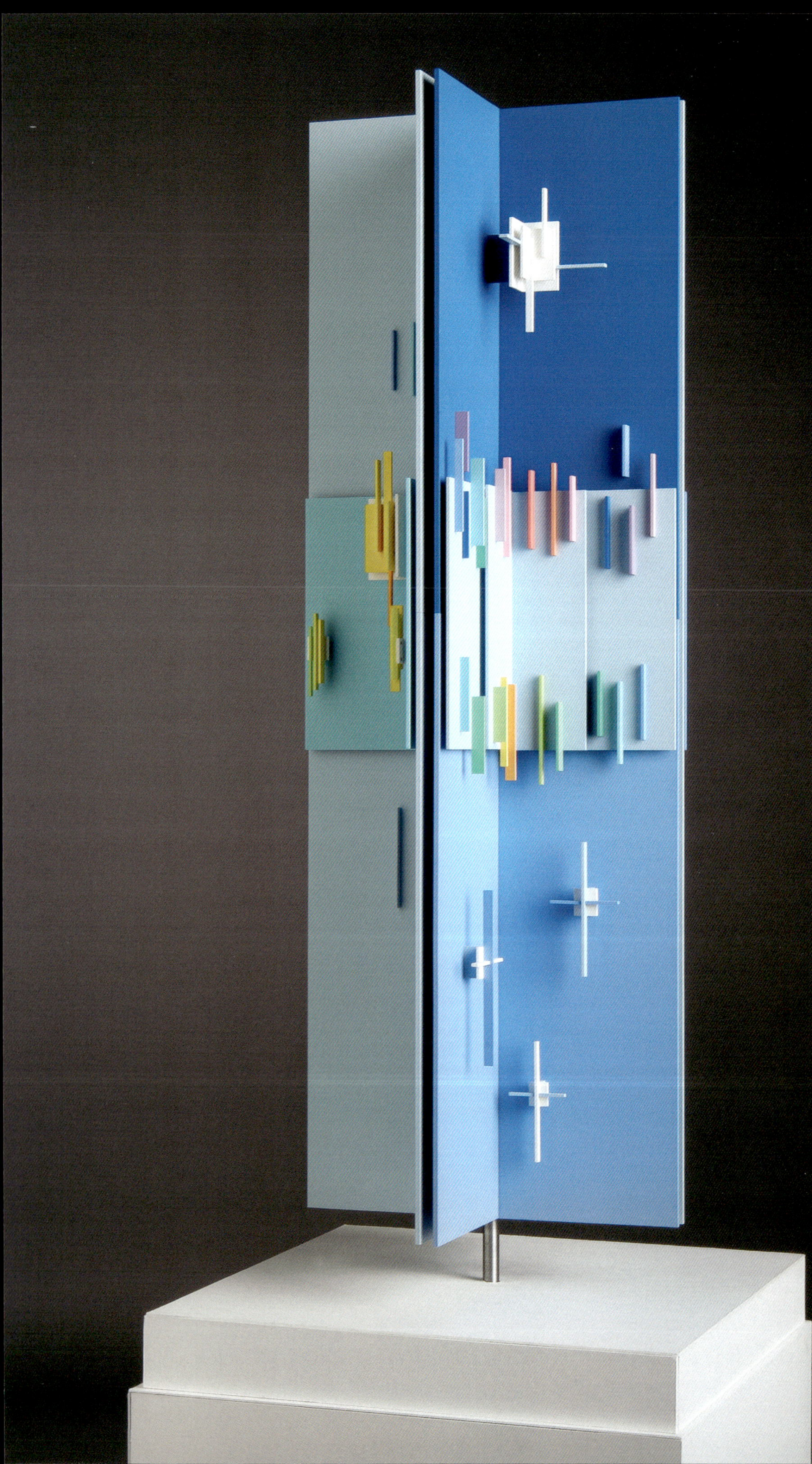

Where to See

The works of Eli Bornstein are held in public and private collections in Canada and internationally. Although the following institutions hold the works listed below, they may not always be on view.

Beaverbrook Art Gallery

703 Queen Street
Fredericton, New Brunswick, Canada
506-458-2028
beaverbrookartgallery.org

Eli Bornstein, *Multiplane Structurist Relief IV, No. 1* (Arctic Series), 1986–87
Enamel on aluminum and Plexiglas
38.1 cm x 38.2 cm

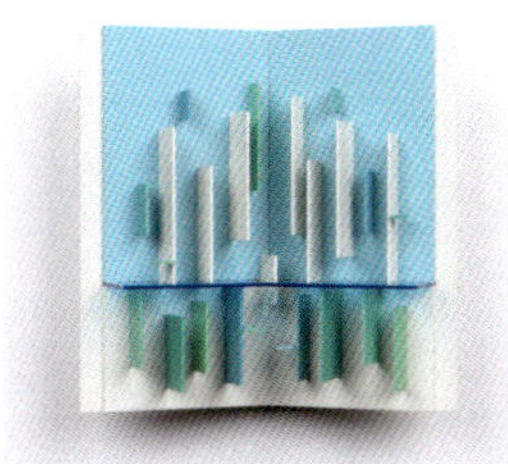

Canadian Centre for Architecture

1920 Baile Street
Montreal, Quebec, Canada
514-939-7026
cca.qc.ca

Eli Bornstein, model of *Four Part Vertical Double Plane Structurist Relief Nos. 14–17* (Winter Sky Series), 1980–83
Enamel on aluminum and Plexiglas on steel frame
104.1 x 38.1 x 38.1 cm

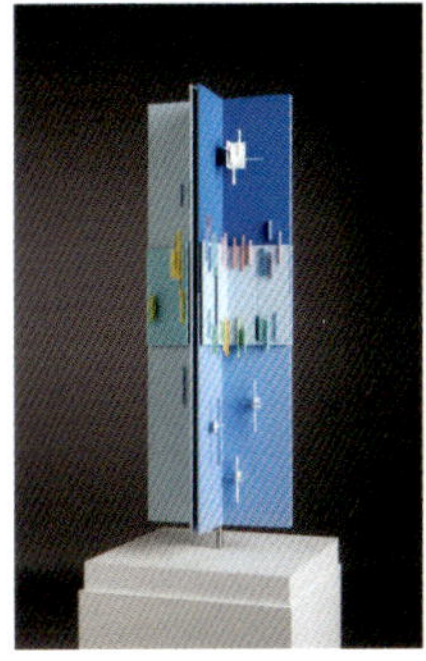

National Gallery of Canada

380 Sussex Drive
Ottawa, Ontario, Canada
613-990-1985
gallery.ca

Eli Bornstein, *Structurist Relief in Five Parts*, Model Version, 1962
Birch relief with oil paint
54.7 x 130.5 x 7.1 cm

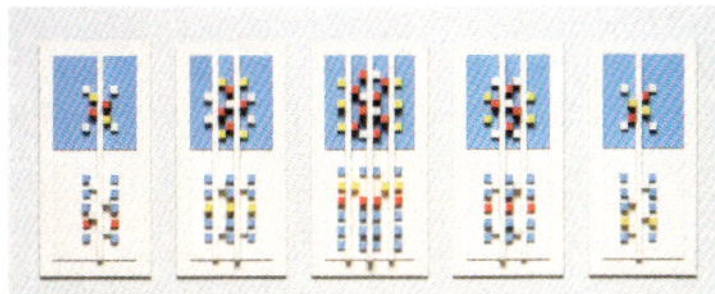

Opposite: Eli Bornstein, model of *Four Part Vertical Double Plane Structurist Relief Nos. 14–17* (Winter Sky Series), 1980–83, enamel on aluminum and, plexiglas on steel frame, 104.1 x 38.1 x 38.1 cm, Canadian Centre for Architecture, Montreal.

Nickle Galleries, University of Calgary

2500 University Drive NW
Calgary, Alberta, Canada
403-210-6201
nickle.ucalgary.ca

Eli Bornstein, *Structurist Relief No. 1*, 1966
Acrylic
86.5 x 61 cm

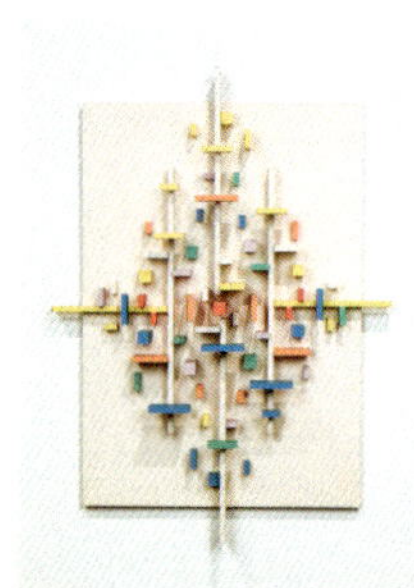

Remai Modern

102 Spadina Crescent East
Saskatoon, Saskatchewan, Canada
306-975-7610
remaimodern.org

1. Eli Bornstein, *Untitled (Murray Adaskin)*, 1953
   Oil on paper
   42.9 x 52.2 cm

2. Eli Bornstein, *Downtown Bridge #4*, 1954
   Etching and serigraph
   33.5 x 41.7 cm

3. Eli Bornstein, *Structurist Relief No. 4–11* (Sea Series), 1965
   Acrylic enamel and Plexiglas on aluminum
   86.5 x 61 cm

4. Eli Bornstein, *Double Plane Structurist Relief No. 8*, 1973
   Acrylic enamel and Plexiglas on aluminum
   43.2 x 43.2 x 27 cm

5. Eli Bornstein, *Multiplane Structurist Relief V, No. 1*, 1993
   Acrylic enamel and Plexiglas on aluminum
   86.5 x 61.1 x 3.1 cm

6. Eli Bornstein, *Tripart Hexaplane Construction No. 3*, 2008–10
   Acrylic enamel on aluminum and anodized aluminum
   73.7 x 43.2 x 43.2 cm

1.
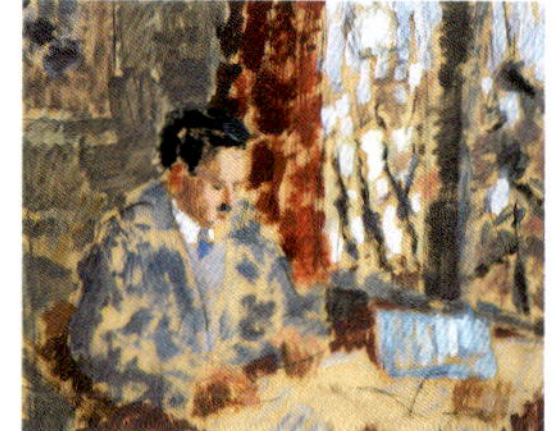

2.
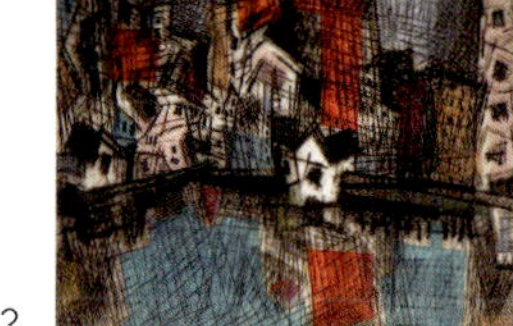

3.
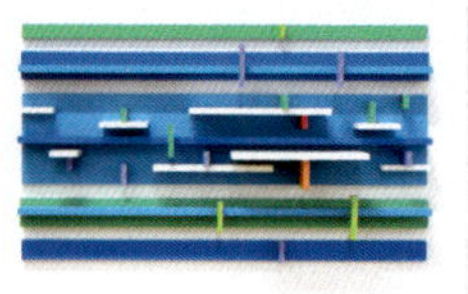

4.
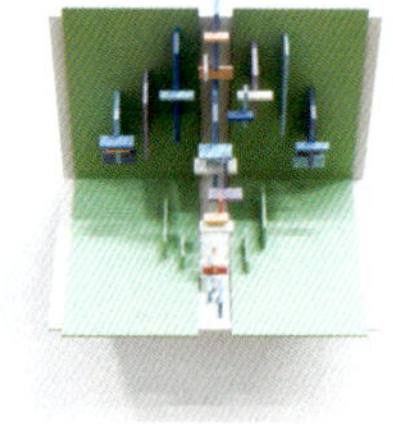

5.
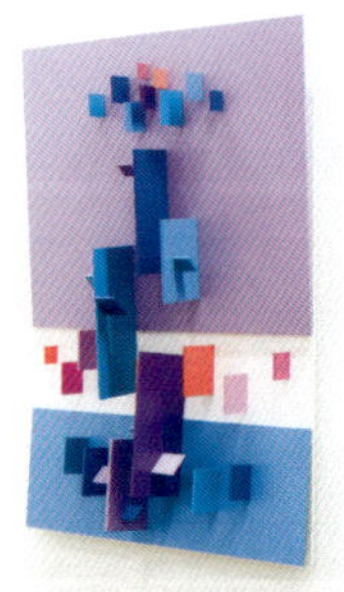

6.
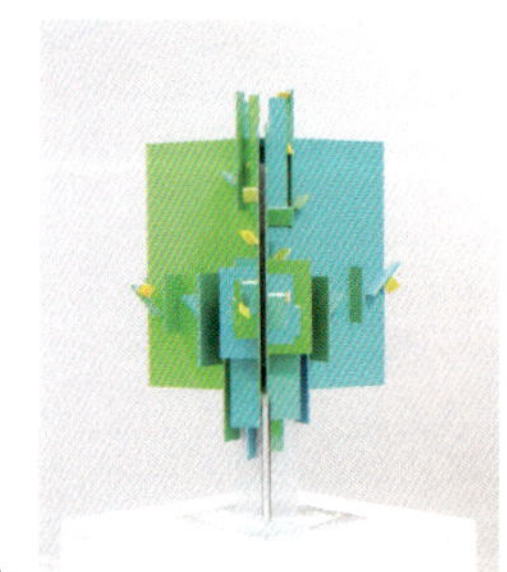

Remai Modern

Continued

7. Eli Bornstein, *Quadriplane Structurist Relief No. 15-II*, 2016–17
   Acrylic enamel on aluminum
   122 x 137 x 15.3 cm

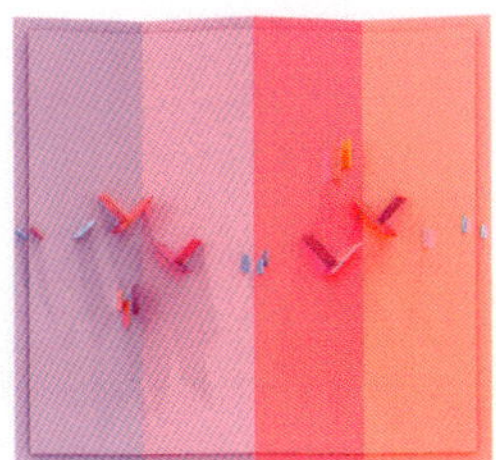

7.

Saskatchewan Teachers' Federation Building

2317 Arlington Avenue
Saskatoon, Saskatchewan, Canada
306-373-1660
stf.sk.ca

Eli Bornstein, *Aluminum Construction (Tree of Knowledge)*, 1956
Welded aluminum on stone base
458 cm (height)

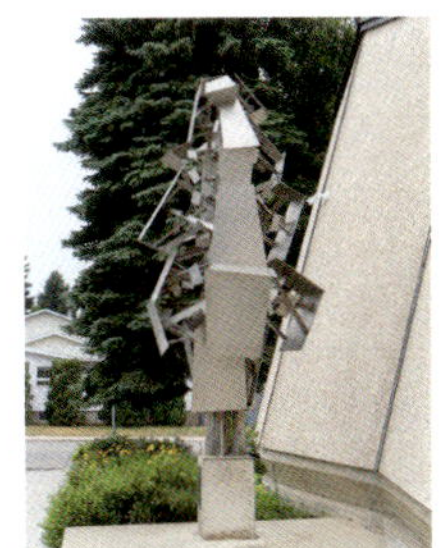

University of Manitoba

66 Chancellors Circle
Winnipeg, Manitoba, Canada
1-800-432-1960
umanitoba.ca

Eli Bornstein, *Tripart Hexaplane Construction No. 2*, 2002–6
Acrylic enamel on anodized aluminum and concrete base
205.25 x 107.8 cm

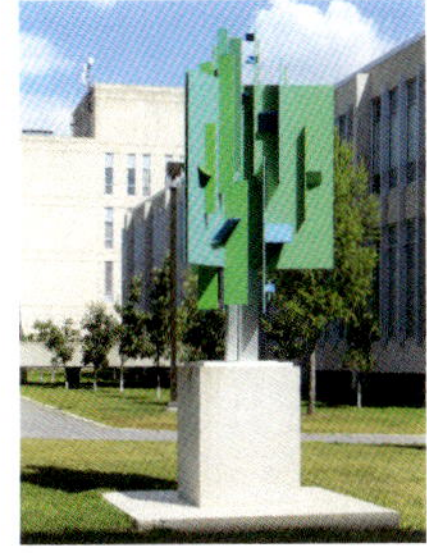

University of Saskatchewan

105 Administration Place
Saskatoon, Saskatchewan, Canada
306-966-4343
kagcag.usask.ca
library.usask.ca/uasc

1. Eli Bornstein, *Downtown*, 1954
   Watercolour on paper
   50 x 70 cm

2. Eli Bornstein, *Structurist Relief No. 18-II*, 1958–60
   Birchwood blocks on aluminum panel over wood panel, painted with acrylic urethane enamel
   259 x 259 x 22.9 cm

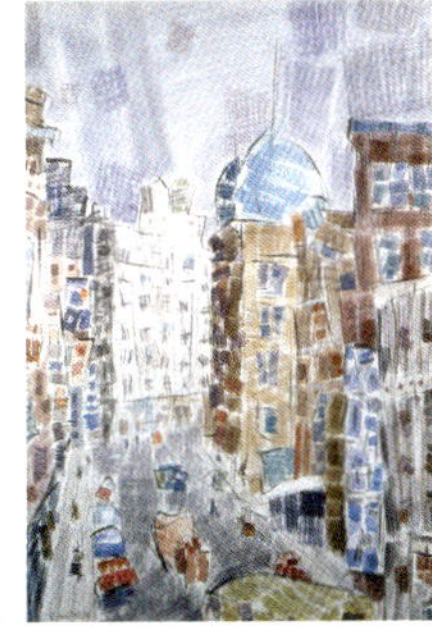

1.

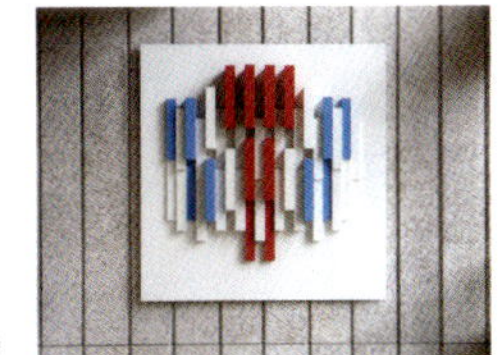

2.

University of Saskatchewan

Continued

3. Eli Bornstein, *Double Plane Structurist Relief No. 3*, 1967–69
   Enamel on Plexiglas and aluminum
   66.7 x 66.7 x 34.3 cm

4. Eli Bornstein, *Hexaplane Structurist Relief No. 2* (Arctic Series), 1995–98
   Acrylic enamel on aluminum and Plexiglas
   67.2 x 182.2 x 15.9 cm

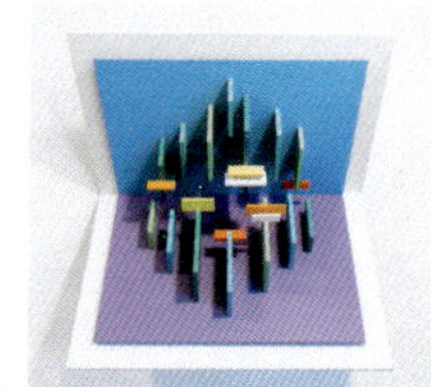

3.

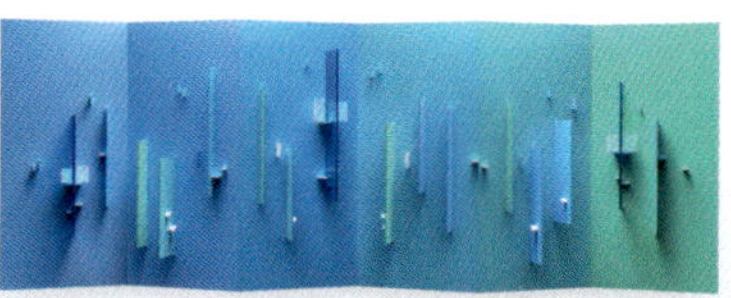

4.

Wascana Centre Authority

2900 Wascana Drive
Regina, Saskatchewan, Canada
306-522-3661
wascana.sk.ca

Eli Bornstein, *Four Part Vertical Double Plane Structurist Relief* (Winter Sky Series), 1980–83
Acrylic lacquer on aluminum and Plexiglas on welded steel
640.1 x 342 cm (diameter)

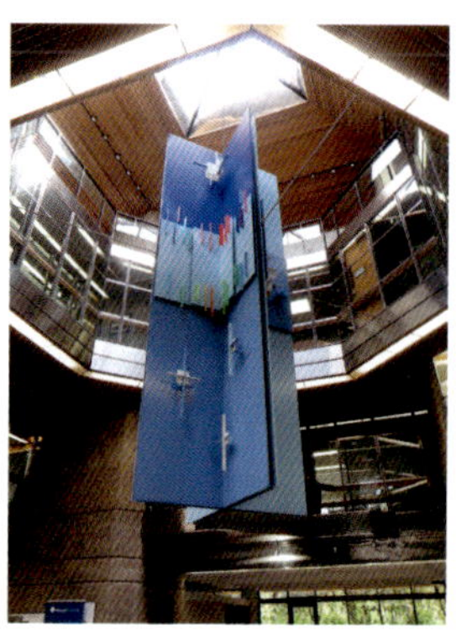

Opposite: Eli Bornstein, *Arctic Study No. 7* (detail), 1986, watercolour on paper, 37.8 x 28.6 cm, collection of the artist.

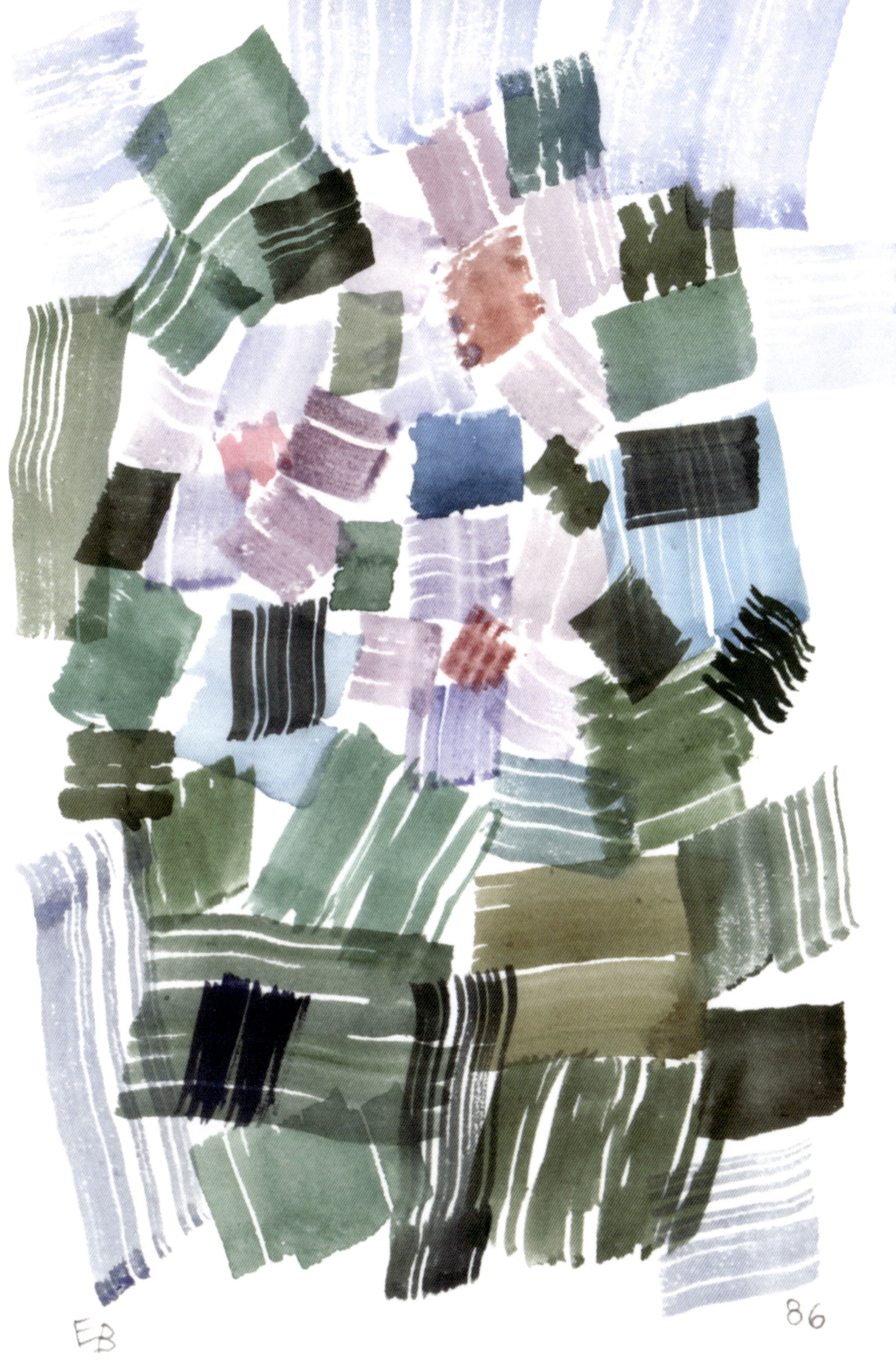
EB
86

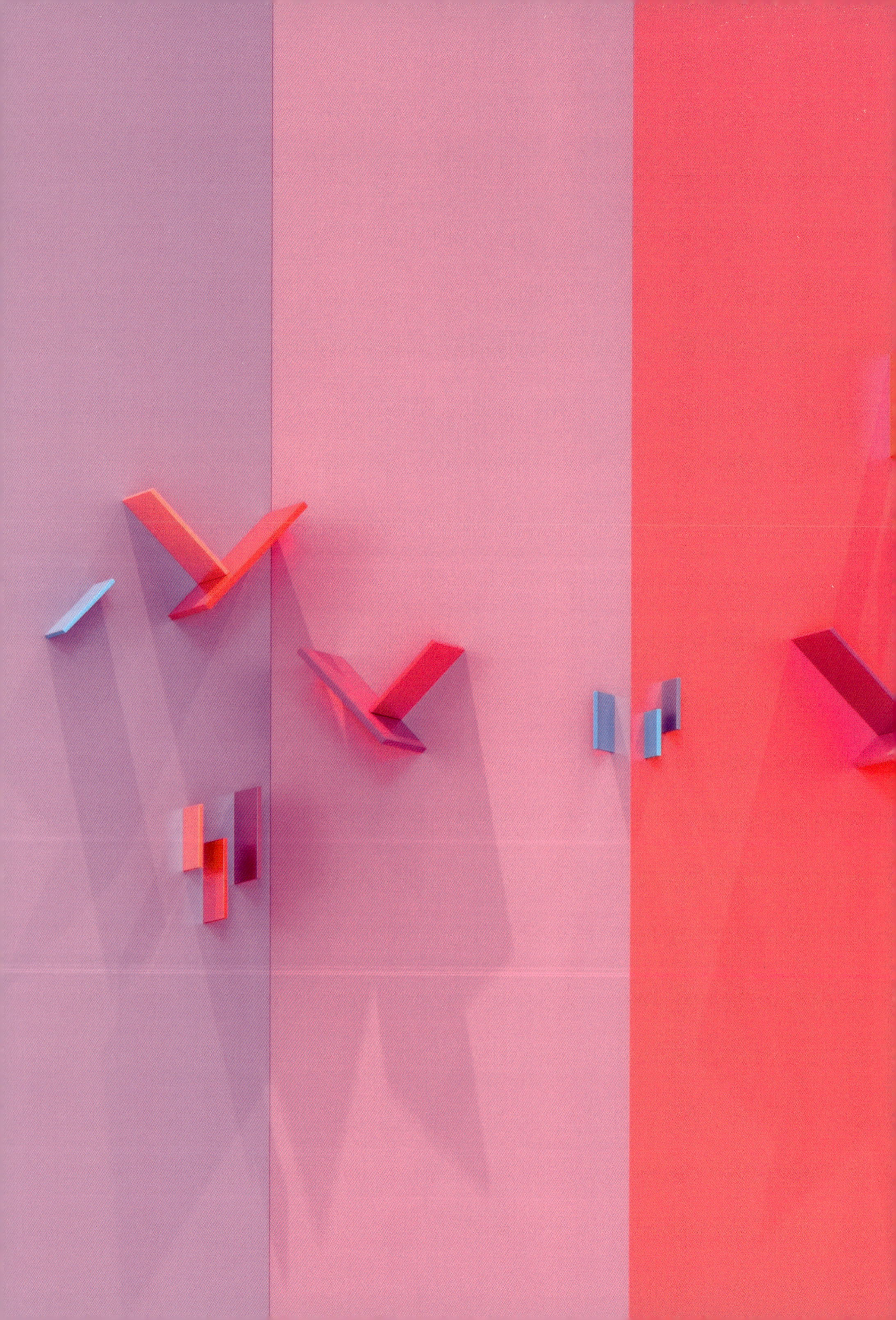

Glossary

abstract art

Also called nonfigurative or nonrepresentational art, abstract art uses form, colour, line, and gestural marks in compositions that do not attempt to represent images of real things. It may interpret reality in an altered form, or depart from it entirely.

Abstract Expressionism

A style that flourished in New York in the 1940s and 1950s, Abstract Expressionism is defined by its combination of formal abstraction and self-conscious expression. The term describes a wide variety of work; among the most famous Abstract Expressionists are Jackson Pollock, Mark Rothko, Barnett Newman, and Willem de Kooning.

Académie Julian

A private art school established by Rodolphe Julian in Paris in 1868. Among the many Canadian artists who studied there are Maurice Cullen, J.W. Morrice, Marc-Aurèle de Foy Suzor-Coté, A.Y. Jackson, and Clarence Gagnon.

Adaskin, Murray (Canadian, 1906–2002)

A member of the Adaskin family (a distinguished Canadian family of artists and musicians), Murray Adaskin began his career as an orchestral and chamber musician before turning to composition. A prolific modernist composer, known for championing Canadian music and musicians, Adaskin was also an influential teacher.

Albers, Josef (German/American, 1888–1976)

A painter and designer who studied and later taught at the Bauhaus, Albers immigrated to the United States after the Nazis closed the school in 1933. As a teacher at Black Mountain College in North Carolina, he attracted future luminaries such as Robert Motherwell and Willem de Kooning. Albers was a pioneer of Op art and Kinetic art.

Art Deco

A decorative style of the early twentieth century, first exhibited in Paris in 1925 at the Exposition internationale des arts décoratifs et industriels modernes. The style had several influences, including Egyptian and Asian motifs, modernist fine art movements, and its design predecessor, Art Nouveau.

Baljeu, Joost (Dutch, 1925–1991)

An abstract painter, sculptor, and theorist, Joost Baljeu was also the editor for the international arts journal *Structure*, which was the touchstone text for artists interested in Concrete art. He is best known for his large painted geometric metal sculptures.

Banff Centre for Arts and Creativity

Established in 1933 as the Banff School of Drama, the Banff Centre for Arts and Creativity is a post-secondary institution located in Banff National Park, Alberta. Founded by the University of Alberta, the Centre offers educational programs in the performing, literary, and visual arts. It is particularly well known for its artist residencies and practicum programs, having served as a site of artistic inspiration and creative practice for many Canadian artists since its founding.

Bauhaus

Open from 1919 to 1933 in Germany, the Bauhaus revolutionized twentieth-century visual arts education by integrating the fine arts, crafts, industrial design, and architecture. Teachers included Josef Albers, Walter Gropius, Wassily Kandinsky, Paul Klee, Ludwig Mies van der Rohe, and László Moholy-Nagy.

Biederman, Charles (American, 1906–2004)

Considered the leading practitioner of Structurist art, Biederman was a painter whose best-known works are shallow, painted relief wall panels. These works are influenced by Biederman's interest in geometric non-objective art, in which he incorporated three-dimensional elements with the use of various materials, including wood, plastic, and aluminum. His works would become influential for the later art movement, Op art.

Opposite: Eli Bornstein, *Quadriplane Structurist Relief No. 15-II* (detail), 2016–17, acrylic enamel on aluminum, 122 x 137 x 15.3 cm, Remai Modern, Saskatoon.

Bloore, Ronald (Canadian, 1925–2009)
A founding member of the abstract painting group the Regina Five, Ronald Bloore was an abstract painter and art teacher. Seeking to achieve a transcendental quality to his art that he saw captured in the ancient architecture of Greece, Turkey, and Egypt, in the early 1960s Bloore destroyed his earlier work and began explorations in black and white, employing bold, organic shapes. Architecture continued to inform his work and he began to link with the practice technically, making small, three-dimensional maquettes of his pieces before creating them in their full size.

Bowman, Richard Irving (American, 1918–2001)
An abstract artist, printmaker, and arts educator whose gestural works are notable for their use of fluorescent coloured paint. He worked in various art schools, including the Chicago Institute of Art—where he taught the Abstract Expressionist Joan Mitchell—the University of Manitoba, and Stanford University.

Brâncuși, Constantin (Romanian, 1876–1957)
An abstract sculptor, with a unique focus on expressing natural forms as simply as possible, Brâncuși influenced later sculptors, including Amedeo Modigliani and Carl Andre. Active for most of his life in Paris, Brâncuși became known in America following his inclusion in the Armory Show, the 1913 International Exhibition of Modern Art.

Bush, Jack (Canadian, 1909–1977)
A member of Painters Eleven, formed in 1953, Bush found his real voice only after critic Clement Greenberg visited his studio in 1957 and focused on his watercolours. Out of these Bush developed the shapes and broad colour planes that would come to characterize a personal colour-field style, parallel to the work of Morris Louis and Kenneth Noland. With them, Bush participated in Greenberg's 1964 exhibition *Post Painterly Abstraction*.

Canadian Art
The national visual-arts periodical *Canadian Art* underwent several name changes from the time of its foundation in 1940. First called *Maritime Art*, it became *Canadian Art* in 1943; in 1967, its editor changed its name to *artscanada*. It became *Canadian Art* again in 1983. The magazine ceased operations in 2021.

Carr, Emily (Canadian, 1871–1945)
A pre-eminent B.C.–based artist and writer, Carr is renowned today for her bold and vibrant images of both the Northwest Coast landscape and its Indigenous peoples. Educated in California, England, and France, she was influenced by a variety of modern art movements but ultimately developed a unique aesthetic style. She was one of the first West Coast artists to achieve national recognition. (See *Emily Carr: Life & Work* by Lisa Baldissera.)

Cézanne, Paul (French, 1839–1906)
A painter of arguably unparalleled influence on the development of modern art, associated with the Post-Impressionist school and known for his technical experiments with colour and form and his interest in multiple-point perspective. In his maturity, Cézanne had several preferred subjects, including his wife, still life, and Provençal landscapes.

Constructivism
Emerging in Russia in the early 1920s, Constructivism was an artistic trend that championed a materialist, non-emotional, utilitarian approach to art and linked art to design, industry, and social usefulness. The term continues to be used generally to describe abstract art that employs lines, planes, and other visual elements in composing abstract geometric images of a precise and impersonal nature.

Cubism
A radical style of painting developed by Pablo Picasso and Georges Braque in Paris between 1907 and 1914, Cubism is defined by the representation of numerous perspectives at once. Cubism is considered crucial to the history of modern art for its enormous international impact; famous practitioners also include Juan Gris and Francis Picabia.

De Stijl (The Style)
An influential Dutch movement in art and architecture founded in 1917 by abstractionists Piet Mondrian, Theo van Doesburg, and Bart van der Leck. De Stijl originated as a publication in which Mondrian elaborated on Neo-Plasticism, a restrained visual language based on primary colours and simple geometric forms that embodied a spiritualism derived from theosophy. After the First World War, De Stijl embraced the utopian potential of art. De Stijl heavily influenced the International Modern style of architecture.

Eckart, Christian (Canadian American, b.1959)
A Calgary-born artist and arts educator, Christian Eckart's often monochromatic works use a Conceptual or meta-painting approach to examine the context that surrounds a work of art and what is included and excluded within a picture's frame. In 2009, he was appointed to the Royal Canadian Academy of Arts.

Emma Lake Artists' Workshops
An annual two-week summer program established by Canadian artists Arthur McKay (1926–2000) and Kenneth Lochhead (1926–2006) in 1955. The goal of the workshops was to connect Saskatchewan artists with the greater art world by inviting art theorists, critics, and artists to conduct workshops at the remote location of Emma Lake in northern Saskatchewan. Throughout the years, the workshop leaders included influential figures such as Clement Greenberg, Barnett Newman, and Will Barnet.

Expressionism
An intense, emotional style of art that values the representation of the artist's subjective inner feelings and ideas. German Expressionism started in the early twentieth century in Germany and Austria. In painting, Expressionism is associated with an intense, jarring use of colour and brush strokes that are not naturalistic.

Feininger, Lyonel (German American, 1871–1956)
A prominent figure in German Expressionism, and a member of several artist groups, including Die Brücke, the Novembergruppe, Gruppe 1919, and Der Blaue Reiter (The Blue Rider). He worked in multiple mediums, including painting, watercolour, and woodcut, and worked as a cartoonist for a portion of his career before becoming an instructor at Bauhaus in 1919 and fleeing the Nazi regime to return to New York City in 1937. Feininger was also a trained musician and composer.

FitzGerald, Lionel LeMoine (Canadian, 1890–1956)
A Winnipeg-born painter and printmaker, FitzGerald was a member of the Group of Seven from 1932 to 1933. He favoured depictions of prairie landscapes and houses, which he executed in pointillist, precisionist, and abstract styles. (See *Lionel LeMoine FitzGerald: Life & Work* by Michael-Parke Taylor.)

Gagnon, Charles (Canadian, 1934–2003)
A Montreal artist who worked across a variety of media, including film, photography, collage, and box constructions, as well as painting. From 1956 to 1960 Gagnon studied in New York, immersing himself in the city's avant-garde world of experimental art. Once he was back in Montreal his painting, especially his use of hard edges, was often associated with that of his Plasticien contemporaries.

Glyde, H.G. (Canadian, 1906–1998)
Trained at the Royal College of Art, London, painter H.G. Glyde is best known for his social-realist depictions of life in the Canadian Prairies. He taught drawing at the Provincial Institute of Technology and Art in Calgary in 1935 and was a painting instructor at the Banff School of Fine Arts between 1936 and 1966. Glyde also established the Division of Fine Art at the University of Alberta, where he taught from 1946 to 1966.

Godwin, Ted (Canadian, 1933–2013)
A painter and arts educator originally from Calgary who, with four other Regina-based artists, was part of the Regina Five—a vanguard group that coalesced through a 1961 exhibition, originally mounted in their hometown, which ultimately became *Five Painters from Regina*, presented that same year at the National Gallery of Canada. Known as both an abstract and a figurative painter, Godwin frequently produced thematic series of works. While he did some work as a commercial artist, he also attended several workshops at the Emma Lake Artists' Workshops and taught at the University of Saskatchewan between 1964 and 1985. He was made a member of the Order of Canada in 2004.

Gorin, Jean (French, 1899–1981)
An abstract artist associated with Neo-Plasticism and known for his three-dimensional relief wall sculptures. A strong follower of Piet Mondrian and the Dutch abstract movement De Stijl, Gorin disrupted the linearity and strict geometric constraints of Neo-Plasticism by including circles and diagonals.

Greenberg, Clement (American, 1909–1994)
A highly influential art critic and essayist known primarily for his formalist approach and his contentious concept of modernism, which he first outlined in his 1960 publication "Modernist Painting." Greenberg was, notably, an early champion of Abstract Expressionists, including Jackson Pollock and the sculptor David Smith.

Group of Seven
A progressive and nationalistic school of landscape painting in Canada, the Group of Seven was active between 1920 (the year of the group's first exhibition, at the Art Gallery of Toronto, now the Art Gallery of Ontario) and 1933. Founding members were the artists Franklin Carmichael, Lawren S. Harris, A.Y. Jackson, Frank H. Johnston, Arthur Lismer, J.E.H. MacDonald, and F.H. Varley.

Harris, Lawren S. (Canadian, 1885–1970)
A founding member of the Group of Seven in Toronto in 1920, Harris was widely considered its unofficial leader. Unlike other members of the group, Harris moved away from painting representational landscapes, first to abstracted landscapes and then to pure abstraction. The Group of Seven broke up in 1933, and when the Canadian Group of Painters was formed in 1933, Harris was elected its first president.

Hart House Gallery
Now the Justina M. Barnicke Gallery, part of the Art Museum at the University of Toronto, Hart House Gallery is an exhibition venue and collecting institution associated with University College at the University of Toronto. Current acquisitions for the collection focus on work by living Canadian artists, especially emerging and mid-career artists of First Nations and culturally diverse backgrounds.

Hayter, Stanley William (British, 1901–1988)
The operator of the Paris printmaking studio Atelier 17, Hayter was a teacher and artist. At his workshop, he welcomed avant-garde European and North American artists, maintaining a social circle and working environment for experimental printmaking techniques as well as discussions about modern art: at various times, Pablo Picasso, Joan Miró, Jean Arp, Max Ernst, Marc Chagall, and Alexander Calder all worked at the atelier. Hayter's background as a research chemist allowed him to develop innovative techniques, bringing printmaking into the vocabulary of modern artists.

Impressionism
A highly influential art movement that originated in France in the 1860s, Impressionism is associated with the emergence of modern urban European society. Claude Monet, Pierre-Auguste Renoir, and other Impressionists rejected the subjects and formal rigours of academic art in favour of scenes of nature and daily life and the careful rendering of atmospheric effects. They often painted outdoors.

International Modern
Emerging around 1920 and reaching its height by the mid-twentieth century, International Modern architecture embraced an unadorned aesthetic of rectilinear structures, with flat surfaces and large planes of glass held in steel frames. Among the most prominent International Modern architects are Walter Gropius, Le Corbusier, Richard Neutra, and Philip Johnson.

Iskowitz, Gershon (Canadian, 1919–1988)
A Toronto-based Polish émigré artist and Holocaust survivor who became internationally renowned for his vibrant abstract paintings, Iskowitz was imprisoned at Auschwitz and Buchenwald during the Second World War. His early figurative works document the horrors he witnessed in the concentration camps. In the late 1960s, inspired by the Canadian landscape, Iskowitz developed the distinctive style of abstract painting for which he is best known. (See *Gershon Iskowitz: Life & Work* by Ihor Holubizky.)

Jackson, A.Y. (Canadian, 1882–1974)
A founding member of the Group of Seven and an important voice in the formation of a distinctively Canadian artistic tradition. A Montreal native, Jackson studied painting in Paris before moving to Toronto in 1913; his northern landscapes are characterized by the bold brush strokes and vivid colours of his Impressionist and Post-Impressionist influences.

Kacere, John (American, 1920–1999)
A painter and printmaker best known for his photorealistic depictions of the lingerie-clad midriffs of female subjects. Born in Iowa, Kacere taught at the University of Manitoba's School of Art from 1950 to 1953. Kacere was originally associated with the Abstract Expressionist movement

but moved away from this painterly style in the 1960s to become a leading practitioner of Photorealism.

Karpuszko, Kazimir (Polish American, 1925–2009)
Associated with the abstract art movement Constructivism, Kazimir Karpuszko was an art dealer, curator, and author. He contributed to the international art journal *Structure*, which was a reference for artists interested in Constructivist art.

Kiyooka, Roy (Canadian, 1926–1994)
Born and raised in the Prairies, Japanese Canadian artist Roy Kiyooka studied under Jock Macdonald at the Provincial Institute of Technology and Art (now Alberta College of Art and Design) in Calgary from 1946 to 1949. A regular presence at the Emma Lake Artists' Workshops, the avant-garde painter developed a hard-edge abstract style. In the 1960s, Kiyooka experimented with a wide range of media and was a central figure in the Vancouver art scene.

Kostyniuk, Ron (Canadian, b.1941)
An artist, sculptor, and arts educator, Ron Kostyniuk is affiliated with the Constructivist movement. His geometric abstraction is informed by his background in biology and interest in organic forms. In 1975, he was elected to the Royal Canadian Academy of Art.

Léger, Fernand (French, 1881–1955)
A leading figure of the Paris avant-garde, whose ideas about modern art, spread through his writing and teaching as well as his own artistic output, would guide a generation of artists. Prolific in media from paint to ceramics to film, Léger was appreciated for his diverse styles, which ranged from Cubist abstraction in the 1910s to realist imagery in the 1950s.

Lochhead, Kenneth (Canadian, 1926–2006)
Although Lochhead's career spanned numerous styles, he is perhaps best known for his colour-field paintings of the 1960s and 1970s. Directly inspired by Barnett Newman and the critic Clement Greenberg, he was instrumental in bringing the principles of modernist abstract painting to Regina, where he was director of the University of Saskatchewan's School of Art.

McKay, Arthur (Canadian, 1926–2000)
A painter and arts educator, whose best-known abstract "mandala" works reflect his interest in Buddhism. A member of the Regina Five, McKay was an associate professor at the University of Regina (formerly the Regina Arts School) and initiated, along with Kenneth Lochhead, the renowned Emma Lake Artists' Workshops in Saskatchewan.

McLuhan, Marshall (Canadian, 1911–1980)
A media theorist and public intellectual, Marshall McLuhan became an international star with his 1964 book *Understanding Media* and garnered a committed following within the 1960s counterculture. His phrase "the medium is the message" has reached the status of popular aphorism. He developed and directed the Centre for Culture and Technology (now the McLuhan Program in Culture and Technology) at the University of Toronto.

McNamee, Don (Canadian, 1938–1994)
A painter, sculptor, and architectural designer, Don McNamee was an activist for the queer community in Saskatoon. He was associated with the first queer organization in the city, the Gay/Lesbian Community Centre of Saskatoon, formerly the Zodiac Friendship Society. He was a founding member of the provincial Conversative government's Coalition for Human Equality (CHE), which campaigned for the legislation to end discrimination against 2SLGBTQI+ people.

Minimalism
A branch of abstract art characterized by extreme restraint in form, Minimalism was most popular among American artists from the 1950s to 1970s. Although Minimalism can be expressed in any medium, it is most commonly associated with sculpture; principal Minimalists include Carl Andre, Donald Judd, and Tony Smith. Among the Minimalist painters were Agnes Martin, Barnett Newman, Kenneth Noland, and Frank Stella.

modernism
A movement extending from the mid-nineteenth to the mid-twentieth century across artistic disciplines, modernism rejected academic traditions in favour of innovative styles developed in response to contemporary industrialized society. Modernist movements in the visual arts have included Gustave Courbet's Realism, and later Impressionism, Post-Impressionism, Fauvism, Cubism, and on to abstraction. By the 1960s, anti-authoritarian postmodernist styles such as Pop art, Conceptual art, and Neo-Expressionism blurred the distinction between high art and mass culture.

Moholy-Nagy, László (Hungarian, 1895–1946)
Hungarian artist László Moholy-Nagy was a professor in the famed Bauhaus school (1923–28) in Germany. Influenced by Constructivism, he explored the integration of life, art, and technology in his radically experimental and wide-ranging practice. Moholy-Nagy is best known for his innovations in photography, notably his camera-less photographs, known as photograms. He led the New Bauhaus in Chicago from 1937 until his death.

Mondrian, Piet (Dutch, 1872–1944)
A leading figure in abstract art, known for his geometric "grid" paintings of straight black lines and brightly coloured squares, whose influence on contemporary visual culture has been called the most far-reaching of any artist. Mondrian saw his highly restrictive and rigorous style, dubbed Neo-Plasticism, as expressive of universal truths.

Montreal Museum of Fine Arts
Founded in 1860 as the Art Association of Montreal, the Montreal Museum of Fine Arts has an encyclopedic collection of artworks and artifacts dating from antiquity to the present day. From its beginnings as a private museum and exhibition space to its current status as a public institution spread over four buildings on Sherbrooke Street, the museum has accumulated a collection of more than forty-three thousand works and hosts historical, modern, and contemporary exhibitions.

Morton, Douglas (Canadian, 1926–2004)
A Winnipeg-born artist, educator, and member of the group of abstract painters known as the Regina Five. Informed by modernist principles from the Emma Lake Workshops, Morton's style features vibrant hues, simplified shapes, and a focus on the interplay of form and colour.

National Gallery of Canada
Established in 1880, the National Gallery of Canada in Ottawa holds the most extensive collection of Canadian art in the country as well as works by prominent international artists. Spearheaded by the Marquis of Lorne (Canada's Governor General from 1878 to 1883), the gallery was created to strengthen a specifically Canadian brand of artistic culture and identity and to build a national collection of art that would match the level of other British Empire institutions. Since 1988, the gallery has been located on Sussex Drive in a building designed by Moshe Safdie.

Newman, Barnett (American, 1905–1970)
A key proponent of Abstract Expressionism, known primarily for his colour-field paintings. In his writing from 1940, Newman argued argue for a break from European artistic traditions in favour of adopting techniques and subject matter more suited to the troubled contemporary moment, and for the expression of truth as he saw it.

O'Keeffe, Georgia (American, 1887–1986)
A critical figure in American modernism, O'Keeffe was encouraged as a young artist by the photographer Alfred Stieglitz, whom she married in 1924. Her expressive and often nearly abstract paintings were inspired by natural forms such as landscapes, flowers, and bones. After Stieglitz's death she settled permanently in northern New Mexico.

Onslow-Ford, Gordon (British, 1912–2003)
A painter, Gordon Onslow-Ford was part of the Surrealist movement led by André Breton in Paris. After the Second World War, he lectured in New York City, influencing the artists that would become associated with Abstract Expressionism. His work explored practices of automatism and levels of consciousness. In 1998, he founded the Lucid Art Foundation in Inverness, Scotland, to support both artists and research on the environment and consciousness.

Panofsky, Erwin (German American, 1892–1968)
An art historian who is known for his developments in the study of iconography. Panofsky's research and methodology of iconology, which was focused on Northern European Renaissance art, linked subject matter with stylistic and culturally informed symbolic analysis of a work of art. Critics argued that iconology, as a tool for grasping art, prioritized symbolic content at the expense of form and substance.

Post-Impressionism
A French-born art movement that was developed in the late nineteenth century and built upon the preceding Impressionist movement. Practitioners rejected the naturalistic use of light and colour and infused their works with more abstract qualities, emphasizing harsher lines and shapes, a heavier use of paint and pigment, and expressive, thickly textured brush strokes. Key figures include Vincent van Gogh, Paul Gauguin, and Paul Cézanne.

realism/Realism
A style of art in which subjects are depicted as factually as possible. The art style "realism" is not to be confused with "Realism," a nineteenth-century art movement, led by Gustave Courbet, concerned with the representation of daily modern life rather than mythological, religious, or historical subjects.

Regina Five
A group of five abstract painters from Regina, Saskatchewan, known for their group exhibition *Five Painters from Regina* at the National Gallery of Canada in 1961. The group included Kenneth Lochhead, Arthur McKay, Douglas Morton, Ted Godwin, and Ronald Bloore. Their works can be characterized as nonfigurative, and they were heavily influenced by the Emma Lake Artists' Workshops and the art critic Barnett Newman.

Remai Modern
An art gallery in Saskatoon, Saskatchewan, located on Treaty Six Territory and the traditional homeland of the Métis. The gallery was established in 2004 after a donation by Ellen Remai, for whom the gallery is named. The gallery collects and showcases local and international modern and contemporary art.

representational
A term used to describe art that is derived from references to real objects and images that are recognizable as depictions of what exists in the real world. A representational work may not be entirely realistic.

Seurat, Georges (French, 1859–1891)
An influential painter, Seurat was a pioneer of the Neo-Impressionist movement, departing from Impressionism's relative spontaneity and practising more formal structure and symbolic content. Along with Paul Signac, he developed Pointillism, a technique adopted by other painters such as Camille Pissarro, Piet Mondrian, and Wassily Kandinsky.

Smith, Gordon (Canadian, 1919–2020)
British-born Smith was a painter living and working in Vancouver. Time spent as a student at the California School of Fine Arts (now the San Francisco Art Institute) influenced his early style, which progressed from Abstract Expressionism through hard-edged abstraction and back to gestural expressionist landscapes through his career. Smith taught at the University of British Columbia and was a prominent figure in Vancouver's postwar art scene.

Snelgrove, Gordon (Canadian, 1898–1966)
A painter, art historian, and professor of art and art history at the University of Saskatchewan. He regularly attended the Emma Lake Artists' Workshops, and upon his death in 1966, the University of Saskatchewan opened the Gordon Snelgrove Gallery in his honour.

Structurist
An art form that refers to nature-based geometric abstraction, developed by leading practitioner Charles Biederman. Key progenitors in the lineage of Structurist art include Édouard Manet, Paul Cézanne, and Piet Mondrian. Artist Eli Bornstein has contributed to the recognition of the genre through the international art journal *The Structurist*, which he established in 1960.

Surrealism
An early twentieth-century literary and artistic movement that began in Paris, Surrealism aimed to express the workings of the unconscious, free of convention and reason, and was characterized by fantastic images and incongruous juxtapositions. The movement spread globally, influencing film, theatre, and music.

Thomas, Howard (American, 1899–1971)
A painter, printmaker, and arts educator. Thomas began painting in the Regionalist style but later met and was highly influenced by the German American abstract artist Carl Holty. Although he taught at the University of Georgia until his retirement, he had continued influence in his hometown as a member of the Wisconsin Painters & Sculptors Association.

Thomson, Tom (Canadian, 1877–1917)
A seminal figure in the creation of a national school of painting, Thomson is known for a bold vision of Algonquin Park—aligned stylistically with Post-Impressionism and Art Nouveau—that has come to symbolize both the Canadian landscape and Canadian landscape painting. Thomson and the members of what would in 1920 become the Group of Seven profoundly influenced one another's work. (See *Tom Thomson: Life & Work* by David P. Silcox.)

Transcendentalism
Transcendentalism is a literary and philosophical movement that originated in the northeastern United States in the 1820s and emphasized the importance of independence and personal insight in uncovering truth and spiritual experience. Developed from the writings of Ralph Waldo Emerson and Henry David Thoreau, among others, the movement had a significant impact on artists including Lawren S. Harris and J.E.H. MacDonald.

Vantongerloo, Georges (Belgian, 1886–1965)
A painter, sculptor, architect, art theorist, and founding member of the Dutch abstract movement De Stijl. He would later move to Paris and become a member of the abstract group Cercle et Carré, which later was assimilated into the group Abstraction-Création. Vantongerloo and the groups he was associated with were all interested in Neo-Plasticism and abstraction through a reduction of form and colour.

von Neumann, Robert (American, 1888–1976)
A painter, watercolourist, printmaker, and teacher, Robert von Neumann was associated with the Regionalist movement in American art during the 1930s and 1940s. He was born and studied in Germany, before moving to the United States and teaching at several art schools. True to the Regionalist movement, his works are known for their depictions of rural American life.

Willmott, Elizabeth (Canadian, b.1928)
Artist, photographer, and writer Elizabeth Willmott is a major Structurist who, for over two decades, created a rich body of three-dimensional colour reliefs. Many of her photographs, as well as her book reviews and articles, were published in the Canada-based and internationally-circulated art journal *The Structurist*.

Winnipeg Art Gallery
Established in 1912, the Winnipeg Art Gallery has the world's largest public collection of Inuit art; it displayed Inuit sculpture for the first time in December 1953, and began systematic purchases for its permanent collection in 1957. In 1960 the gallery made a serious commitment when it purchased 139 major pieces from George Swinton. Over the years, the gallery's Inuit art collection has grown to its present size of close to 14,000 works largely through the donation or purchase of large collections, including the enormous 4,000-piece Jerry Twomey Collection received in 1971. The gallery's other primary collections are dedicated to Canadian historical and contemporary art, decorative art, and contemporary Canadian photography. It has moved several times in its history but has been in its current location since 1971.

Opposite: Eli Bornstein, *Double Plane Structurist Relief No. 8* (detail), 1973, acrylic enamel, Plexiglas on aluminum, 43.2 x 43.2 x 27 cm, Remai Modern, Saskatoon.

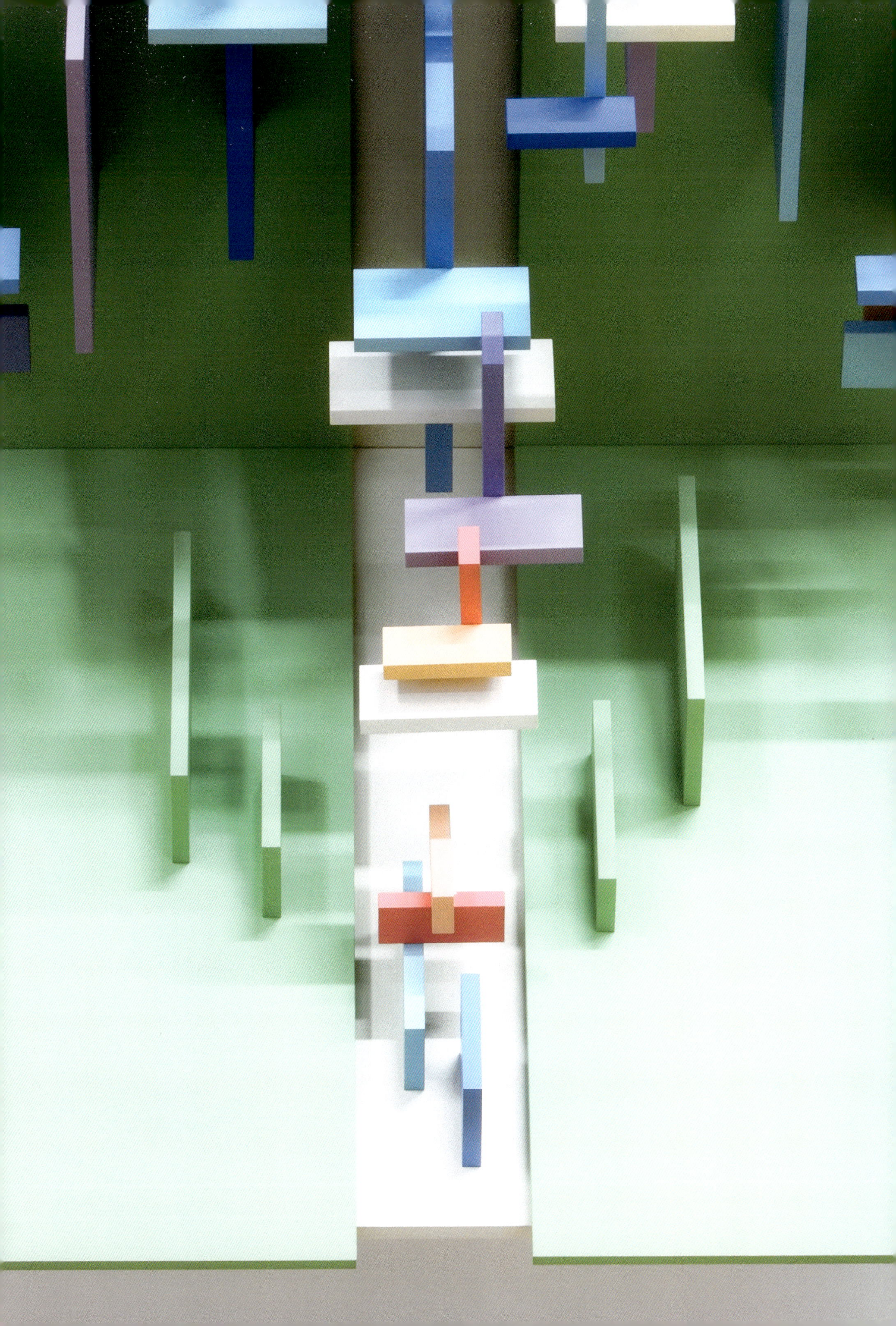

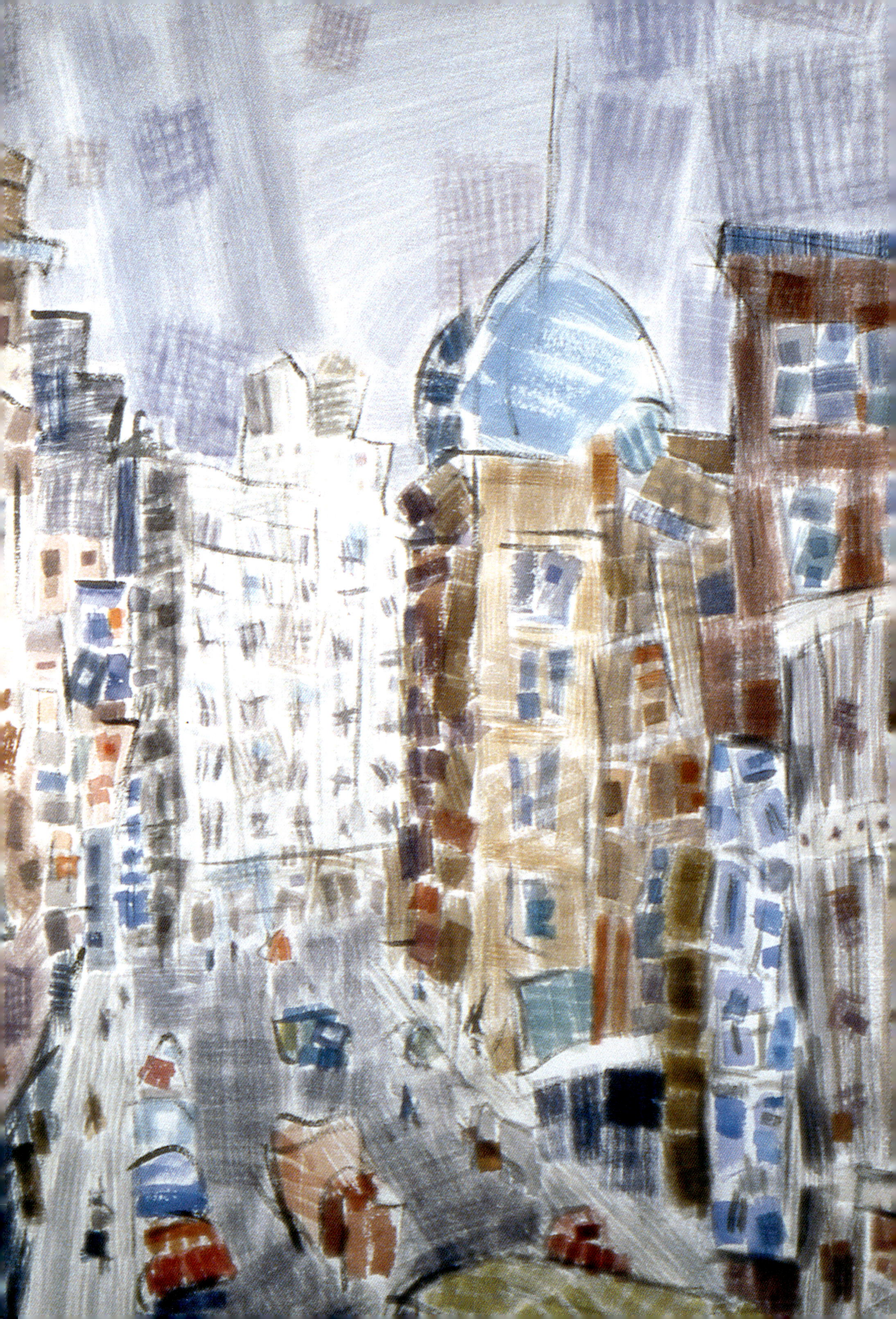

Notes

BIOGRAPHY, PAGES 11–29

1 Eli Bornstein's personal journal, unpublished manuscript, 1997–2017, entry dated January 19, 1997.

2 Jonneke Fritz-Jobse, *Eli Bornstein: Art Toward Nature* (Saskatoon: Mendel Art Gallery, 1996), 5–17.

3 Fritz-Jobse, *Art Toward Nature*, 5.

4 Bornstein's personal journal, entry dated January 23, 2006.

5 Bornstein's personal journal, entry titled "Jazz as an early influence toward abstract art," dated January 23, 2006.

6 One example is Dutch modernist artist Piet Mondrian, who completed his seminal work *Broadway Boogie Woogie* in 1943 after moving to New York.

7 Fritz-Jobse, *Art Toward Nature*, 5.

8 Fritz-Jobse, *Art Toward Nature*, 5.

9 As told to Fritz-Jobse, *Art Toward Nature*, 5.

10 Kazimir Karpuszko in *Eli Bornstein: Selected Works / Œuvres choisies, 1957–1982* (Saskatoon: Mendel Art Gallery, 1982), 5, and in conversation with Roald Nasgaard, August 25, 2020.

11 Bornstein's personal journal, entry dated April 26, 2008.

12 Eli Bornstein, "Abstract Art on the Prairies," in *Perspectives on Saskatchewan*, ed. Jene M. Porter (Winnipeg: University of Manitoba, 2009), 278–80.

13 Bornstein, "Abstract Art on the Prairies," in *Perspectives on Saskatchewan*, 278–80.

14 Bornstein, "Abstract Art on the Prairies," in *Perspectives on Saskatchewan*, 278–80.

15 See Jeffrey Spalding, "IN MY OPINION: In the early '50s Winnipeg Abstraction ruled the roost!," in *gallerieswest*, April 30, 2019. https://www.gallerieswest.ca/magazine/columns/in-the-early-%E2%80%9850s%2C-between-the-automatistes-and-painters-11%2C-winnipeg-abstraction-ruled-the-roos/.

16 *Five Painters from Regina*, 1961, curated by Richard Simmins, organized and presented by the National Gallery of Canada, Ottawa. Kiyooka was not included in the 1961 exhibition because he had by then moved to Vancouver to teach at the Vancouver School of Art.

17 For more on the Emma Lake summer workshops, see John O'Brian, *The Flat Side of the Landscape: The Emma Lake Artists' Workshops* (Saskatoon: Mendel Art Gallery, 1989).

18 Eli Bornstein, "Pioneering Abstract Art on the Prairies," in *A Celebration of Canada's Arts 1930–1970*, ed. Glen Carruthers and Gordana Lazarevich (Toronto: Canadian Scholars' Press, 1996), 149.

19 Bornstein's personal journal, entry dated September 6, 2013.

20 In conversation with the artist, August 2020.

21 Charles Biederman, "Art and Science as Creation," *Structure* no. 1 (1958): 6.

22 Jonneke Fritz-Jobse, *De Stijl Continued: The Journal Structure (1958–1964): An Artists' Debate* (Rotterdam: 010 Publishers, 2005), 151.

23 Bornstein, "Abstract Art on the Prairies," in *Perspectives on Saskatchewan*, 281.

24 The first issue of *Structure* was based in the Department of Art, University of Saskatchewan, with distributors in Toronto (University of Toronto Press), New York (Wittenborn), London, and Amsterdam. Because Bornstein and Baljeu had a falling-out with regard to the publication of *Structure*, Bornstein participated only in the first issue of the periodical. *Structure* ran for six issues, 1958–1964, the other five edited in Amsterdam by Baljeu. See Fritz-Jobse, *De Stijl Continued*, 157.

25 Bornstein personal journal, entry dated January 6, 2009.

Opposite: Eli Bornstein, *Downtown* (detail), 1954, watercolour on paper, 50 x 70 cm, University of Saskatchewan, Saskatoon.

26 Bornstein's personal journal, entry dated September 26, 2008. See also Fritz-Jobse, *De Stijl Continued*, 405–6.

27 Because he was usually out-of-province during summers, Bornstein did not participate in the Emma Lake workshops, a choice that in retrospect he perhaps regrets.

28 Letter from Charles Biederman to Eli Bornstein, March 26, 1958. Cited in Fritz-Jobse, *De Stijl Continued*, 151.

29 Hayton, "The Structurist Movement," *Chicago Omnibus* (May 1967), 59. The location of the illustrated work *Structurist Relief No. 3-II* (Sea Series), 1965, is unknown.

30 Bornstein's personal journal, entry dated November 4, 2013.

31 Eli Bornstein, "Four Conversations on Art and Vision," *The Structurist* no. 17/18 (1977–78), 80.

32 Eli Bornstein, *Eli Bornstein: Arctic Journals 1986 and 1987* (Vancouver: Figure 1 Publishing, 2022).

33 Bornstein, *Arctic Journals*, 105.

34 Bornstein's personal journal, entry dated July 27, 1986.

35 Roald Nasgaard, "Introduction: 'A Very Sacred Experience,'" in Bornstein, *Arctic Journals*, 14–17.

36 See *An Art at the Mercy of Light: Recent Works by Eli Bornstein* (Saskatoon: Mendel Art Gallery, 2013), 18, 24–25, 54.

37 "Mr. Eli Bornstein," Member of the Order of Canada, Governor General of Canada, accessed October 17, 2024, https://www.gg.ca/en/honours/recipients/146-6563.

38 Steven Leyden Cochrane, "Finding His Light: Senior Saskatchewan Artist's Refined Abstractions Celebrate the Natural World," *Winnipeg Free Press*, January 30, 2014. https://www.winnipegfree-press.com/arts-and-life/entertainment/arts/finding-his-light-242707691.html.

KEY WORKS, PAGES 31–57

THE ISLAND

1 1. Eli Bornstein, "Transition toward the New Art," *Structure* no. 1 (1968): 26.

ALUMINUM CONSTRUCTION (TREE OF KNOWLEDGE)

1 The second abstract sculpture was Robert Murray's *Rainmaker*, commissioned by the City of Saskatoon in 1960 for Saskatoon City Hall.

2 Eli Bornstein, "Pioneering Abstract Art on the Prairies," in *A Celebration of Canada's Arts: 1930–1970* (Toronto: Canadian Scholars Press, 1996), 149–50.

3 Clement Greenberg, "Painting and Sculpture in Prairie Canada Today," *Canadian Art* (March–April 1963).

STRUCTURIST RELIEF NO. 2

1 Elizabeth Willmott, "The Relevance for Art of James J. Gibson's Theory of Perception," *The Structurist* no. 51/52 (2019–20), 84.

DOUBLE PLANE STRUCTURIST RELIEF NO. 3

1 Eli Bornstein's personal journal, unpublished manuscript, 1997–2017, entry dated November 4, 2013.

2 Eli Bornstein, "The Oblique in Art: Toward the Oblique in Space," *The Structurist*, no. 9 (1969): 38.

3 Bornstein's personal journal, entry titled "The First Lily," dated June 21, 1991.

4 Eli Bornstein, *Reliefs Structuristes, 1955–1975* (Paris: Centre Culturel Canadien, 1976).

ARCTIC STUDY NO. 38

1 Over the summers of 1986 and 1987, Bornstein also kept a journal that was eventually published in 2022 as *Eli Bornstein: Arctic Journals 1986 and 1987*, whose daily entries recorded in detail his travel and art-making activities, often physically arduous but always wondrous as encounters with the landscape, from the tiniest Arctic flowers to the grandeur of the icebergs.

2 Bornstein's personal journal, unpublished manuscript, 1997–2017, entry dated July 14, 1987.

3 *Eli Bornstein: Arctic Journals 1986 and 1987* (Vancouver: Figure 1, 2022), 78.

4 Adapted from Roald Nasgaard, "Introduction: 'A Very Sacred Experience,'" *Eli Bornstein: Arctic Journals 1986 and 1987*, 14–17.

HEXAPLANE STRUCTURIST RELIEF NO. 2

1 Lawren Harris, "Creative Arts in Canada," *Supplement to the McGill News*, Montreal (December 1928), 184.

2 Adapted from Roald Nasgaard, "Introduction: 'A Very Sacred Experience,'" in *Eli Bornstein: Arctic Journals 1986 and 1987* (Vancouver: Figure 1, 2022), 14–17.

QUADRIPLANE STRUCTURIST RELIEF NOS. 1–3 (RIVER-SCREEN SERIES)

1 Bornstein's personal journal, entry dated November 12, 1994.

2 Akseli Gallen-Kallela, cited in Roald Nasgaard, *The Mystic North* (Toronto: Art Gallery of Ontario by the University of Toronto Press, 1984), 54.

TRIPART HEXAPLANE CONSTRUCTION NO. 2

1 When, in the early 2000s, a proposed commission of a work by Bornstein for the University of Manitoba's new Centre for Music Art and Design, by Patkau Architects, fell through, Oliver A.I. Botar, professor in the School of Art, asked Bornstein if he would consider donating a work instead. (Bornstein had previously made such a donation to Jacobs University, now Constructor University, in Bremen.) Bornstein agreed and made *Tripart Hexaplane Construction No. 2* specially for the University of Manitoba. Bornstein and his wife, Christina, visited a couple of times to oversee its assembly. Botar reports (in an email from November 9, 2023) that "it has been a popular piece on campus ever since."

2 See https://www.jacobs-university.de/drupal_lists/archives/news/11975/index.html.

SIGNIFICANCE & CRITICAL ISSUES, PAGES 59–69

1 Eli Bornstein, "Art and Technology," *The Structurist* no. 6 (1966): 23. Bornstein and co-editor Joost Baljeu, a Dutch relief artist, had a falling-out with regard to the publication of *Structure*. Bornstein participated only in the first issue of the periodical. *Structure* ran for six issues between 1958 and 1964, with the other five edited in Amsterdam by Baljeu. See Jonneke Fritz-Jobse, *De Stijl Continued: The Journal Structure (1958–1964): An Artists' Debate* (Rotterdam: 010 Publishers, 2005), 157.

2 Eli Bornstein, "The Oblique in Art: Toward the Oblique in Space," *The Structurist* no. 9 (1969): 37.

3 In the Arctic in 1986, Bornstein did resume painting in watercolour, picking up from where he had left off with *The Island*, but soon the watercolours evolved toward a more Structurist syntax.

4 See Eli Bornstein, "Structurist Art—Its Origins," *The Structurist* no. 1 (1960–61): 7.

5 Eli Bornstein, "Transition toward the New Art," *Structure: Annual for the New Art* no. 1 (1958): 38.

6 See, for example, Eli Bornstein, "The Oblique in Art: Toward the Oblique in Space," *The Structurist* no. 9 (1969): 37.

7 Eli Bornstein, "The Color 'Molecule' in Art," *The Structurist* no. 13/14 (1973–74), 112–14.

8 Eli Bornstein's personal journal, unpublished manuscript, 1997–2017, entry dated September 14, 1995.

9 Charles Biederman, "Art and Science in Creation," *Structure* no. 1 (1958): 9.

10 Bornstein, "Structurist Art—Its Origins," 4–5.

11 Bornstein, "Transition toward the New Art," 34–35.

12 The following paragraph is adapted from Roald Nasgaard, "Rendering the God-Spirit: Wilderness Landscapes in North America," in *Mystical Landscapes: From Vincent van Gogh to Emily Carr* (Toronto: Art Gallery of Ontario, 2017), 268–69.

13 Walt Whitman, "Preface to the 1955 Edition of Leaves of Grass," in *The American Tradition in Literature*, revised, ed. Sculley Bradley et al. (New York: W.W. Norton, 1962), 832.

14 Hartley's statement for his exhibition at Münchener Graphic-Verlag in Berlin as quoted in "American Artist Astounds Germans," *New York Times*, December 19, 1915, in James Timothy Voorhies, ed., *My Dear Stieglitz: Letters of Marsden Hartley and Alfred Stieglitz, 1912–1915* (Columbia: University of South Carolina, 2022), 209.

15 Eli Bornstein, "Abstract Art on the Prairies," in *Perspectives on Saskatchewan*, ed. Jene M. Porter (Winnipeg: University of Manitoba, 2009), 283.

16 Bornstein's personal journal, entry dated 2012 (month/day unknown).

17 Eli Bornstein, "Art and Morality," *The Structurist* no. 10 (1970): 6.

18 See Roald Nasgaard, *The Mystic North: Symbolist Landscape Painting in Europe and North America* (Toronto: University of Toronto Press, 1984).

19 Akseli Gallen-Kallela, cited in Roald Nasgaard, *The Mystic North* (Toronto: Art Gallery of Ontario by the University of Toronto Press, 1984), 54.

20 Adapted from Roald Nasgaard, "To Invent the Truth," in *Artist in Focus: Eli Bornstein* (Saskatoon: Remai Modern, 2019), 7.

21 Bornstein's personal journal, entry titled "Art and Biology," dated May 17, 2006.

22 Oliver A.I. Botar, "The Structurist," in *An Art at the Mercy of Light: Recent Works by Eli Bornstein* (Saskatoon: Mendel Art Gallery, 2013), 46.

23 Botar, "The Structurist," in *An Art at the Mercy of Light*, 46.

24 Eli Bornstein, "Conflicting Concepts in Art," *The Structurist* (1963), cited by Botar, "The Structurist," in *An Art at the Mercy of Light*, 43.

25 Bornstein, "Conflicting Concepts in Art," *The Structurist* (1963), cited by Botar, "The Structurist," in *An Art at the Mercy of Light*, 43.

26 Botar, "The Structurist," 45.

27 Bornstein's personal journal, January 14, 2012. Slightly edited for clarity.

STYLE & TECHNIQUE, PAGES 71–81

1 Eli Bornstein, "Art Toward Nature," *The Structurist* no. 15/16 (1975–76): 153. The quote has been paraphrased for clarity.

2 Eli Bornstein's personal journal, unpublished manuscript, 1997–2017, entry dated April 2, 1995.

3 Bornstein's personal journal, entry dated April 2, 1995.

4 Bornstein's personal journal, entry dated September 2, 1995.

5 Bornstein's personal journal, entry dated April 1, 1995.

6 Bornstein's personal journal, entry dated September 2, 1995.

7 Adapted from Roald Nasgaard, "To Invent the Truth," *Artist in Focus: Eli Bornstein* (Saskatoon: Remail Modern, 2019), 5–6.

8 Adapted from Nasgaard, "To Invent the Truth," 5–6.

9 Bornstein's personal journal, entry titled "The Varied Processes of Birth in an Artworld" and dated May 14, 2011.

10 A "check" is a long crack that appears as the sapwood of a timber shrinks around the heartwood over time.

11 Eli Bornstein, "Aspects of Transparency and Reflection," *The Structurist* no. 27/28 (1987): 58–59.

12 In conversation with the artist, August 25, 2020.

13 At first, Bornstein used a room inside the house, but later, he built a separate studio building complete with skylights that let natural light flow onto the hanging walls.

14 Bornstein's personal journal, entry dated November 28, 1999.

15 Eli Bornstein, "The Burden of Art Dependent upon Light," cited by Oliver A.I. Botar in his article "The Structurist," in *An Art at the Mercy of Light: Recent Works by Eli Bornstein* (Saskatoon: Mendel Art Gallery, 2013), 35.

16 Bornstein's personal journal, entry titled "The Burden of Art Dependent upon Light" and dated December 19–20, 2001.

17 In conversation with the artist, August 25, 2020.

18 In conversation with the artist, August 25, 2020.

19 Bornstein's personal journal, entry titled "The Burden of Art Dependent upon Light," dated December 19–20, 2001.

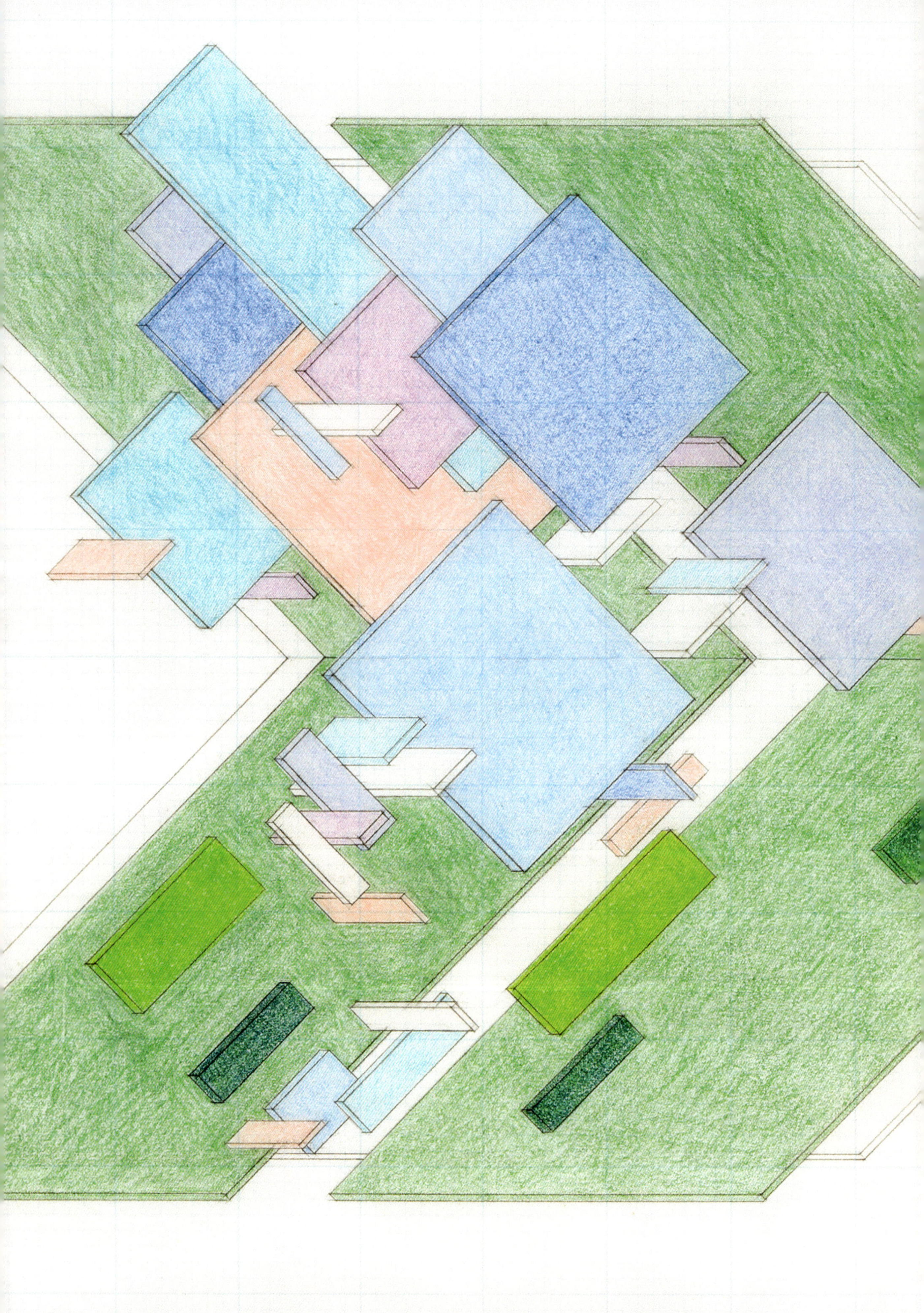

Credits

IMAGE SOURCES

Every effort has been made to secure permissions for all copyrighted material. The Art Canada Institute will gladly correct any errors or omissions.

The Art Canada Institute thanks the following for their assistance: Art Gallery of Ontario (Alexandra Cousins); ARTRES (John Benicewicz); Bauhaus-Archiv Berlin (Erika Babatz, Kai-Annett Becker); Beaverbrook Art Gallery (Dawn Steeves); Canadian Centre for Architecture (Céline Pereira); Copyright Visual Arts (Geneviève Daigneault); Dallas Museum of Art (Paul Molinari); Estate of Charles Gagnon (Eames Gagnon); Estate of Henry George Glyde; Estate of Naum Gabo; Family of Lawren S. Harris (Stew Sheppard); Figure 1 Publishing (Mark Redmayne); Forum Gallery (Asja Gleeson); General Hardware (Niki Dracos); Hirshhorn Museum and Sculpture Garden, Smithsonian Institute (Hannah Green); Kunstmuseum Den Haag (Jolanda Zonderop); Maynards Fine Art and Antiques (Maya Thapa); McMichael Canadian Art Collection (Hanna Broker); Minneapolis Institute of Art (Dan Dennehy); Moholy-Nagy Foundation (Natalia Hug); Mondrian Trust (Madalena Holtzman); Montreal Museum of Fine Arts (Marie-Claude Saia); National Gallery of Canada (Raven Amiro, Philip Dombowsky); Nickle Galleries, University of Calgary (Lisa Tillotson, Christine Sowiak); Ottawa Art Gallery (Jennifer Gilliland); Postmedia (Elena Novikova); Remai Modern (Jillian Cyca); RISD Museum (Nicole Priedemann); Saskatoon Public Library (Jeff O'Brien); Tate Modern (Fintan Ryan); University of Manitoba Art Collection (C.W. Brooks); University of Regina Archives and Special Collections (Alyssa Hyduk); University of Saskatchewan Art Galleries (Blair Barbeau); University of Saskatchewan, University Archives and Special Collections (Cheryl Avery); University of Wisconsin-Milwaukee Libraries (Abigail Nye); Vancouver Art Gallery (Danielle Currie); Walker Art Centre (Kova Walker-Lečič); Weisman Art Museum at the University of Minnesota (MollieRae Miller); Whyte Museum of the Canadian Rockies (Amy Lalonde); Winnipeg Art Gallery (Nicole Fletcher, Sydney Murchison); Eli Bornstein; Oliver A.I. Botar; Christian Eckart; Roald Nasgaard; Liv Valmestad; and Elizabeth Willmott.

CREDITS FOR WORKS BY ELI BORNSTEIN

Aluminum Construction (Tree of Knowledge), 1956. Photo credit: Roald Nasgaard.

Arctic Study No. 7, 1986. Collection of the artist. Courtesy of the University of Saskatchewan, University Archives and Special Collections.

Arctic Study No. 12, 1986. Collection of the artist. Courtesy of the University of Saskatchewan, University Archives and Special Collections.

Arctic Study No. 38, 1987. Collection of the artist. Courtesy of the University of Saskatchewan, University Archives and Special Collections.

Double Plane Structurist Relief No. 2-1, 1966–71. Private collection.

Double Plane Structurist Relief No. 3, 1967–69. Collection of the University of Saskatchewan, Saskatoon, Purchased 1973 (1973.011.001). Courtesy of the University of Saskatchewan.

Double Plane Structurist Relief No. 8, 1973. The Mendel Art Gallery Collection at Remai Modern, Saskatoon, Purchased 1984 (1984.16). Courtesy of Remai Modern. Photo credit: Blaine Campbell.

Downtown, 1954. Collection of the University of Saskatchewan, Saskatoon, Purchased 1956 (1957.011.001). Courtesy of the University of Saskatchewan.

Downtown Bridge #4, 1954. The Mendel Art Gallery Collection at Remai Modern, Saskatoon, Gift of the Picture Sales and Rental Committee, Women's Auxiliary, Saskatoon Art Centre, 1977 (1977.3.2). Courtesy of Remai Modern.

Four Part Vertical Double Plane Structurist Relief Nos. 14–17 (Winter Sky Series), 1980–83, model of commission for Wascana Centre Authority. Collection of the Canadian Centre for Architecture, Montreal, Gift of Eli Bornstein (DR2008:0028). Courtesy of the Canadian Centre for Architecture.

Four Part Vertical Double Plane Structurist Relief (Winter Sky Series), 1980–83. Photo credit: Roald Nasgaard.

Girl Reading, 1948. Collection of the artist. Courtesy of the University of Saskatchewan, University Archives and Special Collections.

Growth Motif No. 4, 1956. Collection of the artist. Courtesy of Eli Bornstein.

Head, c.1947. Collection of the Walker Art Center, Minneapolis, Gift of the T.B. Walker Foundation, 1947 (1947.46). Courtesy of the Walker Art Center.

Opposite: Eli Bornstein, *Isometric Study for Double Plane Structurist Relief* (detail), 1969, colour pencil on paper, dimensions unknown, collection of the artist.

Hexaplane Structurist Relief No. 1 (River-Screen Series), 1989–96. Collection of the artist. Courtesy of Remai Modern. Photo credit: Troy Mamer.

Hexaplane Structurist Relief No. 2 (Arctic Series), 1995–98. Collection of the University of Saskatchewan, Saskatoon, Gift of Dorothea Adaskin, 2005 (2005.001.001). Courtesy of the University of Saskatchewan.

Installation view of *Quadriplane Structurist Relief Nos. 1–3* (River-Screen Series), 1989–96, by Eli Bornstein. Collection of the artist. Courtesy of Roald Nasgaard. Photo credit: Roald Nasgaard.

Installation view of *Structurist Relief No. 6*, 1999–2000, *Structurist Relief No. 7*, 2000–2001, and *Structurist Relief No. 8*, 2000–2002, by Eli Bornstein at the Mendel Art Gallery, Saskatoon, 2013. Courtesy of Remai Modern. Photo credit: Troy Mamer.

Installation view of *Untitled Hexaplane Structurist Relief*, 2004, by Eli Bornstein on the Canadian Light Source Building, University of Saskatchewan, Saskatoon, date unknown. Photographer unknown. Courtesy of Eli Bornstein.

The Island, 1956. Collection of the artist. Courtesy of Eli Bornstein.

Isometric Study for Double Plane Structurist Relief, 1969. Collection of the artist. Courtesy of Remai Modern. Photo credit: Blaine Campbell.

Low Form Relief No. 10, 1957. Collection of the artist. Courtesy of Remai Modern. Photo credit: Blaine Campbell.

Multiplane Structurist Relief IV, No. 1 (Arctic Series), 1986–87. Collection of the Beaverbrook Art Gallery, Fredericton, Gift of the artist (2009.143). Courtesy of the Beaverbrook Art Gallery.

Multiplane Structurist Relief IV, No. 2 (Arctic Series) (detail), 1987–88. Collection of the artist. Courtesy of the University of Saskatchewan, University Archives and Special Collections.

Multiplane Structurist Relief V, No. 1, 1993. The Mendel Art Gallery Collection at Remai Modern, Saskatoon, Gift of Dorothea Larsen Adaskin, 2004 (2004.17.25). Courtesy of Remai Modern. Photo credit: Blaine Campbell.

Multiplane Structurist Relief VI, No. 1 (Sunset Series), 1998–99. Collection of the artist. Courtesy of Remai Modern. Photo credit: Troy Mamer.

Quadriplane Structurist Relief No. 1 (River-Screen Series), 1989–96. Collection of the artist. Courtesy of Roald Nasgaard. Photo credit: Roald Nasgaard.

Quadriplane Structurist Relief No. 2 (River-Screen Series), 1989–96. Collection of the artist. Courtesy of Roald Nasgaard. Photo credit: Roald Nasgaard.

Quadriplane Structurist Relief No. 3 (River-Screen Series), 1989–96. Collection of the artist. Courtesy of Roald Nasgaard. Photo credit: Roald Nasgaard.

Quadriplane Structurist Relief No. 8, 2000–2002. Collection of the artist. Courtesy of the University of Saskatchewan, University Archives and Special Collections.

Quadriplane Structurist Relief No. 9, 2000–2001. Private collection, Toronto. Courtesy of Remai Modern. Photo credit: Troy Mamer.

Quadriplane Structurist Relief No. 15-II, 2016–17. The Mendel Art Gallery Collection at Remai Modern, Saskatoon, Gift of the artist, 2017 (2017.12). Courtesy of Remai Modern. Photo credit: Blaine Campbell.

Saskatoon, 1954. Private collection. Courtesy of Eli Bornstein.

Structurist Relief in Five Parts, Model Version, 1962. Collection of the National Gallery of Canada, Ottawa, Purchased 1965 (14754). Courtesy of the National Gallery of Canada. Photo credit: NGC.

Structurist Relief No. 1, 1965. Private collection.

Structurist Relief No. 1, 1966. Collection of the Nickle Galleries, University of Calgary (NG.1970.060.002). Courtesy of the Nickle Galleries. Photo credit: Andy Nichols, LCR Photo Services.

Structurist Relief No. 1-1 (Sea Series), 1966. Collection of Forum Gallery, New York. Courtesy of Forum Gallery.

Structurist Relief No. 2, 1966. Private collection.

Structurist Relief No. 3 (Sea Series), 1966–67. Collection of the artist. Courtesy of the University of Saskatchewan, University Archives and Special Collections.

Structurist Relief No. 3-1 (Canoe Lake Series), 1964. Private collection.

Structurist Relief No. 4, 1957. Private collection.

Structurist Relief No. 4-11 (Sea Series), 1965. The Mendel Art Gallery Collection at Remai Modern, Saskatoon, Gift of Dorothea Larsen Adaskin, 2004 (2004.17.26). Courtesy of Remai Modern. Photo credit: Blaine Campbell.

Structurist Relief No. 14, 1957. Private collection.

Structurist Relief No. 18-II, 1958–60. Collection of the University of Saskatchewan, Saskatoon, Commissioned 1958 (1958.003.001). Courtesy of the University of Saskatchewan. Photo credit: Roald Nasgaard.

Tripart Hexaplane Construction No. 2, 2002–6. Collection of the University of Manitoba, Gift of Eli Bornstein, 2007. Courtesy of Liv Valmestad. Photo credit: Liv Valmestad.
Tripart Hexaplane Construction No. 2 (model), 2002–6. Collection of the artist. Courtesy of Remai Modern. Photo credit: Troy Mamer.
Tripart Hexaplane Construction No. 3, 2008–10. Collection of Remai Modern, Saskatoon, Purchased with the support of the Frank and Ellen Remai Foundation, 2019 (2019.11). Courtesy of Remai Modern. Photo credit: Blaine Campbell.
Untitled (Murray Adaskin), 1953. The Mendel Art Gallery Collection at Remai Modern, Saskatoon, Gift of Dorothea Larsen Adaskin, 2004 (2004.17.19). Courtesy of Remai Modern.

CREDITS FOR PHOTOGRAPHS AND WORKS BY OTHER ARTISTS

Above Bow Falls, 1952, by H.G. Glyde. Collection of Whyte Museum of the Canadian Rockies, Banff, Gift of Fred Burghardt, Edmonton, 2018 (GyH.02.15). Courtesy of the Whyte Museum of the Canadian Rockies.
Abstract: Green and Gold, 1954, by Lionel LeMoine FitzGerald. Collection of the Winnipeg Art Gallery, Gift of Mr. and Mrs. Joseph Harris (G-63-287). Courtesy of WAG-Qaumajuq. Photo credit: Ernest Mayer.
Beaver Lake, Combermere, 1961, by A.Y. Jackson. Firestone Collection of Canadian Art, the Ottawa Art Gallery, Donated to the City of Ottawa by the Ontario Heritage Foundation (FAC 1617). Courtesy of the Ottawa Art Gallery. © A.Y. Jackson / CARCC Ottawa 2025. Photo credit: Tim Wickens.
Billboard advertising the exhibition *Artist in Focus: Eli Bornstein* at Remai Modern, Saskatoon, 2019. Courtesy of Roald Nasgaard. Photo credit: Roald Nasgaard.
Bird's-eye view of 21st Street East, Saskatoon, 1955. Hillyard Photograph Collection, Saskatoon Public Library (B-2051). Courtesy of the Saskatoon Public Library. Photographer unknown.
The Bornstein family, 1938–39. Courtesy of Eli Bornstein. Photographer unknown.
Composition with Color Planes 2, 1917, by Piet Mondrian. Collection of Museum Boijmans Van Beuningen, Rotterdam, Netherlands, Gift of A.P. van Hoey Smith, 1928 (1543 (MK)). Courtesy of the Mondrian Trust. © Mondrian/Holtzman Trust 2025.
Composition with Large Red Plane, Yellow, Black, Gray, and Blue, 1921, by Piet Mondrian. Collection of the Kunstmuseum Den Haag (333329). Courtesy of Kunstmuseum Den Haag.
Constructed Head No. 2, 1923–34, by Naum Gabo. Collection of the Dallas Museum of Art, Edward S. Marcus Memorial Fund, 1981 (1981.35). Courtesy of the Dallas Museum of Art. © Estate of Naum Gabo.
Cover of *Artist in Focus: Eli Bornstein*, with contributions by Sandra Fraser and Roald Nasgaard (Saskatoon: Remai Modern, 2019). Courtesy of Remai Modern.
Cover of *Eli Bornstein: Arctic Journals 1986 and 1987*, by Eli Bornstein, with contributions by Roald Nasgaard (Vancouver: Figure 1 Publishing, 2022). Courtesy of Figure 1 Publishing.
Cover of *Nature* by Ralph Waldo Emerson (Boston: James Munroe and Company, 1836). Courtesy of Christie's.
Cover of *Structure: Annual on the New Art*, no. 1, edited by Eli Bornstein and Joost Baljeu (Saskatoon: University of Saskatchewan, 1958). Courtesy of the University of Saskatchewan, University Archives and Special Collections.
Cover of *The Structurist*, no. 1, "Structurist Origins/Developments," edited by Eli Bornstein (Saskatoon: University of Saskatchewan, 1960). Courtesy of the University of Saskatchewan, University Archives and Special Collections.
Cover of *The Structurist*, no. 2, "Art in Architecture," edited by Eli Bornstein (Saskatoon: University of Saskatchewan, 1962). Courtesy of the University of Saskatchewan, University Archives and Special Collections.
Cover of *The Structurist*, no. 4, "Art and Music," edited by Eli Bornstein (Saskatoon: University of Saskatchewan, 1964). Courtesy of the University of Saskatchewan, University Archives and Special Collections.
Eli and Christina Bornstein's dining room with skylight, 2020. Photograph by Roald Nasgaard. Courtesy of Roald Nasgaard.
Eli and Christina Bornstein in the artist's studio, date unknown, Saskatoon. Courtesy of Oliver A.I. Botar. Photo credit: Oliver A.I. Botar.
Eli Bornstein and A.Y. Jackson at Murray Adaskin's cabin, Canoe Lake, Ontario, 1964. Courtesy of Eli Bornstein. Photographer unknown.
Eli Bornstein and Gordon Snelgrove, c.1950–51. Courtesy of Eli Bornstein. Photographer unknown.
Eli Bornstein and his first dog, Skippy, 1932. Courtesy of Eli Bornstein. Photographer unknown.
Eli Bornstein and Murray Adaskin at a party hosted by Fred Mendel in Saskatoon, c.1954. Courtesy of Eli Bornstein. Photographer unknown.

Eli Bornstein in his studio, date unknown. Courtesy of Oliver A.I. Botar. Photo credit: Oliver A.I. Botar.

Eli Bornstein on the occasion of his graduation from the Milwaukee State Teachers College, 1945. Courtesy of Eli Bornstein. Photographer unknown.

Eli Bornstein painting at Ellesmere Island, 1986. Courtesy of the University of Saskatchewan, University Archives and Special Collections. Photo credit: Hans Dommasch.

Eli Bornstein playing the drums, date unknown. Courtesy of Eli Bornstein. Photographer unknown.

Eli Bornstein posing with the maquette for *Tree of Knowledge*, 1979. Courtesy of Eli Bornstein. Photo credit: Sandra Semchuk.

Eli Bornstein with one of his Structurist reliefs in *An Art at the Mercy of Light: Recent Works by Eli Bornstein* at the Mendel Gallery, Saskatoon, 2013. Courtesy of Saskatoon StarPhoenix, a division of Postmedia Network Inc. © Postmedia Network Inc. Photo credit: Michelle Berg.

Eli Bornstein with *Structurist Relief No. 18-II* in the Arts and Science Building at the University of Saskatchewan, Saskatoon, 1961. University of Saskatchewan Photograph Collection, University of Saskatchewan, University Archives and Special Collections (A-8368). Courtesy of the University of Saskatchewan, University Archives and Special Collections. Photographer unknown.

Eli Bornstein with *Untitled Hexaplane Structurist Relief*, date unknown. Courtesy of the University of Saskatchewan, University Archives and Special Collections. Photographer unknown.

Ellesmere Island—Otto Fjord, 1986, by Hans Dommasch. University of Saskatchewan, University Archives and Special Collections, Hans Dommasch fonds, box 25, file F.5 folder 2 (MG 172). Courtesy of the University of Saskatchewan, University Archives and Special Collections.

Exterior of the Layton Art Gallery, Milwaukee, 1895. Collection of the University of Wisconsin-Milwaukee Library. Courtesy of the University of Wisconsin-Milwaukee Library. Photographer unknown.

Forest, British Columbia, 1931–32, by Emily Carr. Collection of the Vancouver Art Gallery, Emily Carr Trust (VAG 42.3.9). Courtesy of the Vancouver Art Gallery.

Frank Lloyd Wright, 1954. Photograph by Al Ravenna. Collection of the Library of Congress, Washington, D.C. Courtesy of the Library of Congress.

Gardanne, 1885–86, by Paul Cézanne. Collection of The Metropolitan Museum of Art, New York, Gift of Dr. and Mrs. Franz H. Hirschland, 1957 (57.181). Courtesy of The Metropolitan Museum of Art.

Icebergs, Davis Strait, 1930, by Lawren S. Harris. McMichael Canadian Art Collection, Kleinburg, Gift of Mr. and Mrs. H. Spencer Clark (1971.17). Courtesy of the McMichael Canadian Art Collection. © Family of Lawren S. Harris.

In the Northland, 1915, by Tom Thomson. Collection of the Montreal Museum of Fine Arts, Purchase, Gift of Dr. Francis J. Shepherd, Sir Vincent Meredith, Drs. Lauterman and W. Gardner and Mrs. Hobart Molson (1922.197179). Courtesy of the Montreal Museum of Fine Arts. Photo credit: MMFA, Denis Farley.

Installation view of *Artist in Focus: Eli Bornstein* at Remai Modern, Saskatoon, 2019. Courtesy of Remai Modern. Photo credit: Blaine Campbell.

The Market Church at Halle, 1930, by Lyonel Feininger. Sammlung Moderne Kunst, Pinakothek der Moderne/ Bayerische Staatsgemäldesammlungen, Munich. Courtesy of Pinakothek der Moderne / Art Resource, NY. © Estate of Lyonel Feininger / Bild-Kunst, Bonn / CARCC Ottawa 2025.

Mount Katahdin (Maine), Autumn #2, 1939–40, by Marsden Hartley. Collection of The Metropolitan Museum of Art, New York, Bequest of Edith Abrahamson Lowenthal, 1991 (1992.24.3). Courtesy of The Metropolitan Museum of Art and Wikimedia Commons / CC BY 1.0.

Mount Thule, Bylot Island, 1930, by Lawren S. Harris. Collection of the Vancouver Art Gallery, Gift of the Vancouver Art Gallery Women's Auxiliary (VAG 49.6). Courtesy of the Vancouver Art Gallery. © Family of Lawren S. Harris.

Page 36 of the inaugural issue of *Structure: Annual on the New Art* (1958), illustrating one of Eli Bornstein's first Structurist reliefs alongside Piet Mondrian's *Composition with Color Planes 2*, 1917. Courtesy of the University of Saskatchewan, University Archives and Special Collections.

Paris Houses, 1920, by Lyonel Feininger. Collection of the RISD Museum, Providence, Museum Works of Art Fund (50.237). Courtesy of the RISD Museum. © Estate of Lyonel Feininger / Bild-Kunst, Bonn / CARCC Ottawa 2025.

Spatio-Temporelle #23, 1966, by Jean Gorin. Collection of the University of Saskatchewan, Saskatoon, Purchased 1972 (1972.008.001). Courtesy of the University of Saskatchewan.

View of an unfinished Structurist relief in Eli Bornstein's studio, Saskatoon, 2020. Courtesy of Roald Nasgaard. Photo credit: Roald Nasgaard.

View of Eli Bornstein's studio featuring a collection of colour swatches for enamel paints, date unknown, Saskatoon. Courtesy of Oliver A.I. Botar. Photo credit: Oliver A.I. Botar.

View of Eli Bornstein's studio featuring an unpainted aluminum Structurist relief, date unknown, Saskatoon. Courtesy of Oliver A.I. Botar. Photo credit: Oliver A.I. Botar.

View of the South Saskatchewan River Valley from Eli Bornstein's house, date unknown. Courtesy of Eli Bornstein. Photographer unknown.

Walt Whitman, c.1860–65. Photograph by Matthew Brady. Collection of the National Archive and Records Administration, Photographs and Graphic Materials, Washington, D.C. Courtesy of the National Archives and Records Administration.

Winter Night in the Mountains, 1914, by Harald Sohlberg. Collection of the National Museum of Art, Architecture and Design, Oslo. Courtesy of the National Museum of Art, Architecture and Design and Wikimedia Commons / CC BY 1.0.

#26, Red Wing, 1956–68, 1956–68, by Charles Biederman. Collection of Minneapolis Institute of Art, Gift of Mrs. Anna Biederman Brown (2003.107). © Weisman Art Museum at the University of Minnesota. Photo credit: Minneapolis Institute of Art.

#36–1950, 1950, by Charles Biederman. Collection of Minneapolis Institute of Art, Gift of Mr. and Mrs. John P. Anderson (74.29). © Weisman Art Museum at the University of Minnesota. Photo credit: Minneapolis Institute of Art.

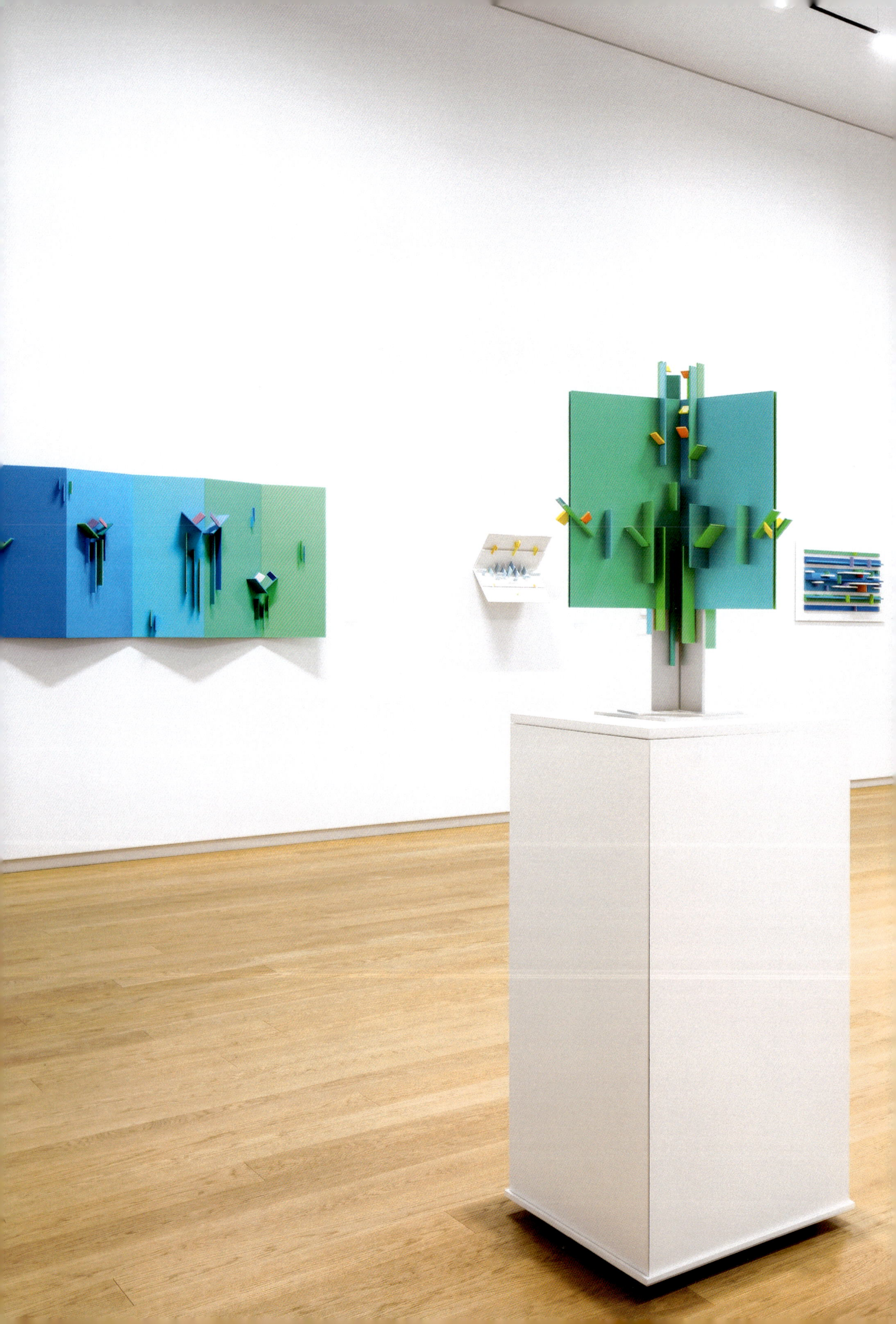

Acknowledgements

Eli Bornstein: Life & Work was made possible thanks to the Season Sponsorship of the Power Corporation of Canada. Through their generosity, it was first published online at www.aci-iac.ca, where it is available in English and French as an open-access book.

From the Author

I am deeply indebted to Eli Bornstein for many studio visits and long conversations. I am grateful to both Eli and his wife, Christina, for crucial background stories and biographical details, as well as for delightful lunches and dinners, and so much more. My other indispensable partner in Saskatoon has been Cheryl Avery, archivist at the University of Saskatchewan, who has been tireless in her pursuit of the images for the book and of archival information. At Remai Modern I thank Sandra Fraser and also Troy Mamer, who has been an essential source not only of his own photography of Eli's art, but also for his work in scanning and cleaning Eli's personal photographs and collection of old slides. Valuable advice has come from artist Elizabeth Willmott, and from art historian Oliver A.I. Botar, who has long been an astute writer on and curator of Eli's work. The hospitality of Norman Zepp and Judith Varga, Bob and Susanne Christie, and Cathy Perehudoff and Graham Fowler during my many visits has made Saskatoon one of my favourite Canadian cities. Also my thanks to the several Art Canada Institute editors, including Sara Angel, Emma Doubt, Tara Ng, Victoria Nolte, and Ray Cronin, who helped shape my prose for a general reader. And finally, endless kisses to my wife, Lori Walters, always a patient reader and rereader of my writings.

Opposite: Installation view of *Artist in Focus: Eli Bornstein* at Remai Modern, Saskatoon, 2019, photograph by Blaine Campbell.

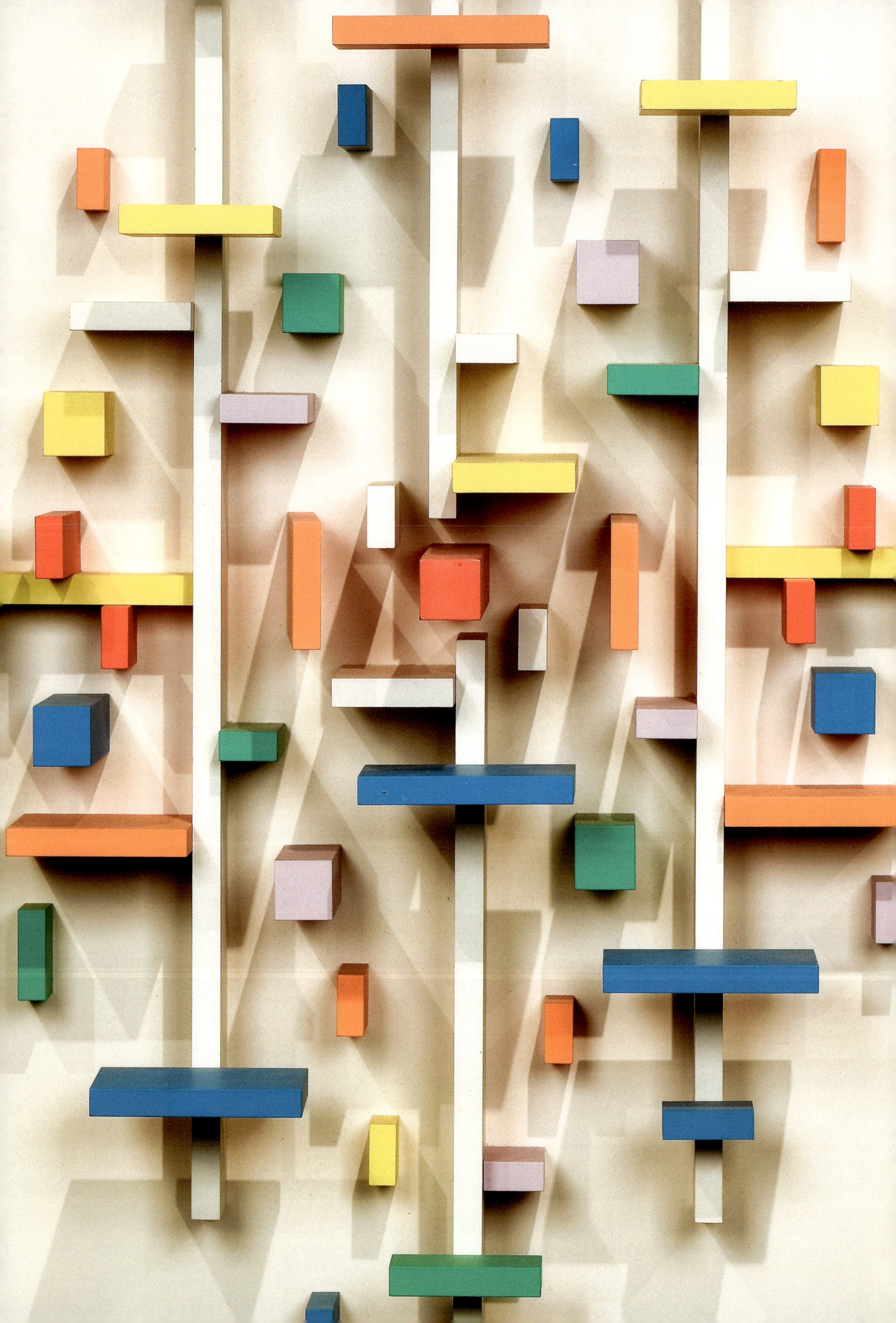

About the Author

I have long thought Eli Bornstein a major artist, but perhaps my real revelation came in 2013, when I was setting up my exhibition The Automatiste Revolution *at the Mendel Art Gallery in Saskatoon. As it happened, an exhibition of Eli's recent work had just been installed in the adjacent galleries, which were—and this was the crux—illuminated by natural light flowing down from the skylights above. Here was affirmation that Eli's work was truly, as in the words of the title of that show, "an art at the mercy of light."*

—ROALD NASGAARD

Roald Nasgaard, OC, is a teacher, writer, and curator. The publication of the present book brings together his long-standing commitments to both abstract art and landscape painting. He is the author of the critically acclaimed *Abstract Painting in Canada* (2007). His major exhibitions and accompanying books include *The Mystic North: Symbolist Landscape Painting in Northern Europe and North America 1890–1940* (1984); the first Gerhard Richter retrospective in North America (1988); *The Automatiste Revolution: Montreal 1941–1960* (2009); and *The Plasticiens and Beyond: Montreal 1955–1970* (2013). He co-curated *Mystical Landscapes: Masterpieces from Monet, Van Gogh and More* for the Art Gallery of Ontario and the Musée d'Orsay (2016–17), and *Higher States: Lawren Harris and His American Contemporaries* (2017) for the McMichael Canadian Art Collection. In 2022, he shepherded into publication *Eli Bornstein: Arctic Journals 1986 and 1987*. Nasgaard's extended essay "Charles Gagnon: A Painter of Paradoxes" appears in the book *Charles Gagnon: The Colour of Time, the Sound of Space* (2025).

Opposite: Eli Bornstein, *Structurist Relief No. 1* (detail), 1966, acrylic and wood on a wood support, 86.5 x 61 cm, Nickle Galleries, University of Calgary.

Eli Bornstein
Life & Work

This book is part of the Canadian Art Library Series, published by the Art Canada Institute.

Cover and half-title image: Eli Bornstein, *Multiplane Structurist Relief V, No. 1* (detail), 1993, acrylic enamel, Plexiglas on aluminum, 86.5 x 61.1 x 3.1 cm, Remai Modern, Saskatoon.
Title page and back cover image: Eli Bornstein posing with the maquette for *Tree of Knowledge*, 1979, photograph by Sandra Semchuk.
Contents image: Eli Bornstein, *Quadriplane Structurist Relief No. 2* (River-Screen Series) (detail), 1989–96, acrylic enamel on aluminum and Plexiglas, 60.4 x 137.8 x 14.6 cm, collection of the artist.

Art Canada Institute
Massey College, University of Toronto
4 Devonshire Place
Toronto, ON M5S 2E1

Library and Archives Canada Cataloguing in Publication

Eli Bornstein : life & work / by Roald Nasgaard.
Names: Nasgaard, Roald, author. | Container of (work) : Bornstein, Eli. Works. Selections. | Art Canada Institute, publisher.
Identifiers: Canadiana (print) 20250167131 | Canadiana (ebook) 20240402626 | ISBN 9781487103682 (hardcover) | ISBN 9781487103477 (HTML) | ISBN 9781487103484 (PDF)
Subjects: LCSH: Bornstein, Eli. | LCSH: Bornstein, Eli—Criticism and interpretation. | LCSH: Artists—Canada—Biography. | LCGFT: Biographies.
Classification: LCC NB249.B66 N33 2025 | DDC 730.92—dc23